POSTCARD HISTORY SERIES

Troy

IN VINTAGE POSTCARDS

Postcard History Series

Troy in Vintage Postcards

Brian and Becky Nielsen

Arcadia Publishing

ISBN 978-0-7385-0903-7

Published by Arcadia Publishing
Charleston, South Carolina

Printed in the United States of America

Library of Congress Catalog Card Number: 2001090272

For all general information contact Arcadia Publishing at:
Telephone 843-853-2070
Fax 843-853-0044
E-mail sales@arcadiapublishing.com
For customer service and orders:
Toll-Free 1-888-313-2665

Visit us on the Internet at www.arcadiapublishing.com

Contents

INTRODUCTION

Troy was established in 1786 in Rensselaer County. It is a 215-year-old city that is rich in history and incredible architecture.

Today, the three city communities of Albany, Schenectady, and Troy are called the Capital District. Troy is known as the Collar City for the invention of the detachable collar by Hannah Lord Montague. It is also known as the home of Uncle Sam (Samuel Wilson).

Every fall, the population of Troy rises with the return of the students to Rensselaer Polytechnic Institute, Russell Sage College, Hudson Valley Community College, and Emma Willard, which is a private school.

I was born in Troy in the late 1950s and grew up in Waterford. My fondest memories are of my mother and grandmother going shopping. They would come home with bags and boxes from Frear's, Peerless, Denby's, Smith's Meat Market on Fourth Street, and baked goods from Nelligan's Bakery. These are just a few of the stores they shopped at. Each year on my birthday, I would get a fresh-baked pie from the Tim Pie Club, located at Wells and Coverly. Then we would go to Grant's or Woolworth's. Next, we were off to Andy's Sporting Goods for a new gym bag or school jacket. The last and best part of the shopping trip would be to go to Paul's Restaurant for lunch or an ice-cream sundae—both if I was lucky. During my high school years, we would go to the Red Front or the Knotty Pine, which would be standing-room-only after a game.

Today, most of these places are gone. However, when we come home for a visit, my wife and I relive my childhood through food. We go to Bella Napoli, Verdiles, Ted's Fish Fry, and, of course, De Fazio's for their homemade sauce and pasta.

In closing, I would like to thank the following people for their help and generosity: Bob and Marion Nielsen, Mark Kane, Edna Kane, Alma Walsh, Steve Reynolds, my brother Robert Nielsen, the staff at the Troy Public Library, and the National Baseball Hall of Fame Library.

—Brian Nielsen

One

GREETINGS FROM TROY

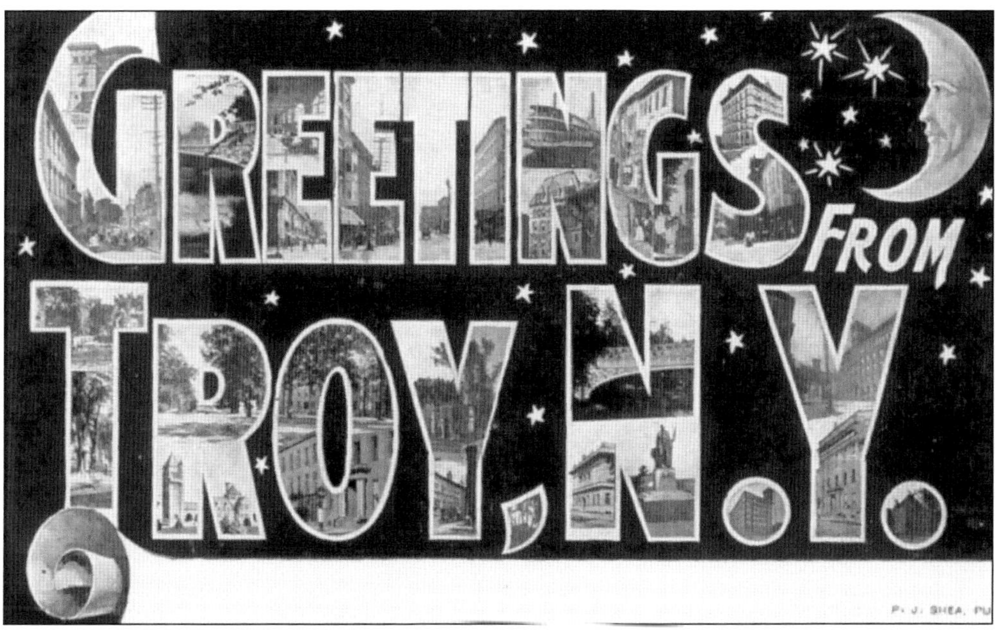

"GREETINGS FROM TROY, N.Y." This was a very common phrase used on postcards in the early 1900s and is still used today.

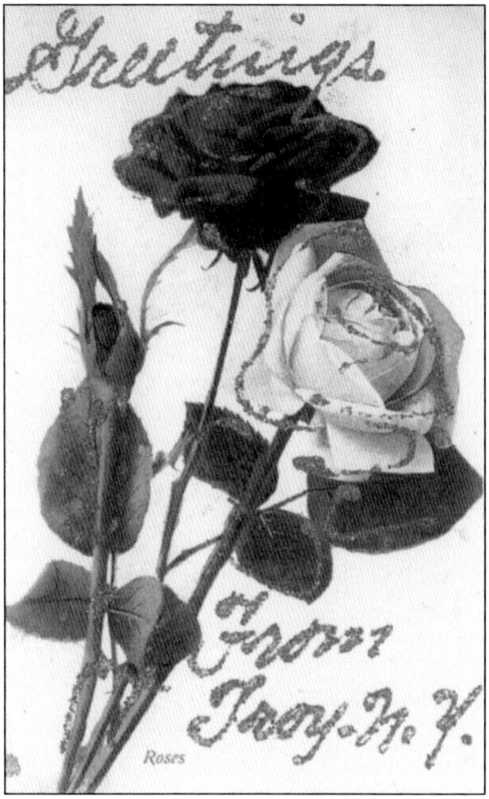

"GREETINGS FROM TROY, N.Y." This card has glitter glued to the roses. Many people decorated and personalized the postcards they sent, as did the postcard companies.

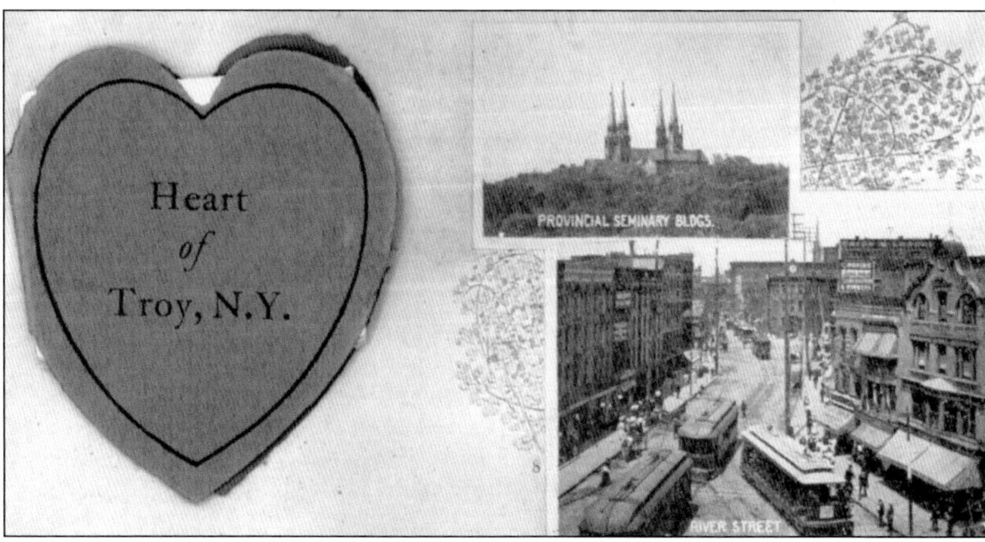

"HEART OF TROY, N.Y." This special Valentine, done in the accordion style, shows different miniature views of the city when the heart is opened.

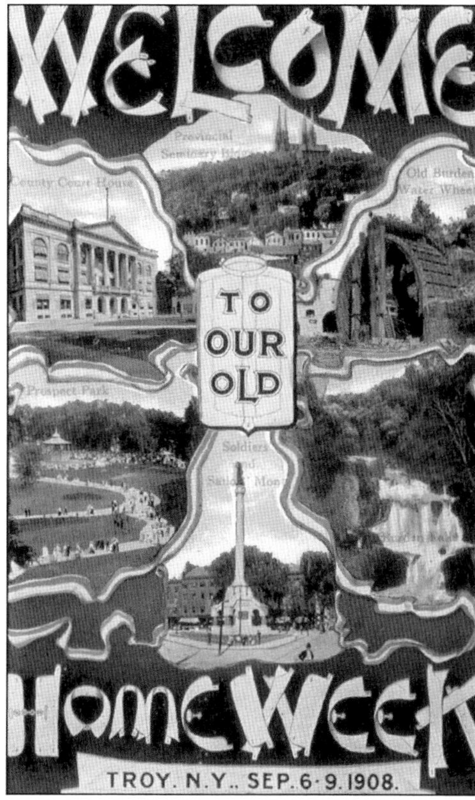

"WELCOME TO OUR OLD HOME WEEK." This creative view spells out the phrase in shirt collars. The card also shows some of Troy's special places, such as Burden Falls, Prospect Park, and the Soldiers and Sailors' Monument.

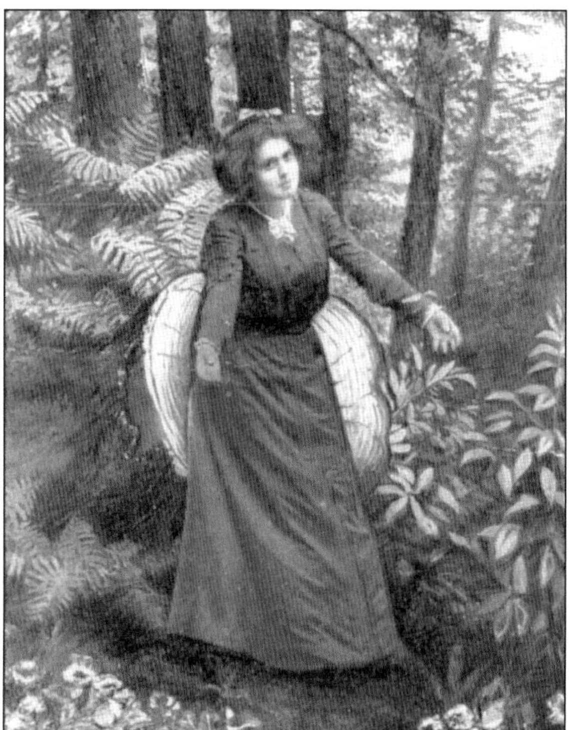

"COME MAKE YOURSELF AT HOME." This young lady is inviting you to Troy with open arms.

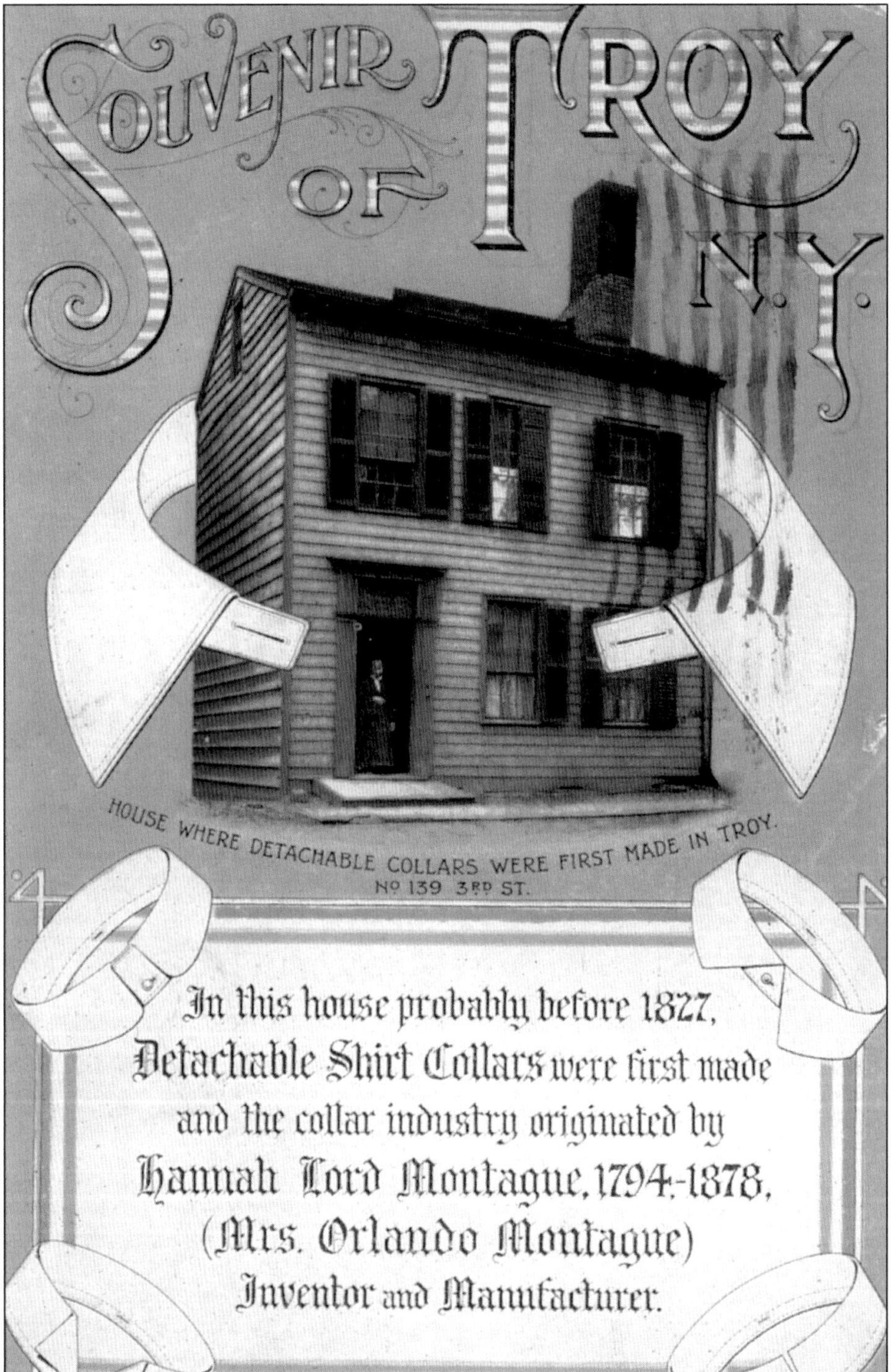

"SOUVENIR OF TROY, N.Y." This card shows the many detachable collars that were invented and manufactured by Hannah Lord Montague at 139 Third Street. Hence came the name of the Collar City. A few years ago, First Lady Hillary Rodham Clinton unveiled a plaque in honor of Montague.

"Do you remember what you told me 'in Troy, N.Y.'" It must have been something special. We can only hope he remembered.

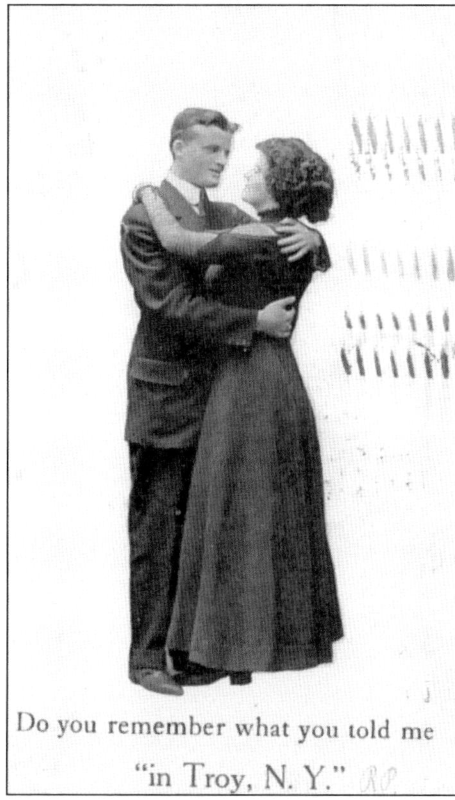

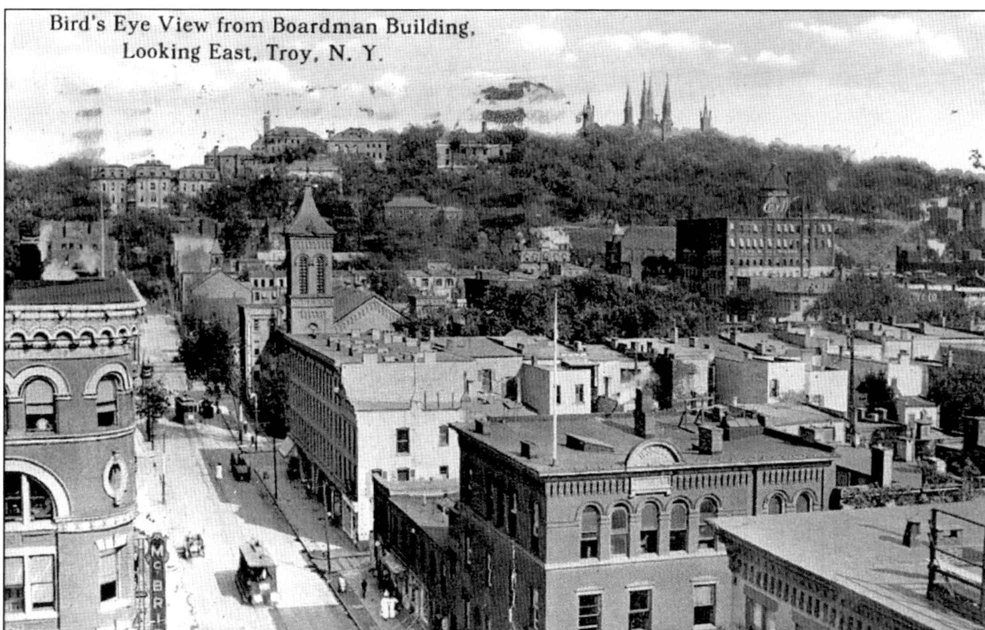

"Bird's Eye View from Boardman Building, Looking East." Panoramic postals, also known as bird's-eye views, have always been popular. This one, taken from the Boardman Building, shows the Rensselaer Polytechnic Institute buildings in the background.

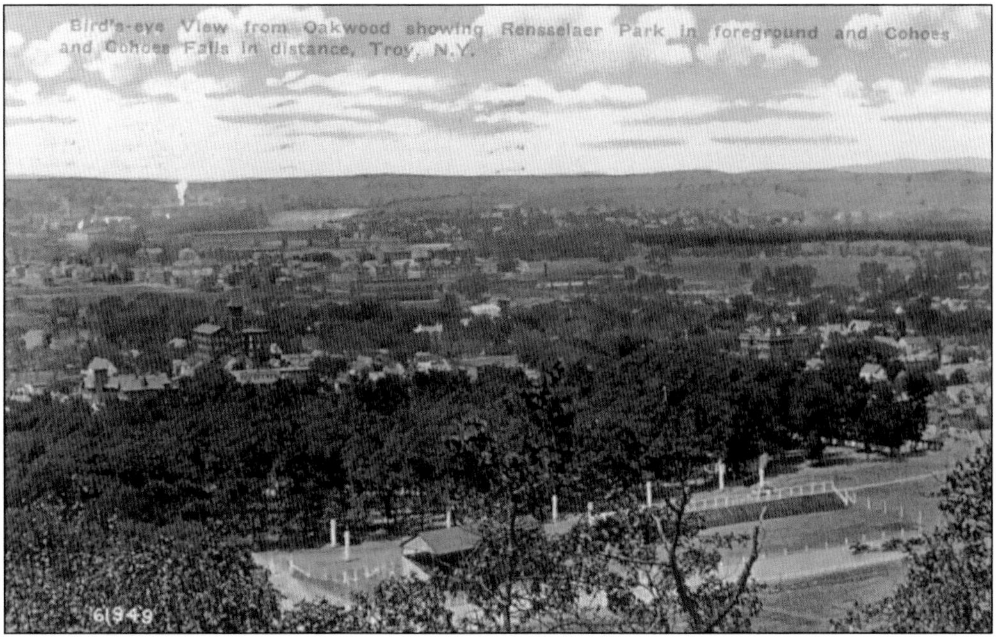

"BIRD'S-EYE VIEW FROM OAKWOOD." This view, taken from Oakwood Cemetery, shows Lansingburgh's Rensselaer Park in the foreground and the city of Cohoes in the background.

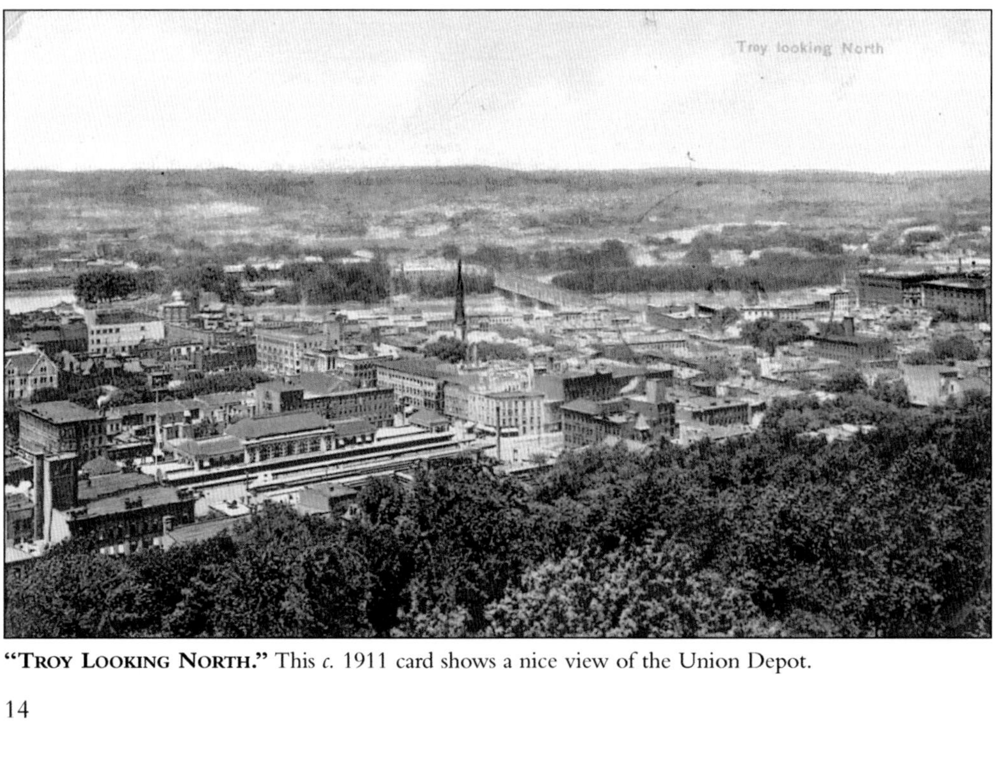

"TROY LOOKING NORTH." This *c.* 1911 card shows a nice view of the Union Depot.

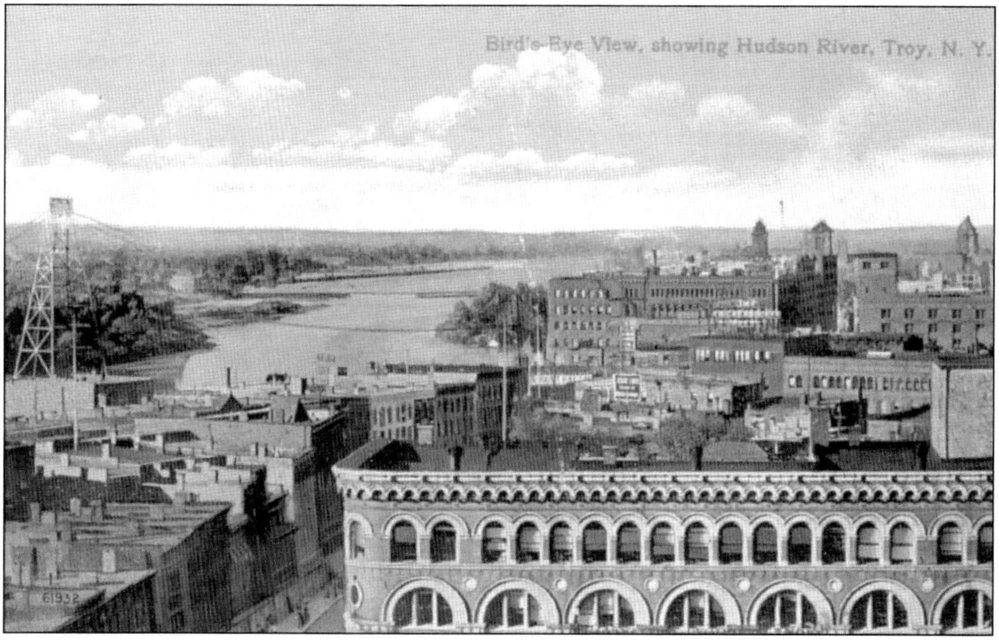

"BIRD'S EYE VIEW, SHOWING HUDSON RIVER" AND "HUDSON RIVER PANORAMA." These two views show Troy by the Hudson River.

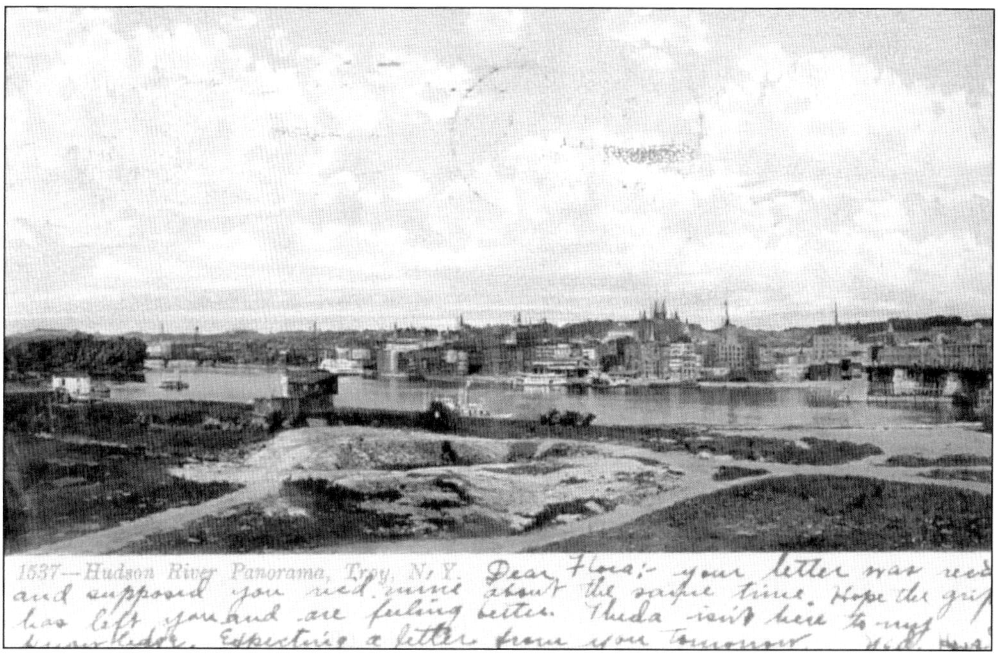

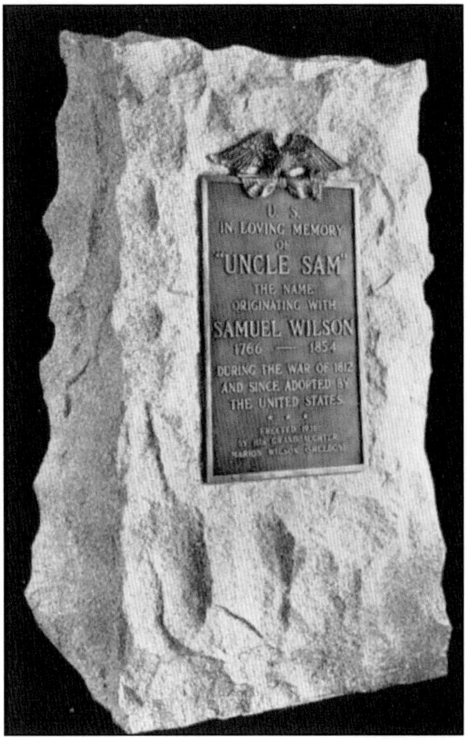

UNCLE SAM MONUMENT. Troy is known as the home of Uncle Sam. This monument was erected in Oakwood Cemetery by Sam Wilson's granddaughter in his memory. Every year, a parade is held in his honor. Congress adopted Uncle Sam as a national symbol in 1961. Sam Wilson was originally from Mason, New Hampshire.

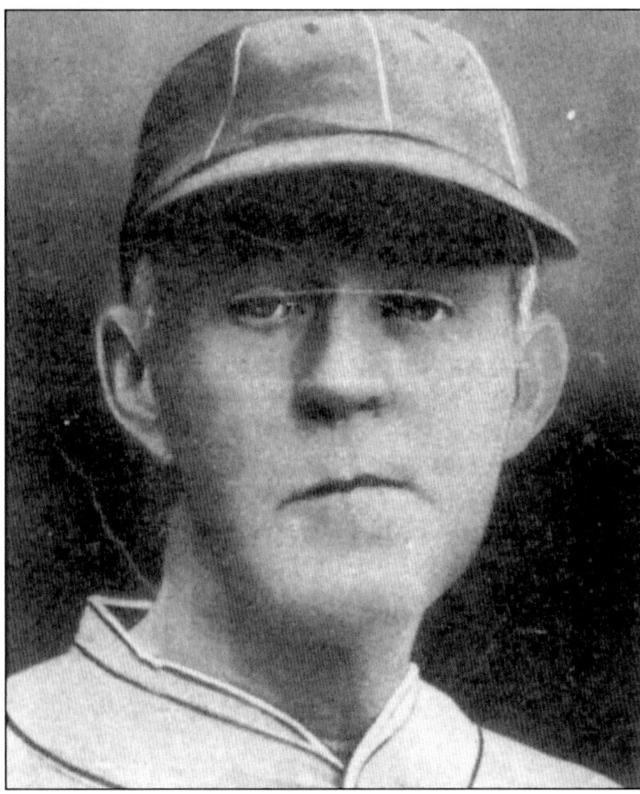

"JOHNNY" EVERS. Seen here is John Joseph "Johnny, the Trojan" Evers. He was born in 1881 and grew up to become a great second baseman. He was famous for the double-play combination of Tinker to Evers to Chance. His lifetime batting average was .270. Evers had 324 stolen bases—21 of them for stealing home. He was elected to the National Baseball Hall of Fame before his death in 1947. Evers is not the only Hall of Famer from Troy. Michael Joseph "King" Kelly, who started his career with the Troy Haymakers in 1873, is another. He was a great base stealer. The crowds were heard to say, "Slide, Kelly, slide." His .313 lifetime average earned him a place in Cooperstown.

Two

Time to Eat

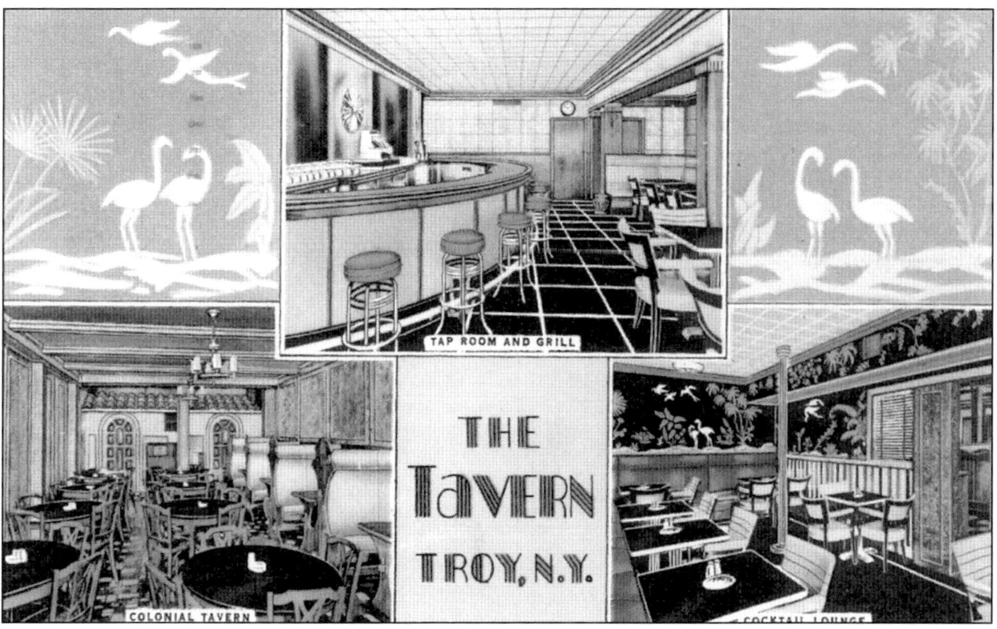

The Tavern. The card describes the Tavern as "an Eating Place for the Epicure." It was located at 211 Broadway and was known for its four dining rooms. They were the Tap Room and Grill, Colonial Tavern, Cocktail Lounge, and Banquet Lodge. Remember when you could get a prime rib dinner for 90¢, a lobster for $1.10, or a Martini for 25¢? You could do just that at the Tavern in 1938. It has had many names over the years. In the 1980s, when it was called Billy's on Broadway, the name Tavern was still spelled out in tile on the floor in the foyer.

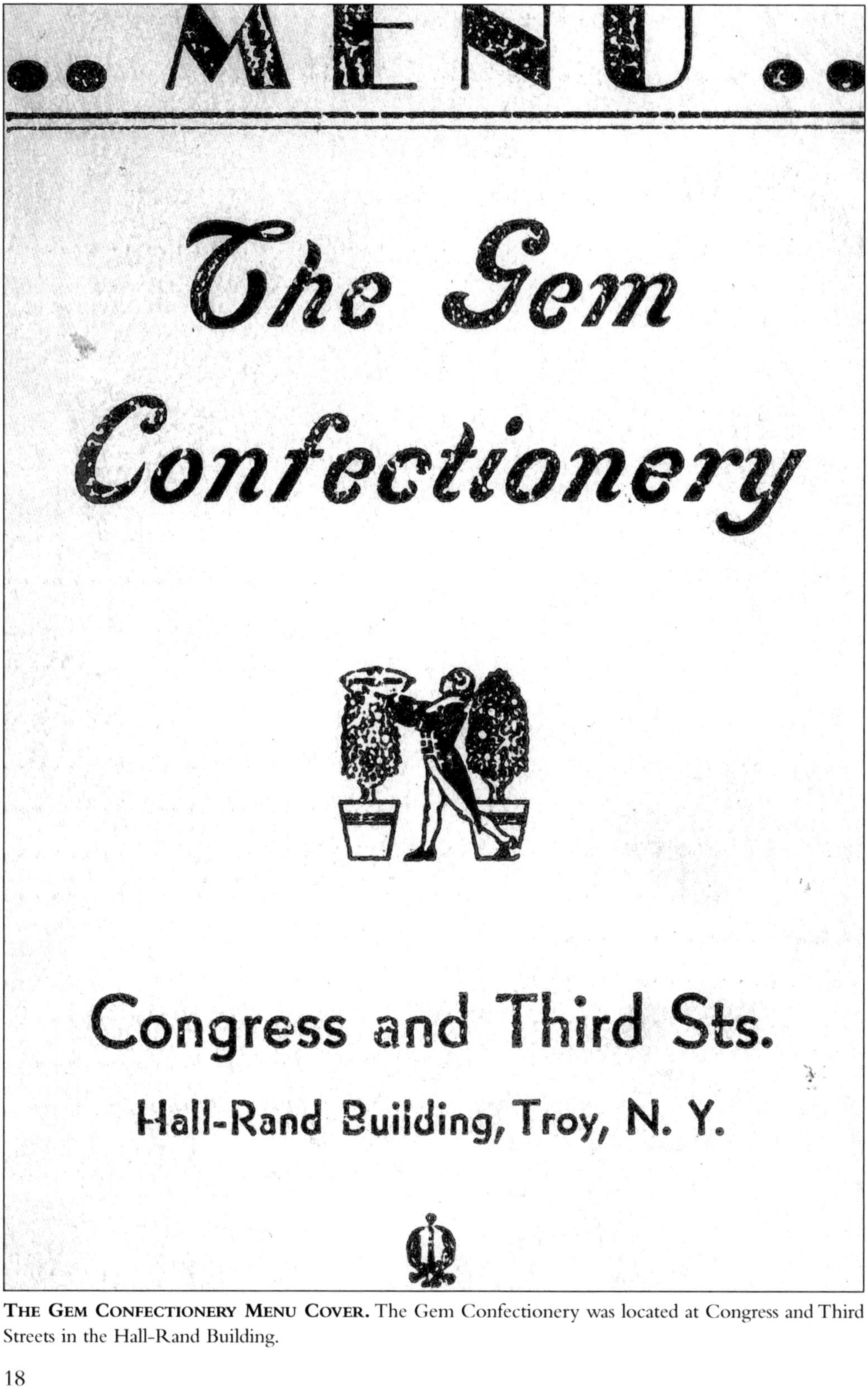

THE GEM CONFECTIONERY MENU COVER. The Gem Confectionery was located at Congress and Third Streets in the Hall-Rand Building.

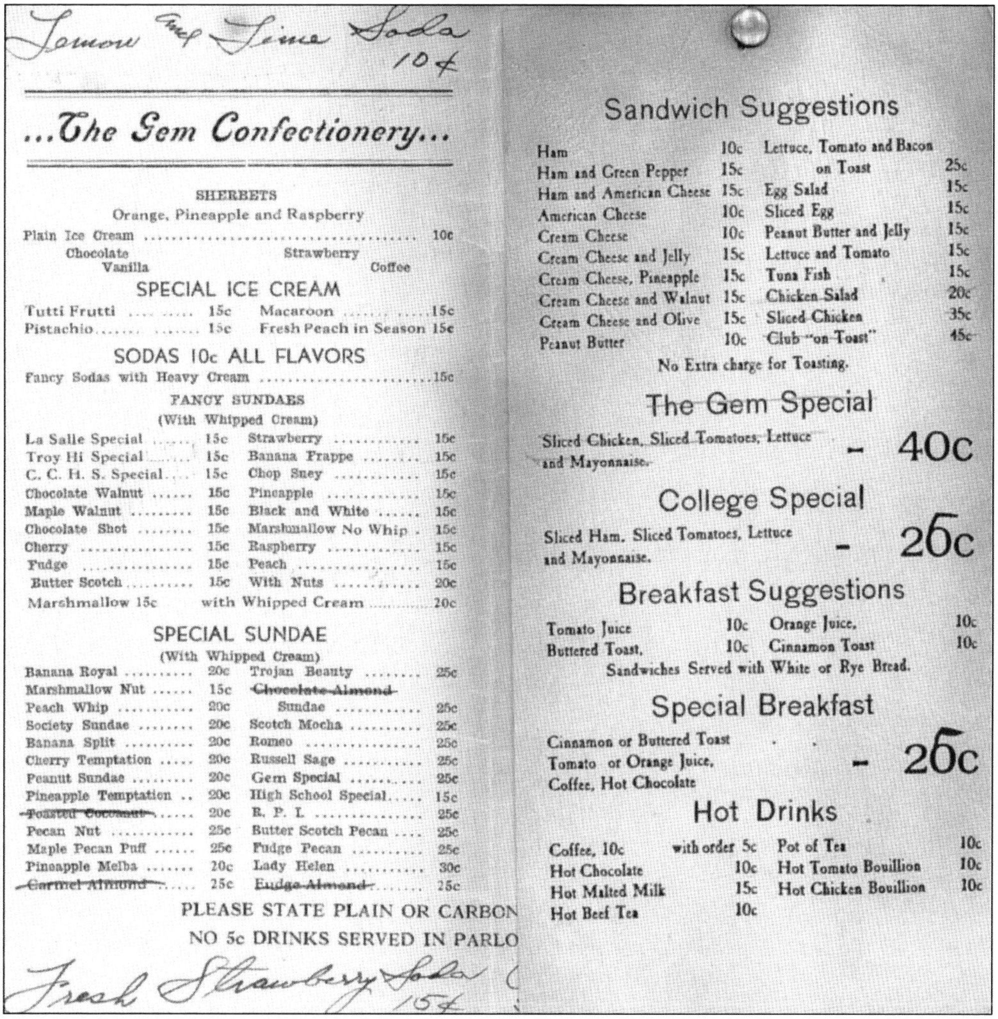

Lemon ~~Lime~~ Lime Soda 10¢

...The Gem Confectionery...

SHERBETS

Orange, Pineapple and Raspberry

Plain Ice Cream 10c

Chocolate — Strawberry — Vanilla — Coffee

SPECIAL ICE CREAM

Tutti Frutti	15c	Macaroon	15c
Pistachio	15c	Fresh Peach in Season	15c

SODAS 10c ALL FLAVORS

Fancy Sodas with Heavy Cream 15c

FANCY SUNDAES

(With Whipped Cream)

La Salle Special	15c	Strawberry	15c
Troy Hi Special	15c	Banana Frappe	15c
C. C. H. S. Special	15c	Chop Suey	15c
Chocolate Walnut	15c	Pineapple	15c
Maple Walnut	15c	Black and White	15c
Chocolate Shot	15c	Marshmallow No Whip	15c
Cherry	15c	Raspberry	15c
Fudge	15c	Peach	15c
Butter Scotch	15c	With Nuts	20c
Marshmallow 15c		with Whipped Cream	20c

SPECIAL SUNDAE

(With Whipped Cream)

Banana Royal	20c	Trojan Beauty	25c
Marshmallow Nut	15c	~~Chocolate Almond~~ Sundae	25c
Peach Whip	20c		
Society Sundae	20c	Scotch Mocha	25c
Banana Split	20c	Romeo	25c
Cherry Temptation	20c	Russell Sage	25c
Peanut Sundae	20c	Gem Special	25c
Pineapple Temptation	20c	High School Special	15c
~~Toasted Cocoanut~~	20c	R. P. I.	25c
Pecan Nut	25c	Butter Scotch Pecan	25c
Maple Pecan Puff	25c	Fudge Pecan	25c
Pineapple Melba	20c	Lady Helen	30c
~~Carmel Almond~~	25c	~~Fudge Almond~~	25c

PLEASE STATE PLAIN OR CARBON

NO 5c DRINKS SERVED IN PARLO

Fresh Strawberry Soda 15¢

Sandwich Suggestions

Ham	10c	Lettuce, Tomato and Bacon on Toast	25c
Ham and Green Pepper	15c	Egg Salad	15c
Ham and American Cheese	15c	Sliced Egg	15c
American Cheese	10c	Peanut Butter and Jelly	15c
Cream Cheese	10c	Lettuce and Tomato	15c
Cream Cheese and Jelly	15c	Tuna Fish	15c
Cream Cheese, Pineapple	15c	~~Chicken Salad~~	20c
Cream Cheese and Walnut	15c	~~Sliced Chicken~~	35c
Cream Cheese and Olive	15c	~~Club "on Toast"~~	45c
Peanut Butter	10c		

No Extra charge for Toasting.

The Gem Special

~~Sliced Chicken, Sliced Tomatoes, Lettuce and Mayonnaise.~~ - 40c

College Special

Sliced Ham, Sliced Tomatoes, Lettuce and Mayonnaise. - 26c

Breakfast Suggestions

Tomato Juice	10c	Orange Juice	10c
Buttered Toast	10c	Cinnamon Toast	10c

Sandwiches Served with White or Rye Bread.

Special Breakfast

Cinnamon or Buttered Toast

Tomato or Orange Juice,

Coffee, Hot Chocolate - 26c

Hot Drinks

Coffee, 10c	with order 5c	Pot of Tea	10c
Hot Chocolate	10c	Hot Tomato Bouillion	10c
Hot Malted Milk	15c	Hot Chicken Bouillion	10c
Hot Beef Tea	10c		

THE GEM CONFECTIONERY MENU. Now these were great prices—there is nothing over 60¢. Notice the high school specials for La Salle, Troy, and Catholic Central High School.

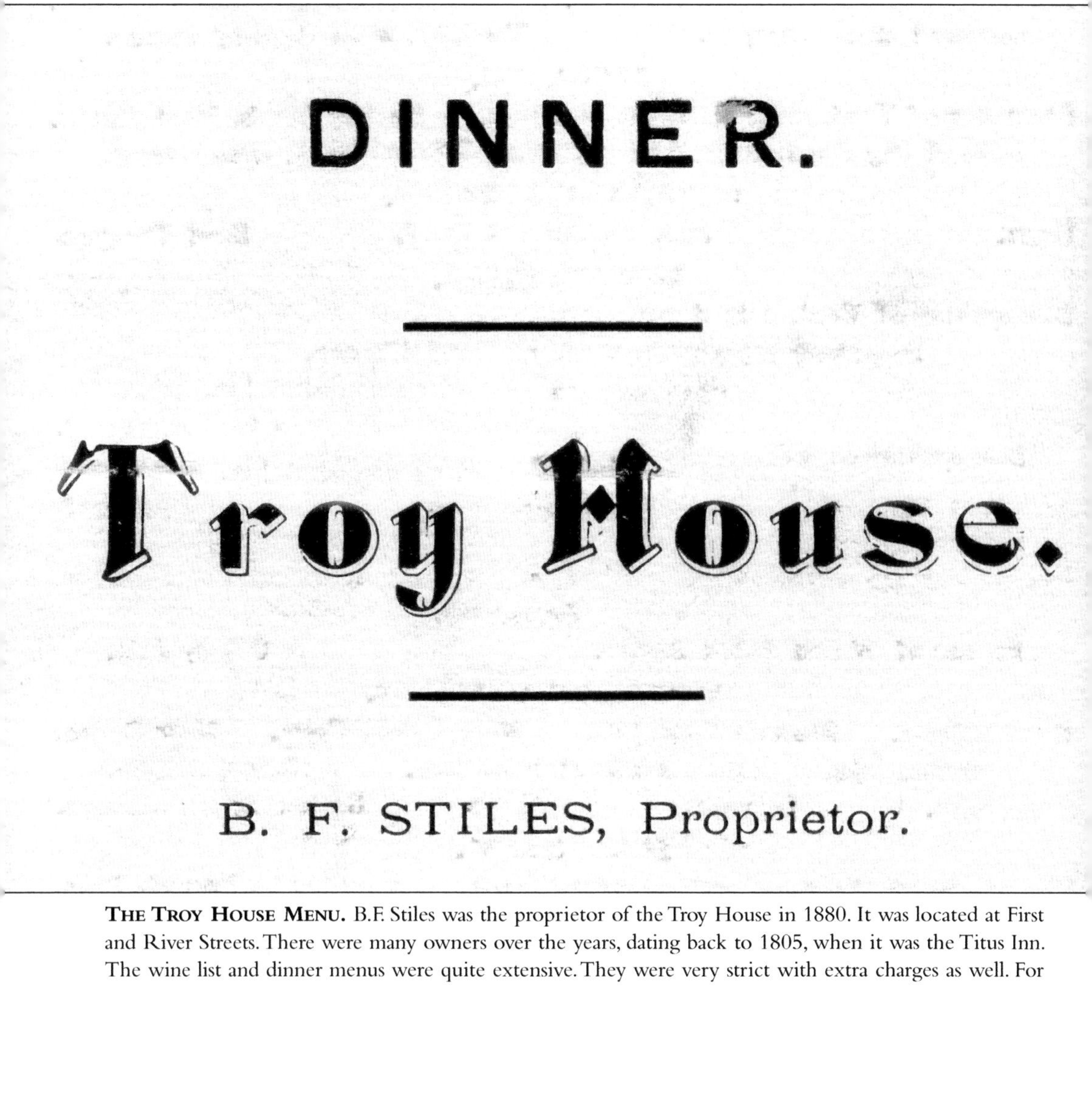

DINNER.

Troy House.

B. F. STILES, Proprietor.

The Troy House Menu. B.F. Stiles was the proprietor of the Troy House in 1880. It was located at First and River Streets. There were many owners over the years, dating back to 1805, when it was the Titus Inn. The wine list and dinner menus were quite extensive. They were very strict with extra charges as well. For

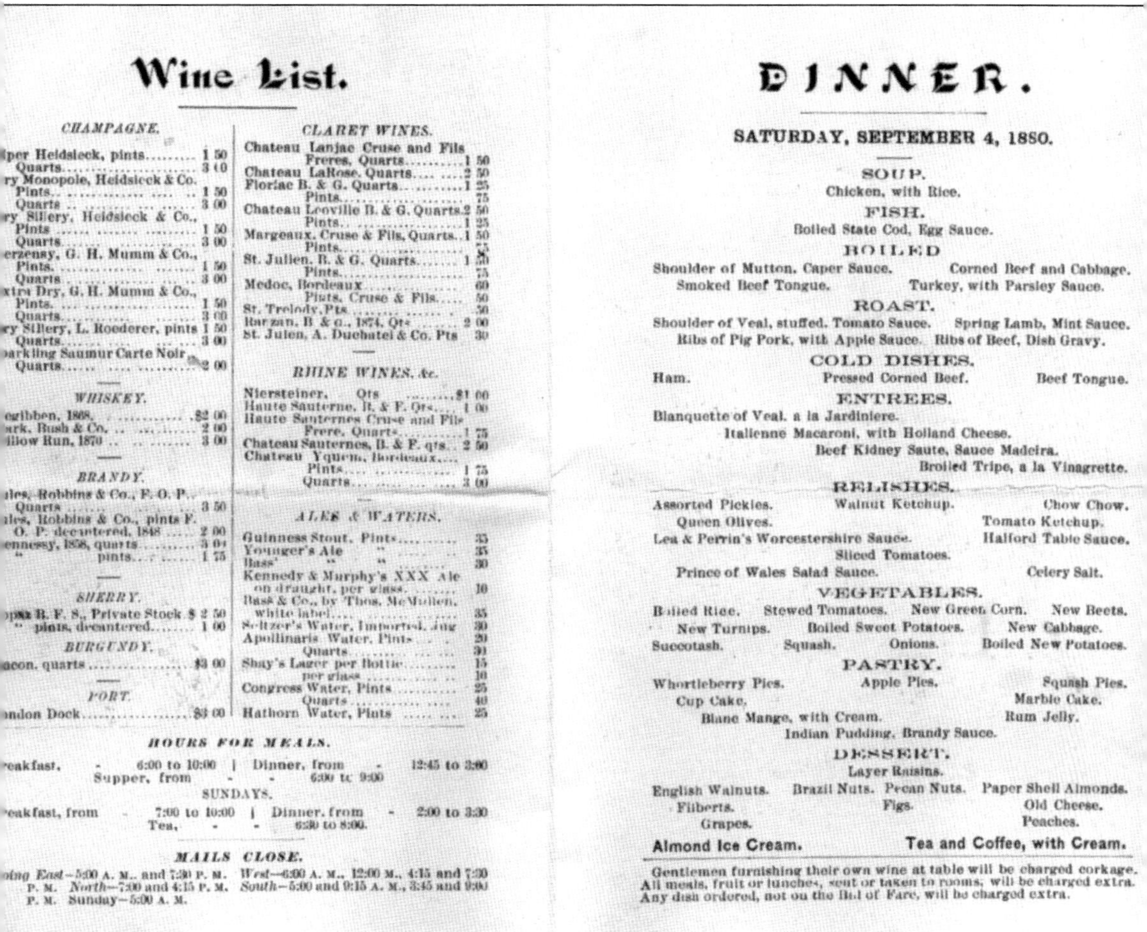

Wine List.

CHAMPAGNE.

per Heidsieck, pints......... 1 50
Quarts.......................... 3 00
ry Monopole, Heidsieck & Co.
Pints.............................. 1 50
Quarts............................ 3 00
ry Sillery, Heidsieck & Co.,
Pints.............................. 1 50
Quarts............................ 3 00
erzenay, G. H. Mumm & Co.,
Pints.............................. 1 50
Quarts............................ 3 00
xtra Dry, G. H. Mumm & Co.,
Pints.............................. 1 50
Quarts............................ 3 00
ry Sillery, L. Roederer, pints 1 50
Quarts............................ 3 00
parkling Saumur Carte Noir,
Quarts............................ 2 00

WHISKEY.

egibben, 1868, ...$2 00
ark, Bush & Co. 2 00
illow Run, 1870 .... 3 00

BRANDY.

les, Robbins & Co., F. O. P.,
Quarts............................ 3 50
les, Robbins & Co., pints F.
O. P. decantered, 1848 ...... 2 00
ennessy, 1858, quarts......... 3 00
" pints.......................... 1 75

SHERRY.

pas B. F. S., Private Stock $ 2 50
" pints, decantered........ 1 00

BURGUNDY.

acon, quarts.................. $3 00

PORT.

ondon Dock..................... $3 00

CLARET WINES.

Chateau Lanjac Cruse and Fils
Freres, Quarts............1 50
Chateau LaRose, Quarts........2 50
Floriac B. & G. Quarts..........1 25
Pints.................................. 75
Chateau Leoville B. & G. Quarts 2 50
Pints.................................1 25
Margeaux, Cruse & Fils, Quarts..1 50
Pints.................................. 75
St. Julien, B. & G. Quarts.......1 50
Pints.................................. 75
Medoc, Bordeaux.................... 60
Pints, Cruse & Fils.............. 50
St. Trelody, Pts...................... 50
Barzan, B & G., 1874, Qts........ 2 00
St. Julen, A. Duchatel & Co. Pts 30

RHINE WINES, &c.

Niersteiner, Qts $1 00
Haute Sauterne, B. & F. Qts..... 1 00
Haute Sauternes Cruse and Fils
Frere, Quarts....................1 75
Chateau Sauternes, B. & F. qts.. 2 50
Chateau Yquem, Bordeaux....
Pints..................................1 75
Quarts................................ 3 00

ALES & WATERS.

Guinness Stout, Pints.............. 35
Younger's Ale " 35
Bass' " " 30
Kennedy & Murphy's XXX Ale
on draught, per glass........... 10
Bass & Co., by Thos. McMullen,
white label........................ 35
Seltzer's Water, Imported, Jug 30
Apollinaris Water, Pints......... 20
Quarts................................ 30
Shay's Lager per Bottle........... 15
per glass............................ 10
Congress Water, Pints............ 25
Quarts................................ 40
Hathorn Water, Pints............. 25

HOURS FOR MEALS.

eakfast, - 6:00 to 10:00 | Dinner, from - 12:45 to 3:00
Supper, from - - 6:00 to 9:00

SUNDAYS.

eakfast, from - 7:00 to 10:00 | Dinner, from - 2:00 to 3:30
Tea, - - 6:30 to 8:00.

MAILS CLOSE.

oing *East*—5:00 A. M., and 7:30 P. M. *West*—6:00 A. M., 12:00 M., 4:15 and 7:30 P. M. *North*—7:00 and 4:15 P. M. *South*—5:00 and 9:15 A. M., 3:45 and 9:00 P. M. Sunday—5:00 A. M.

DINNER.

SATURDAY, SEPTEMBER 4, 1880.

SOUP.
Chicken, with Rice.

FISH.
Boiled State Cod, Egg Sauce.

BOILED
Shoulder of Mutton, Caper Sauce. Corned Beef and Cabbage.
Smoked Beef Tongue. Turkey, with Parsley Sauce.

ROAST.
Shoulder of Veal, stuffed, Tomato Sauce. Spring Lamb, Mint Sauce.
Ribs of Pig Pork, with Apple Sauce. Ribs of Beef, Dish Gravy.

COLD DISHES.
Ham. Pressed Corned Beef. Beef Tongue.

ENTREES.
Blanquette of Veal, a la Jardiniere.
Italienne Macaroni, with Holland Cheese.
Beef Kidney Saute, Sauce Madeira.
Broiled Tripe, a la Vinagrette.

RELISHES.
Assorted Pickles. Walnut Ketchup. Chow Chow.
Queen Olives. Tomato Ketchup.
Lea & Perrin's Worcestershire Sauce. Halford Table Sauce.
Sliced Tomatoes.
Prince of Wales Salad Sauce. Celery Salt.

VEGETABLES.
Boiled Rice. Stewed Tomatoes. New Green Corn. New Beets.
New Turnips. Boiled Sweet Potatoes. New Cabbage.
Succotash. Squash. Onions. Boiled New Potatoes.

PASTRY.
Whortleberry Pies. Apple Pies. Squash Pies.
Cup Cake. Marble Cake.
Blanc Mange, with Cream. Rum Jelly.
Indian Pudding, Brandy Sauce.

DESSERT.
Layer Raisins.
English Walnuts. Brazil Nuts. Pecan Nuts. Paper Shell Almonds.
Filberts. Figs. Old Cheese.
Grapes. Peaches.

Almond Ice Cream. Tea and Coffee, with Cream.

Gentlemen furnishing their own wine at table will be charged corkage.
All meals, fruit or lunches, sent or taken to rooms, will be charged extra.
Any dish ordered, not on the Bill of Fare, will be charged extra.

example, "Gentlemen furnishing their own wine at the table will be charged corkage." You don't see broiled tripe on a menu as much as you used to.

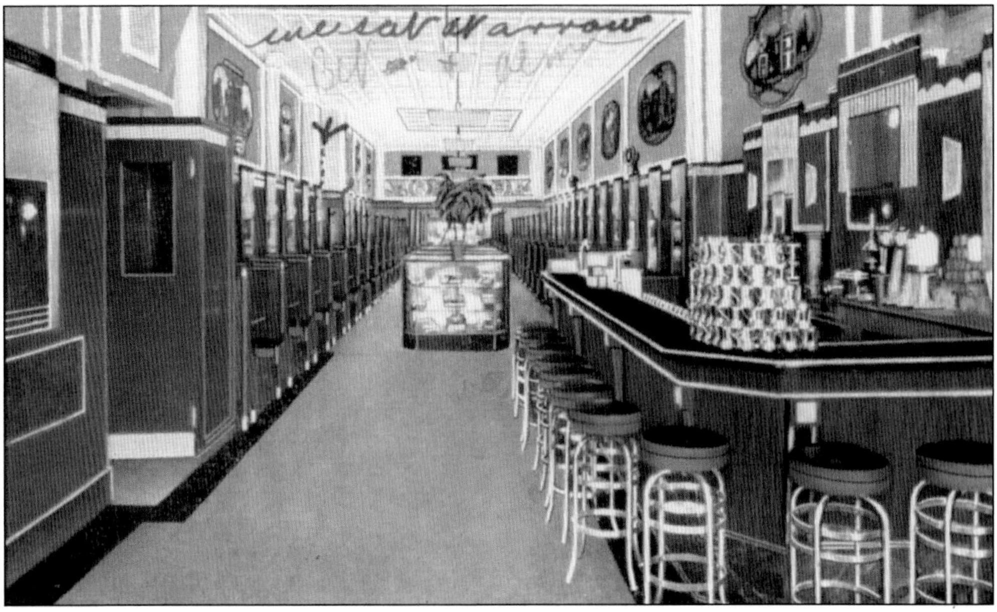

The Puritan Restaurant and Luncheonette. This classic restaurant was located in the heart of the city at Broadway and Third Street. Lunch and dinner was served, and for dessert there was homemade ice cream and pies. In later years, it was called the Puritan Tea Room.

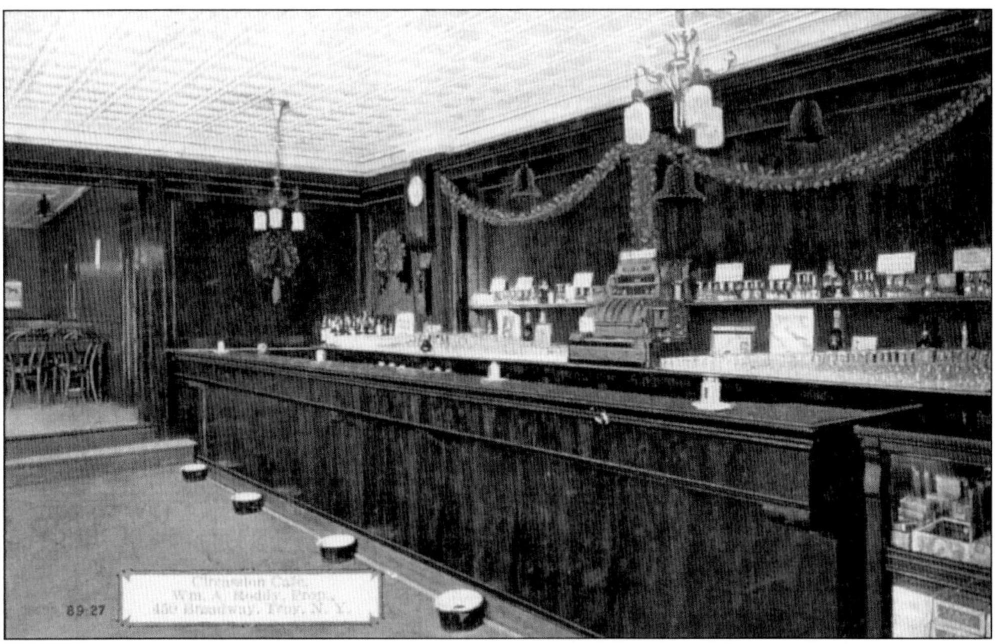

The Circassion Café. William A. Roddy was the proprietor at the Circassion Café, which was located at 450 Broadway. The bar was decorated for the Christmas holiday with bells, garland, and a spittoon next to each customer's foot. With the tables to the left and the cigar display to the right, what more could you ask for?

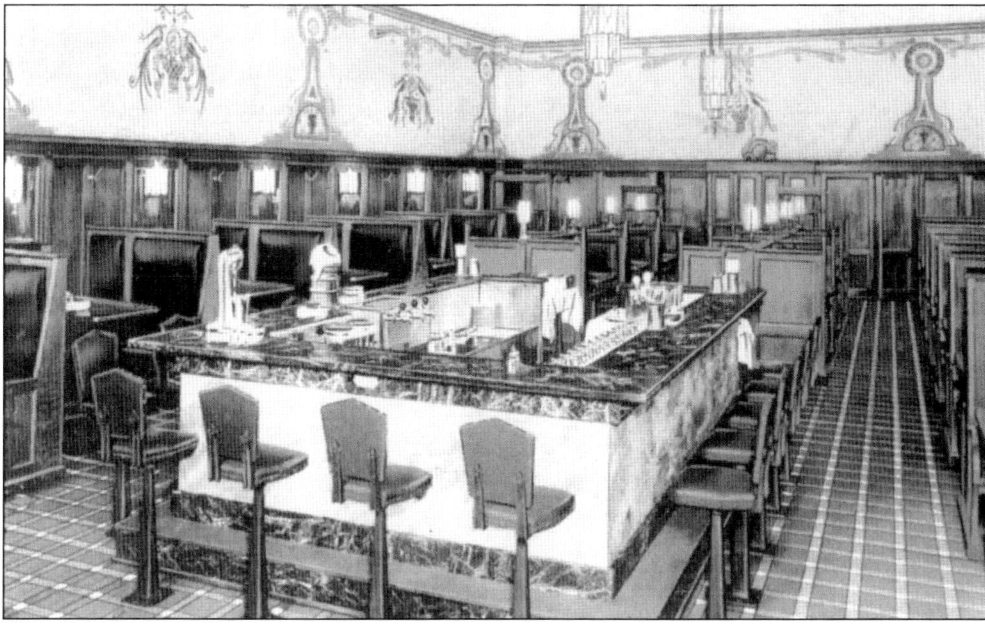

Paul's Luncheonette. Paul's Luncheonette was located at 295 River Street. Whether called a luncheonette or a restaurant, it was always known as the "Restaurant Unusual." It was known for its luncheons and homemade ice cream. The Saratoga Lounge was famous for cocktails, the Georgian Room for dining and dancing, and the Rendezvous Room was a place for the young and old.

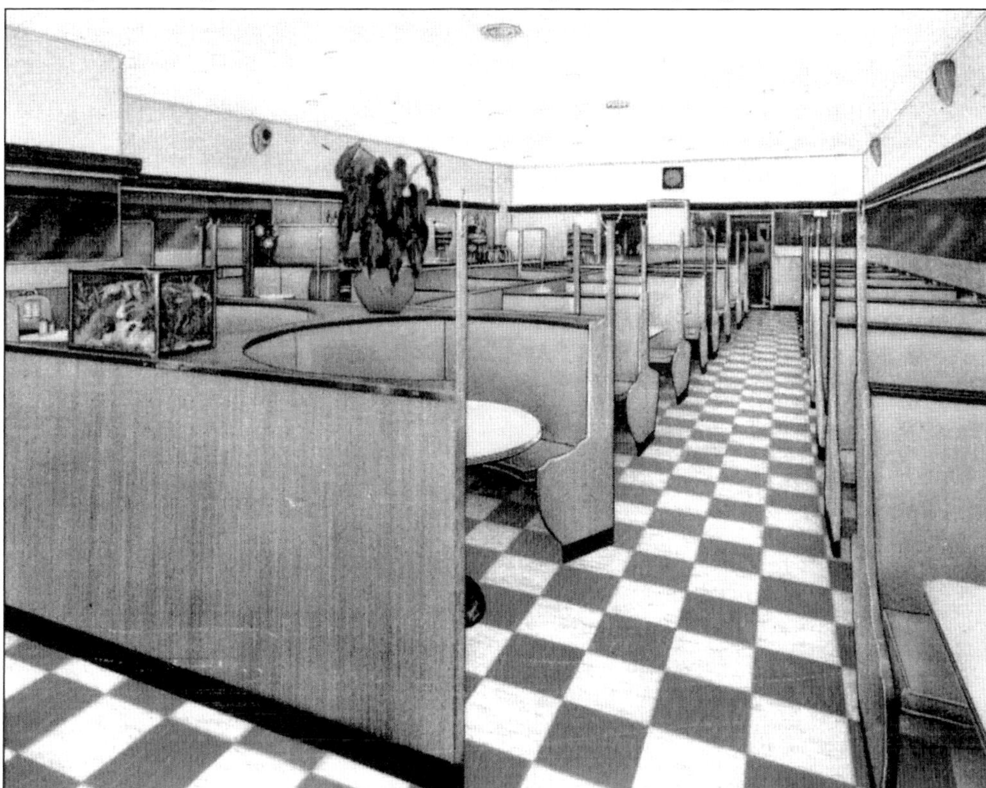

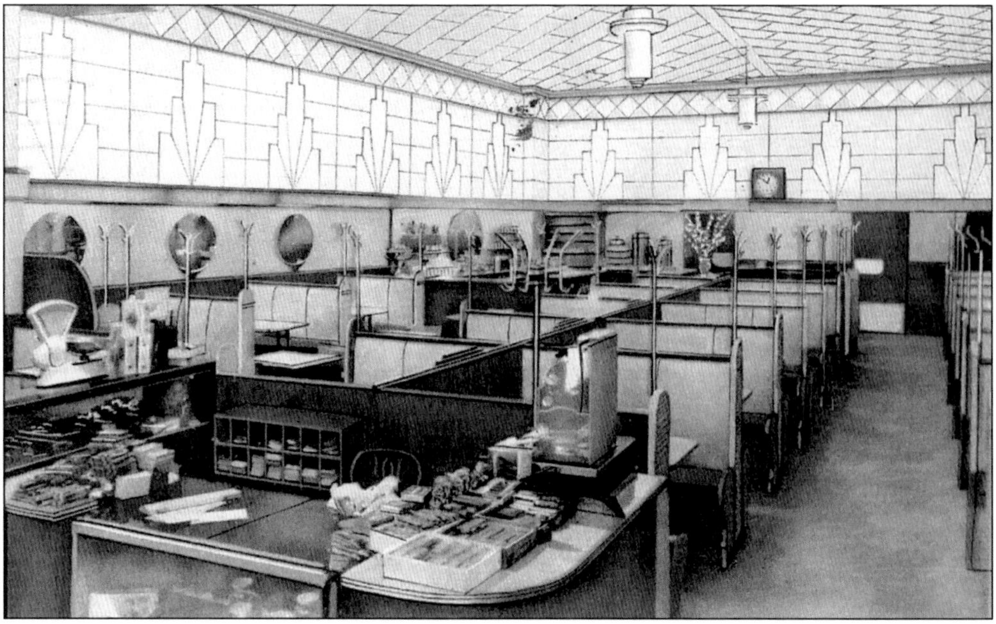

PAUL'S LUNCHEONETTE. Here is another interior view of Paul's.

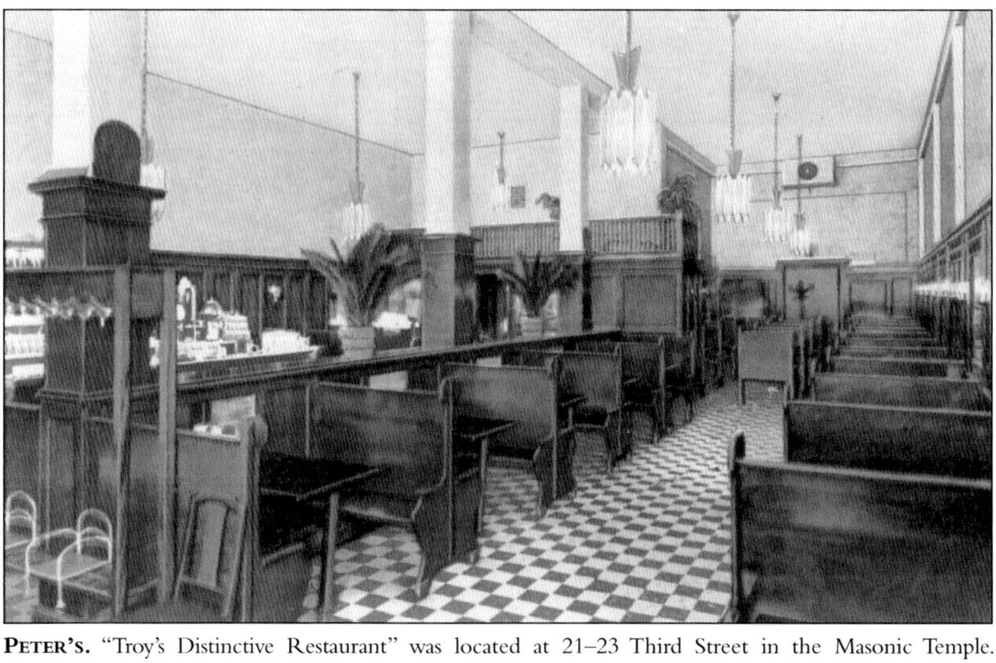

PETER'S. "Troy's Distinctive Restaurant" was located at 21–23 Third Street in the Masonic Temple. Peter's was another one of Troy's fine restaurants with great atmosphere and friendly service. Peter's sold Schrafft's Candies exclusively. They had a soda fountain and offered blue plate specials—dinners were from 40¢ to 75¢.

Three

TAKING IT TO THE STREETS

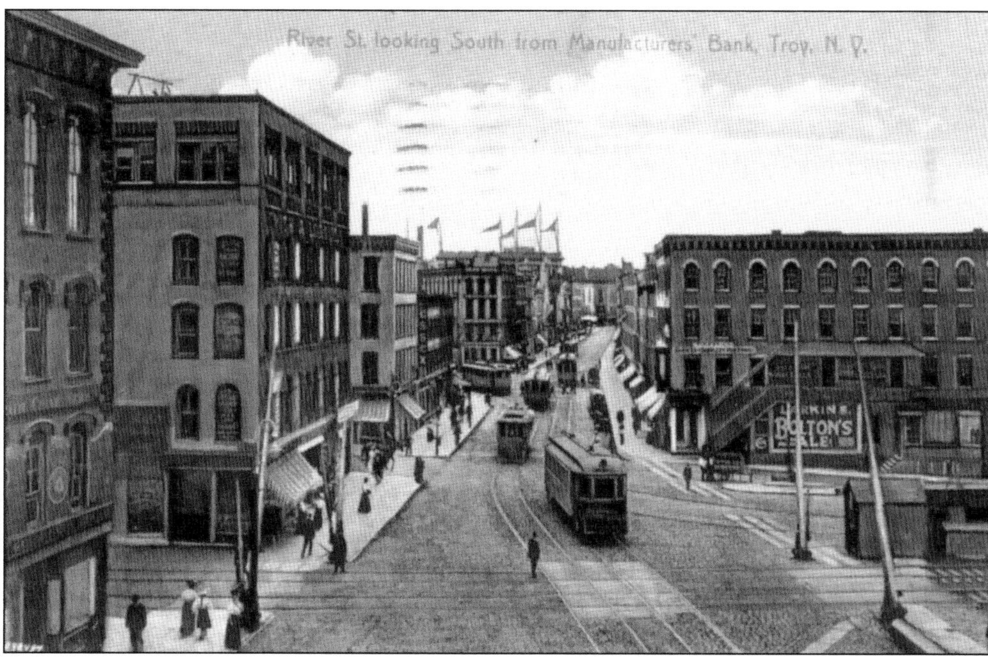

"RIVER ST. LOOKING SOUTH FROM MANUFACTURERS' BANK." Seen here are several electric trolleys coming down the street. The first electric trolley cars ran in 1899. Before using electricity to move them, the trolleys were drawn by horses. In 1934, we saw the last of the trolleys; they were replaced by buses.

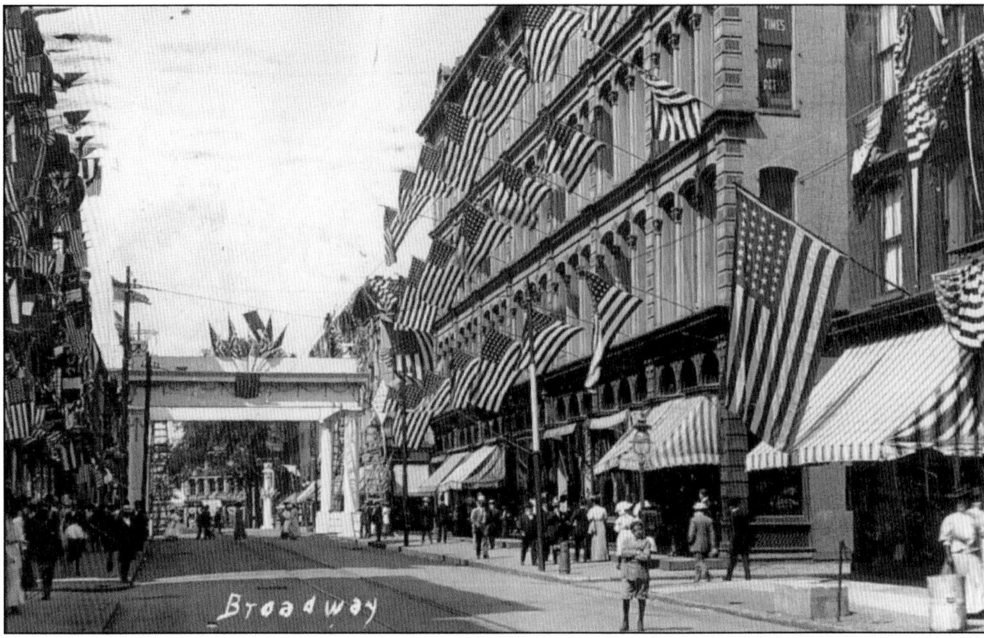

BROADWAY. In this *c.* 1908 view looking up Broadway, there appears to be a big celebration, possibly the Fourth of July. The Troy Times Building is on the right.

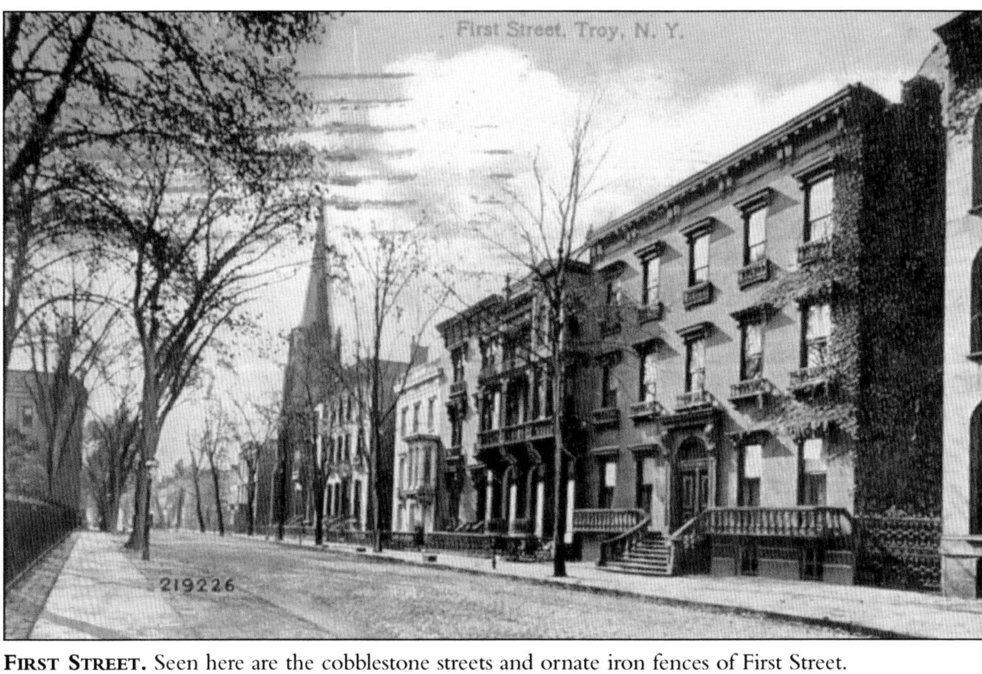

FIRST STREET. Seen here are the cobblestone streets and ornate iron fences of First Street.

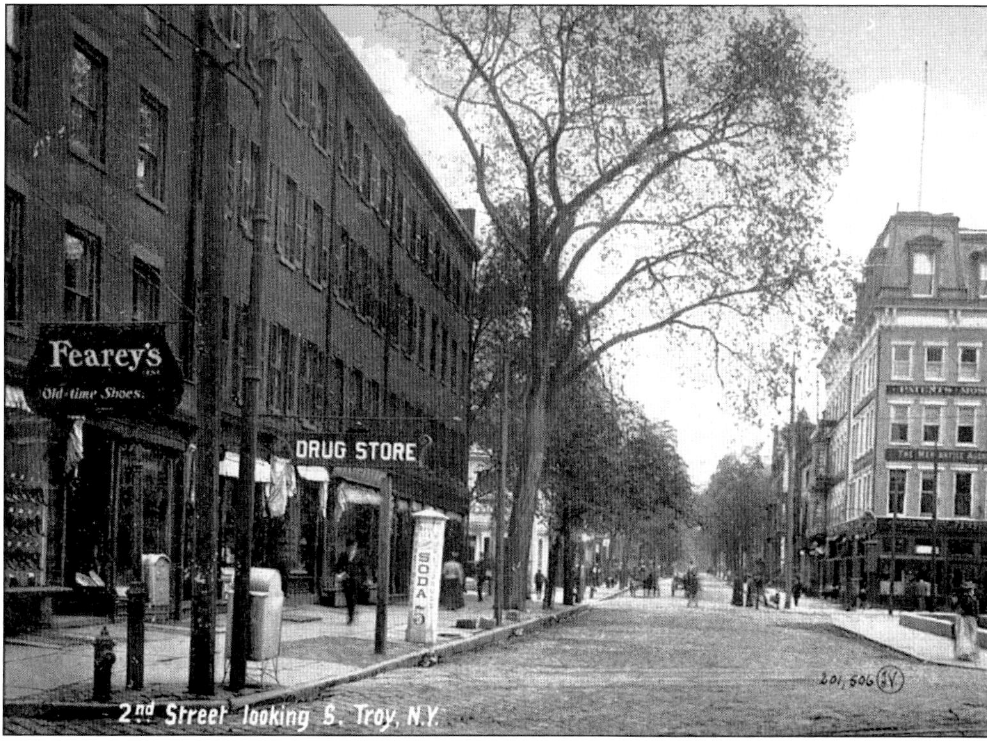

SECOND STREET, LOOKING SOUTH. Seen here are Fearey's Old Time Shoes, on the left, and the Cannon Building, on the right. When was the last time you saw a drugstore selling soda for a nickel?

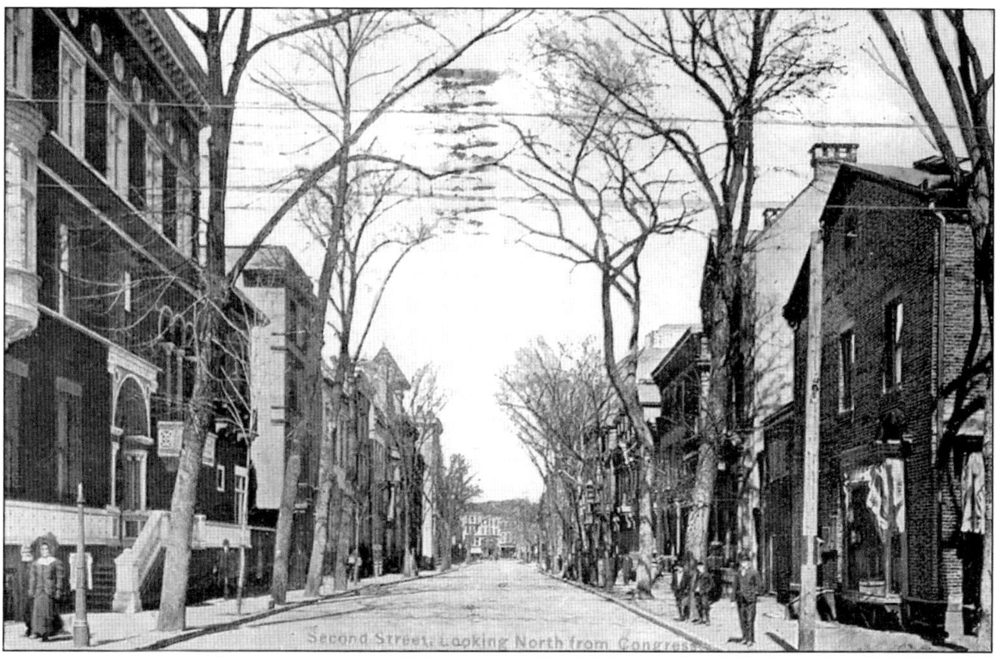

SECOND STREET, LOOKING NORTH. The folks in this postal seem to be posing for the photographer. If you look closely, you can see the roof of the Troy Music Hall in the middle of the block on the right.

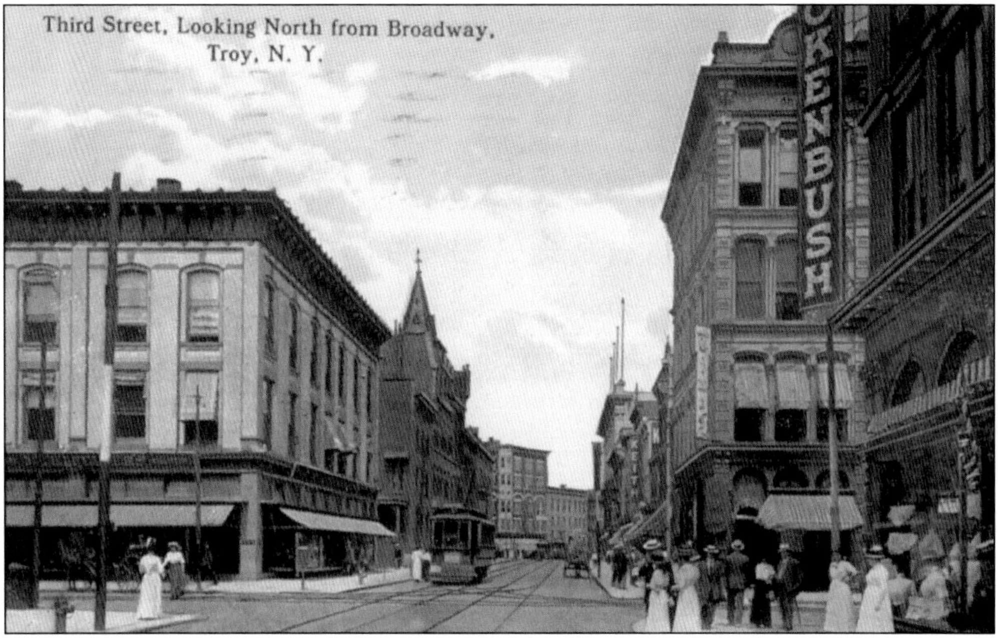

"THIRD STREET, LOOKING NORTH FROM BROADWAY." Notice Quackenbush's, on the right.

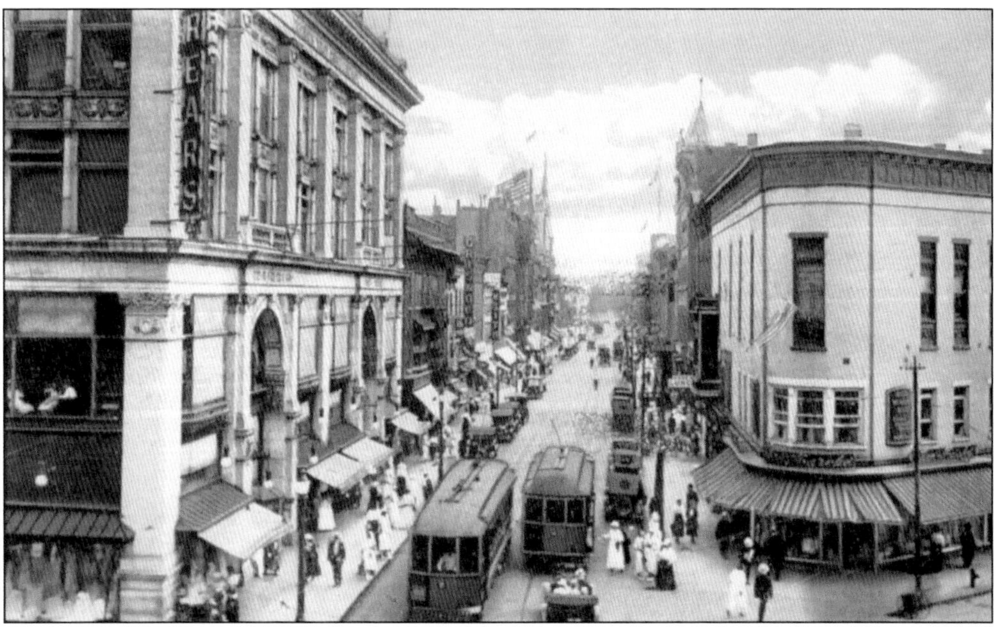

"THIRD STREET, TROY, N.Y." This postcard, looking south on Third Street, shows the hustle and bustle of streetcars and people milling about. Frear's department store is on the left, and the Griswold Theater is just down the street.

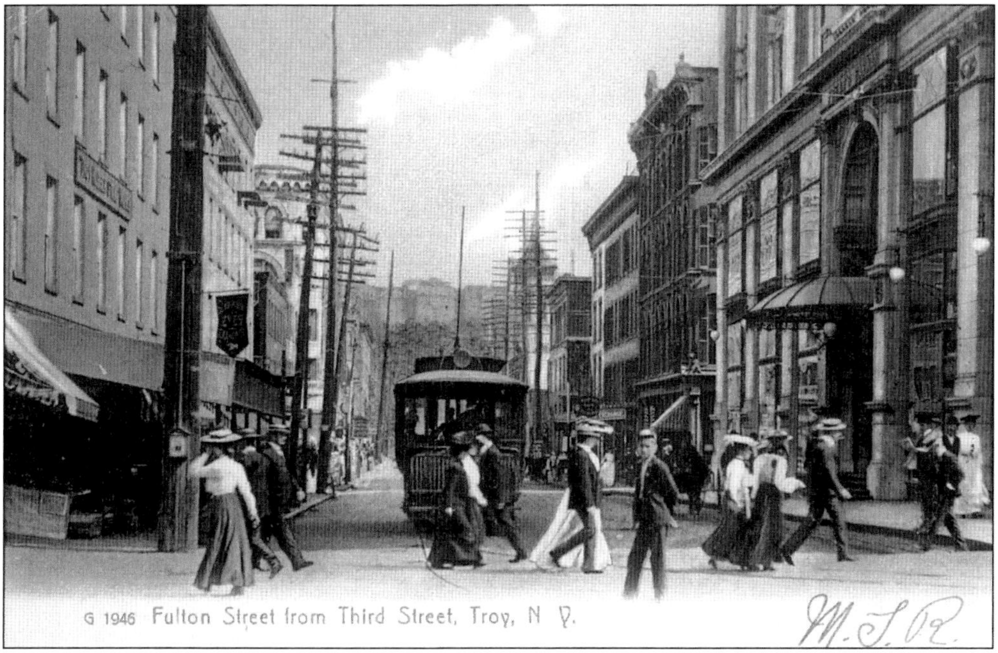

FULTON STREET. These people do not seem to be afraid of the streetcar coming at them. Perhaps they were thinking about the big sale at Frear's, on the right.

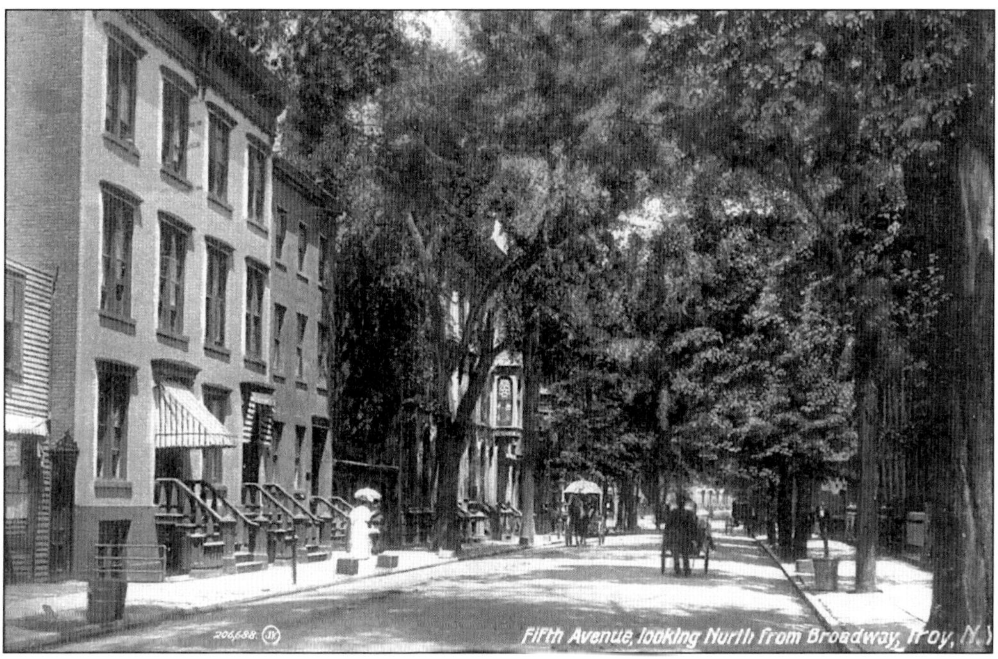

FIFTH AVENUE, LOOKING NORTH. Horse-drawn carriages were a common sight in Troy. Note that on both sides of the street there are stone step-ups that passengers used to get in and out of their coaches.

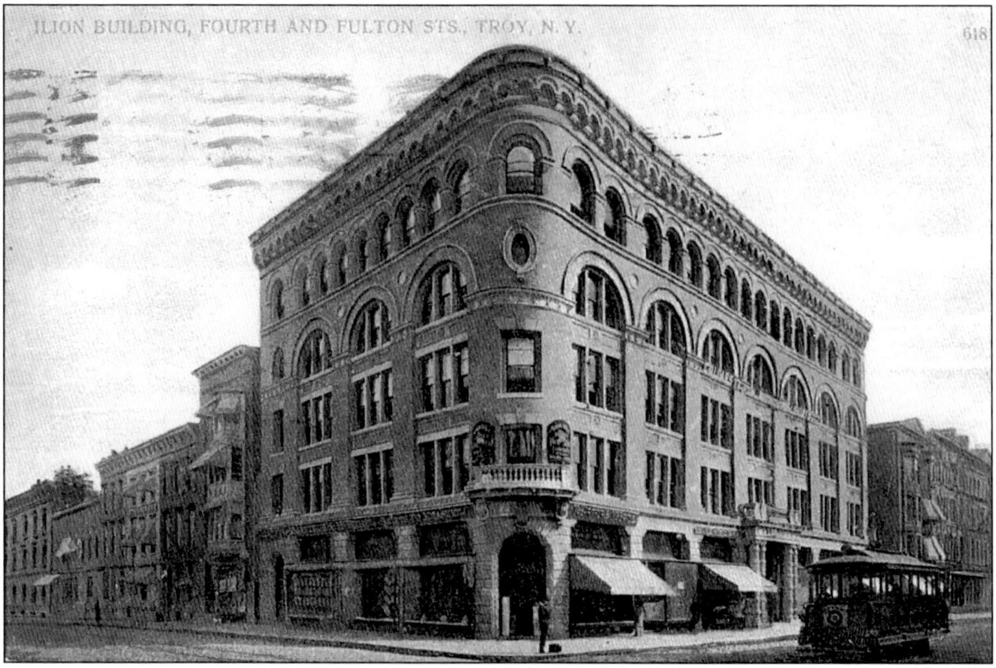

FULTON STREET AND THE ILLIUM BUILDING. On the corner of Fourth and Fulton Streets is the Illium Building, the home of Wagar's (Troy's leading confectionery store), Prudential Incorporated, and the Artistic Shirt Company. Wagar's, established in 1885, was said to have "the very best ice cream in town." The architect for the Illium Building was Frederick M. Cummings. It was built in 1904.

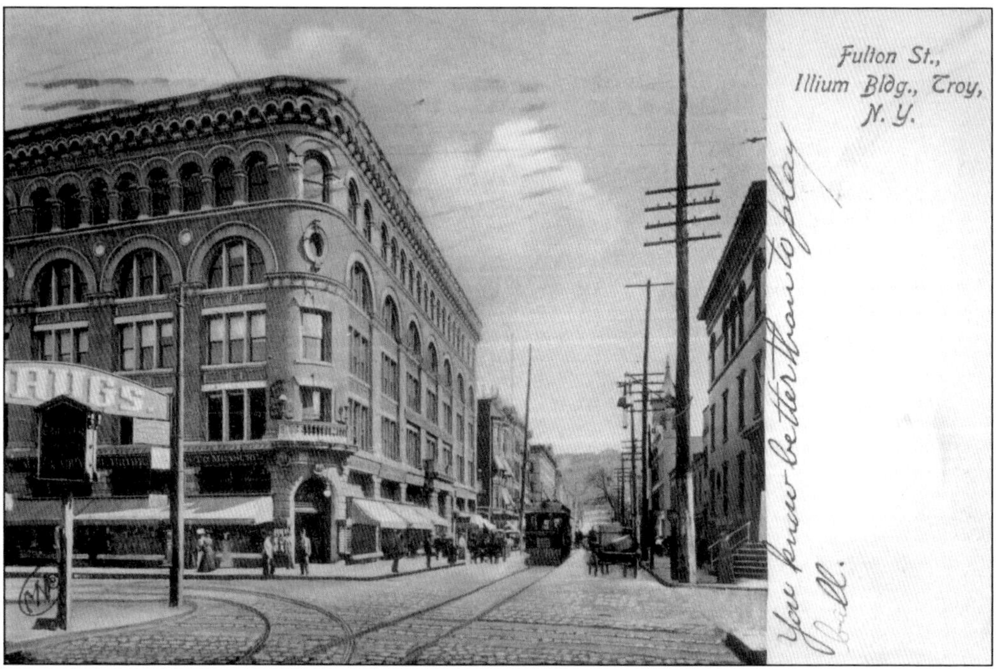

THE SOLDIERS AND SAILORS' MONUMENT. Located at Monument Square, the monument was built for the soldiers and sailors of Rensselaer County in 1891 at a cost of $50,000. The granite rises 93 feet in the air plus the 13-foot bronze figure at the top, which is known as *A Call to Arms.* On the base are historical bronze scenes. The Doring Band played at the dedication of this monument.

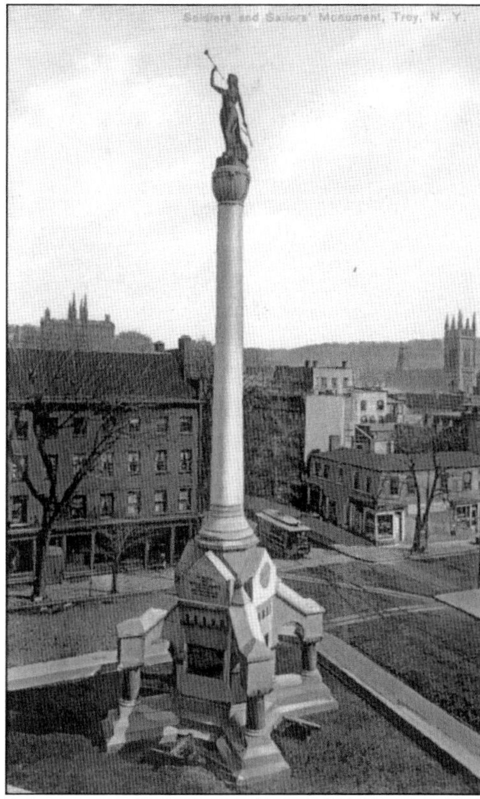

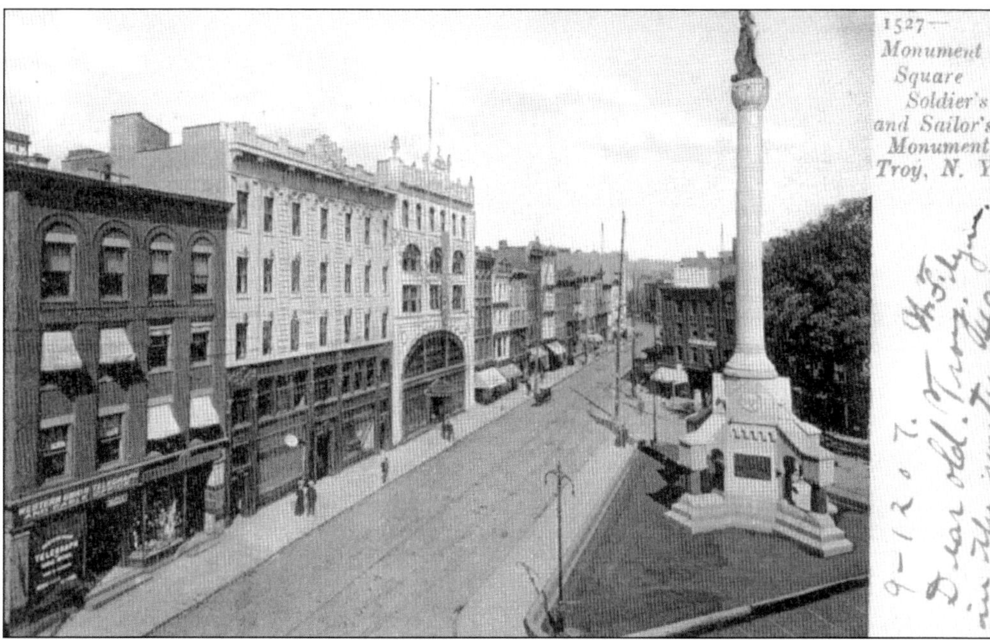

MONUMENT SQUARE. Seen on the left is Western Union along with R.C. Reynolds in the McCarthy Building. Peter McCarthy built the building in 1883. R.C. Reynolds, "where a visit requires no obligation," claimed to have everything for the home, including furniture, rugs, and draperies.

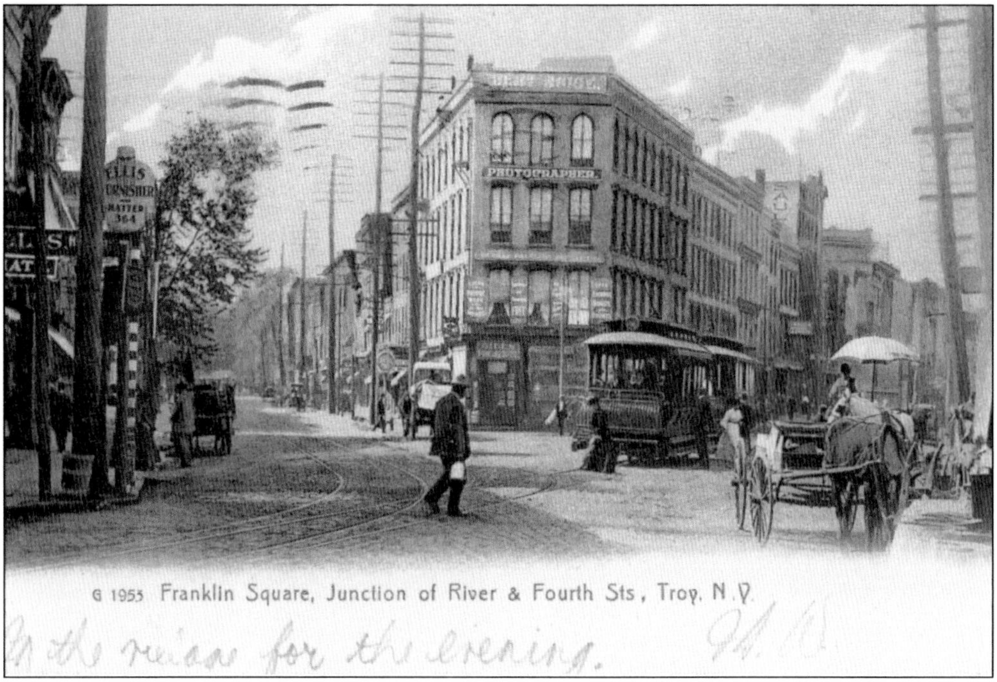

FRANKLIN SQUARE. Bert Boice's studio was located in the Flat Iron Building. He was an expert photographer of his time and, since 1895, was well known throughout the city.

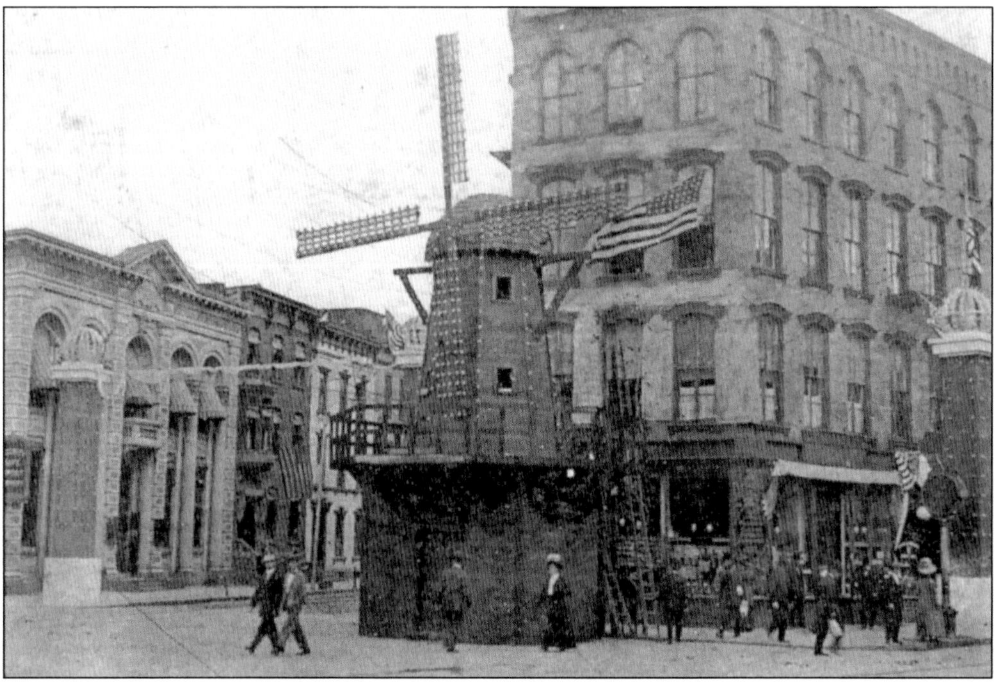

"THE OLD DUTCH WINDMILL AT FRANKLIN SQUARE." In this view, there is a celebration of Troy's Dutch heritage. They pulled out all the stops for the Hudson-Fulton Celebration.

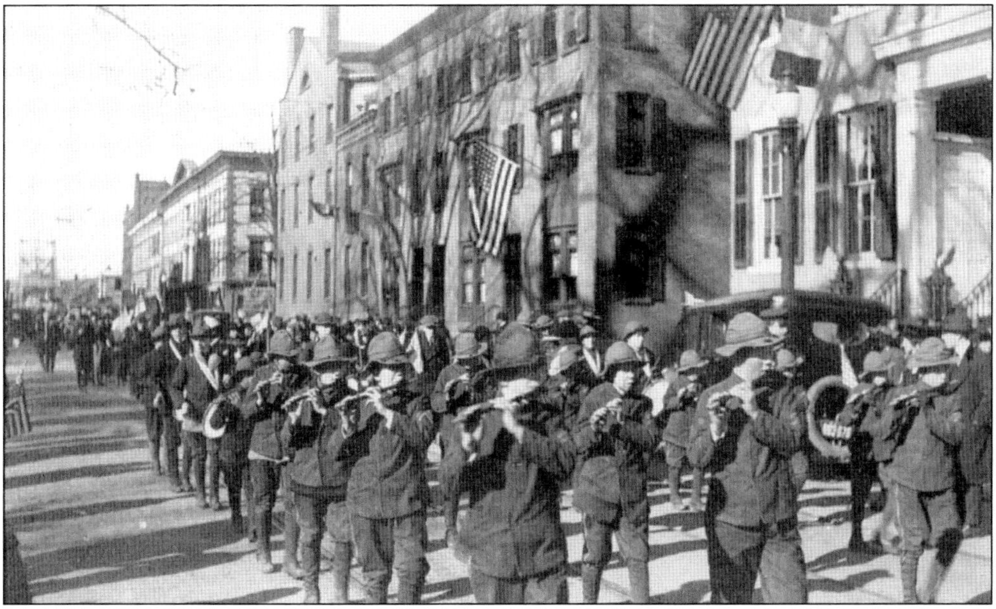

TIME FOR A PARADE. This parade is in celebration of the end of World War I. From St. Patrick's Day to Flag Day, parades are always popular in Troy.

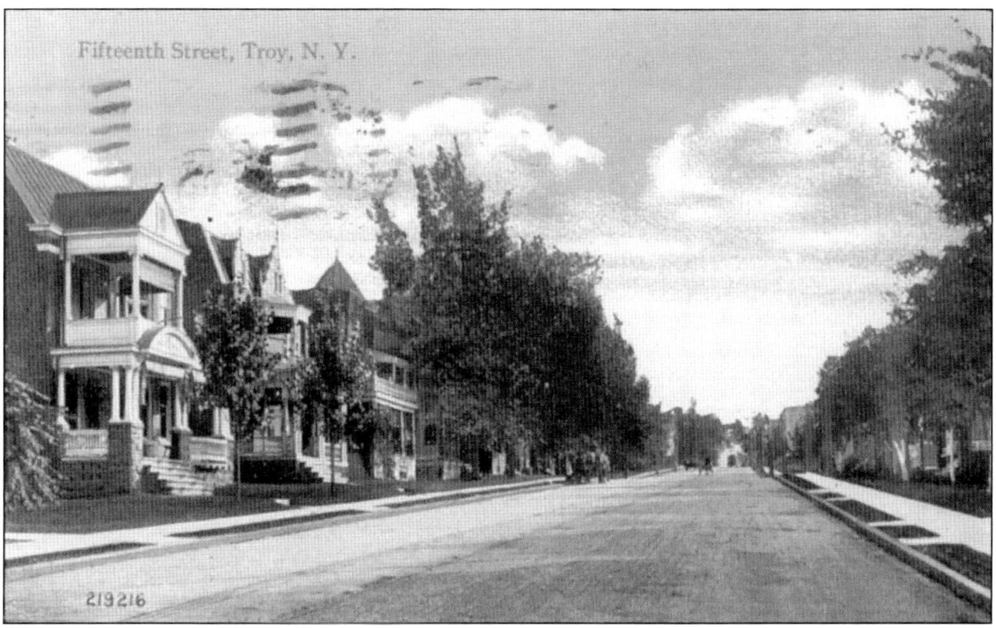

FIFTEENTH STREET. No parking problems here. Except for a few teams of horses, Fifteenth Street was vacant the day this view was taken in 1915. It is much busier today.

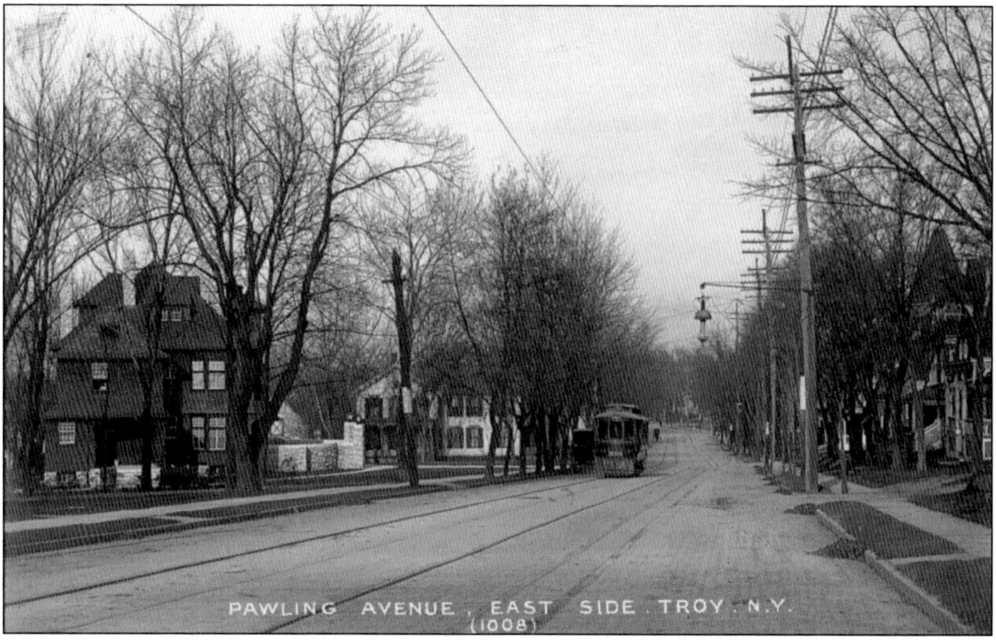

"PAWLING AVENUE, EAST SIDE." A streetcar traveling up Pawling Avenue was not an unusual site in the early 1900s.

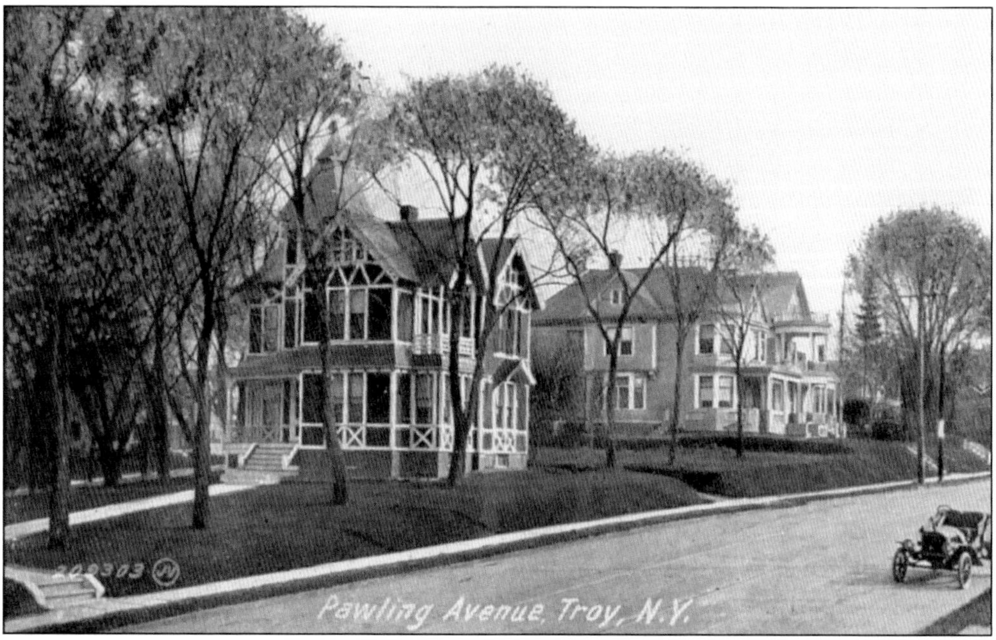

PAWLING AVENUE. Seen in this postcard is Pawling Avenue, with its small mansion-like homes lining the street.

Four

Taking Care of Business

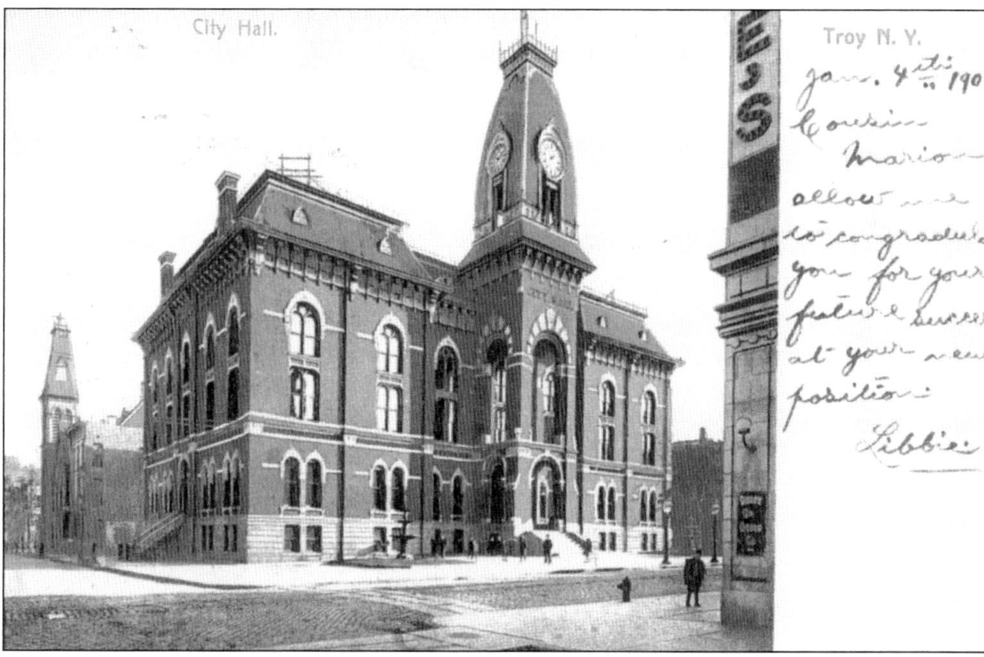

City Hall. Troy's former city hall was on the corner of Third and State Streets. It was built of Philadelphia pressed brick in 1876. The building was home to the Common Council as well as the mayor's office. The cost to build it was $300,000. City hall burned down in 1938. Today, it is the site of Barker Park, which was built in 1938.

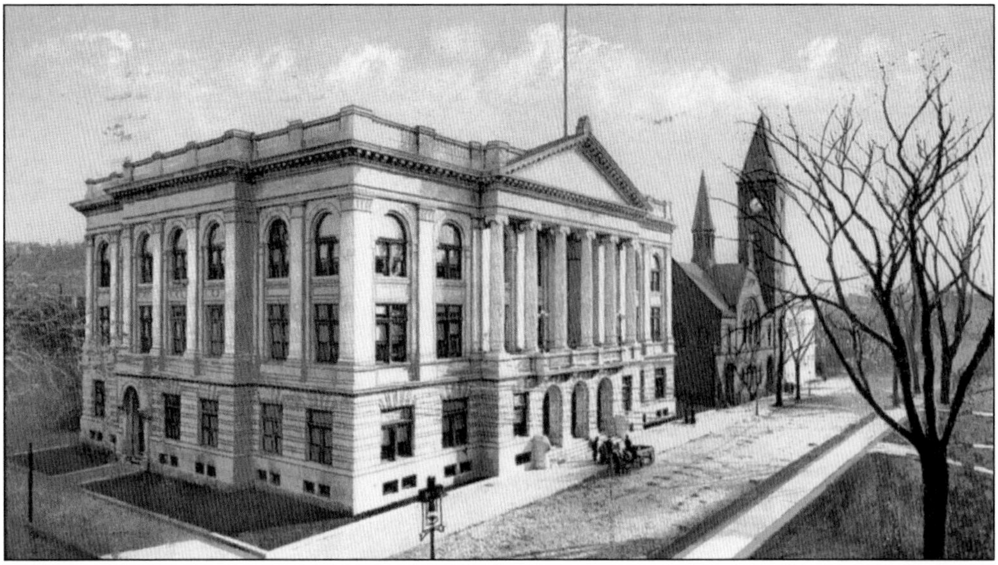

THE COURTHOUSE. The Rensselaer County Court House is located at the corner of Second and Congress Streets, just across from Seminary Park. It was built in 1898 at a cost of $350,000. Today, it looks much the same, with its stately lions guarding the entrance.

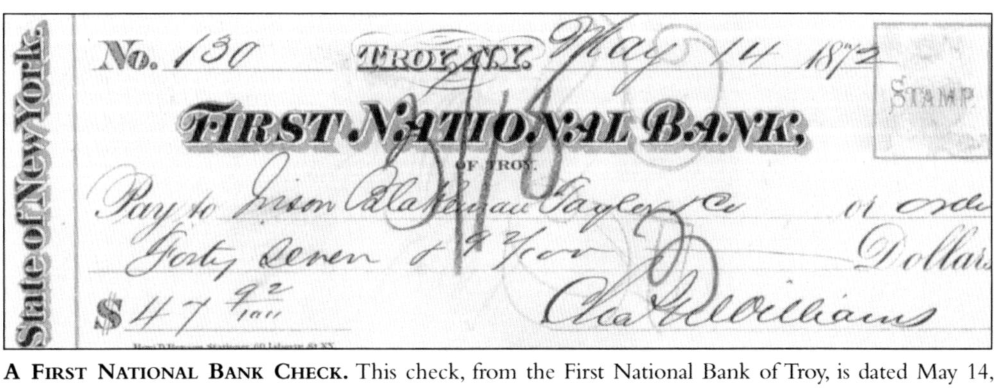

A FIRST NATIONAL BANK CHECK. This check, from the First National Bank of Troy, is dated May 14, 1872. The bank opened for business at 218 River Street in 1864. Shortly after, it moved to 15 First Street. The bank was taken over by the National Bank of Troy in 1883.

THE TROY POST OFFICE. The old Troy post office was on the corner of Fourth and Broadway. It was built in 1894 at a cost of $500,000.

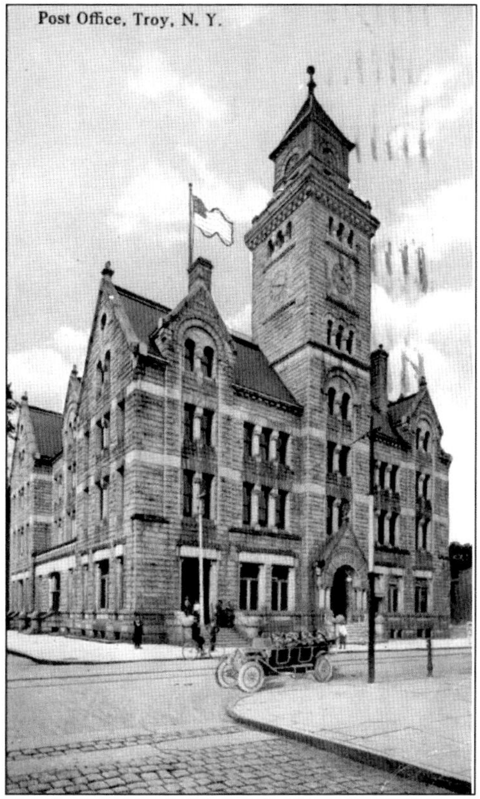

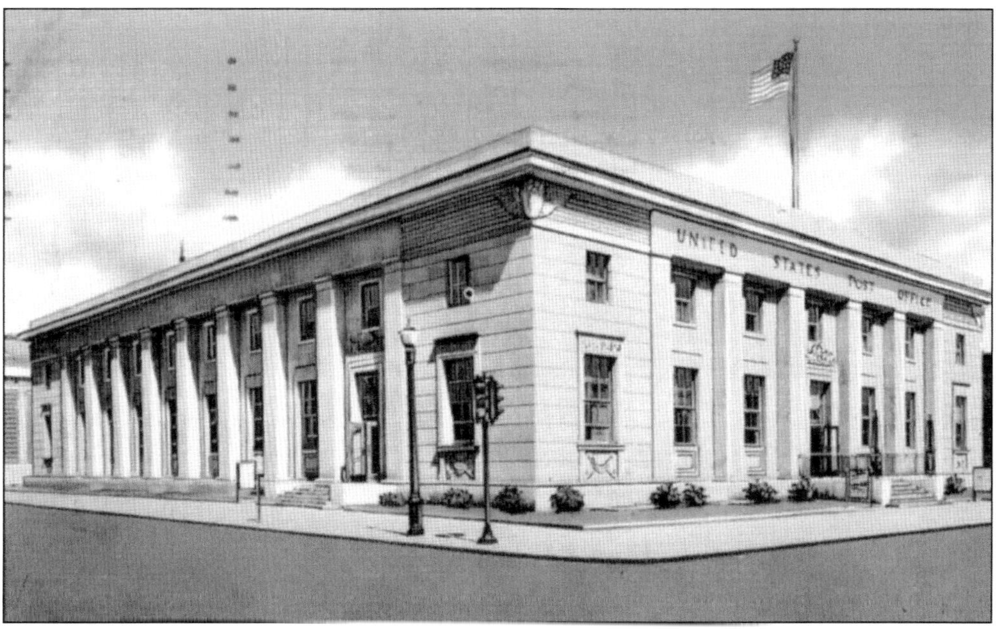

THE NEW POST OFFICE. The new post office on Broadway was built between 1936 and 1938 in the Classical Revival style.

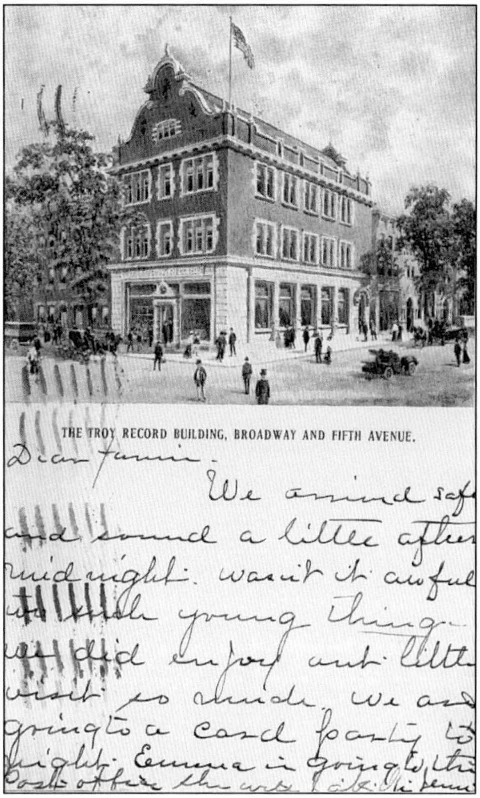

THE TROY RECORD BUILDING. Located at Broadway and Fifth, the Troy Record Building was built in 1909. In 1935, the Troy Record merged with the Troy Times.

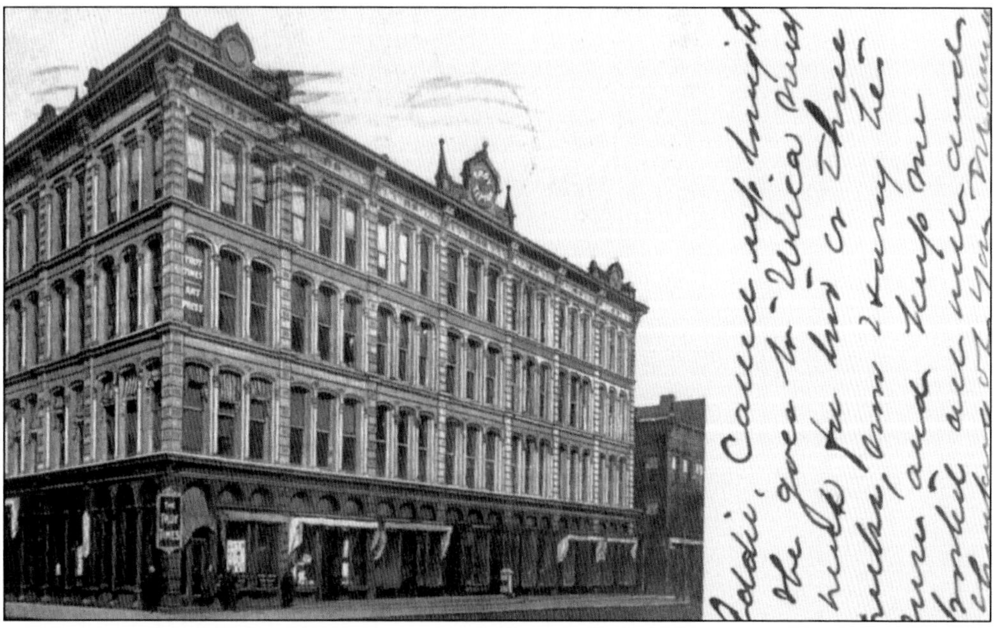

THE TROY TIMES BUILDING. This building was located at the intersection of Broadway and Third Street. It has been said that at the turn of the century, a man actually scaled the corner of this building, using only his hands and feet. There were many newspapers in Troy over the years, with names like the *Troy American,* the *Trojan,* and the *Troy Daily Herald*.

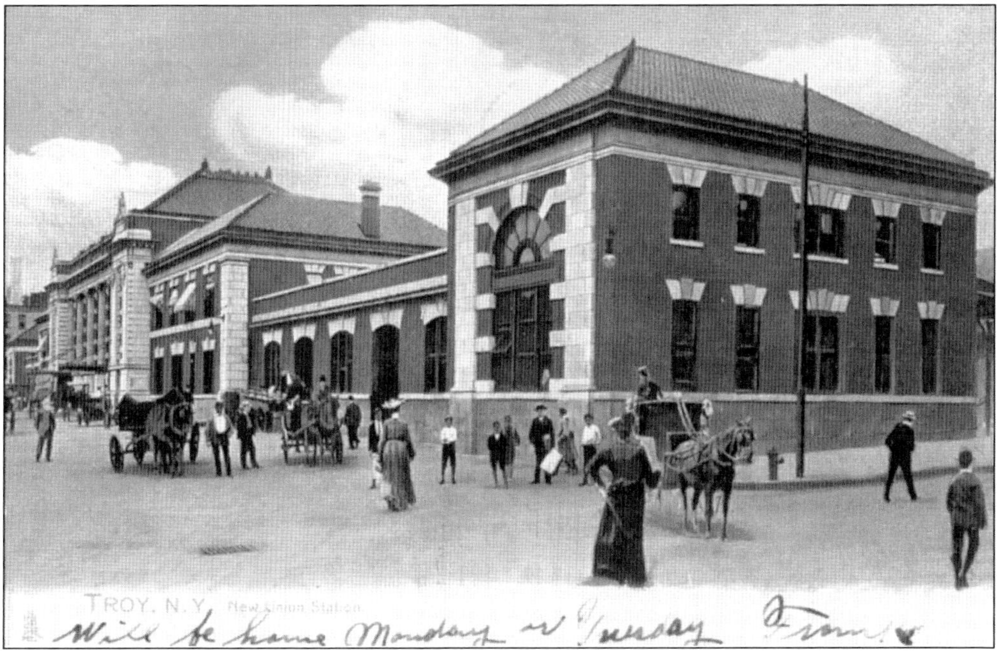

NEW UNION STATION. The New Union Station opened in 1903 on Sixth Avenue. The station was built with the combined effort of the Boston & Maine, New York Central, and the Delaware & Hudson companies at a cost of $300,000. Inside the station was a shoeshine and a newspaper stand. Train announcers called the arrivals and departures without the use of loudspeakers. Unfortunately, with the demise of the railroads, this beautiful building was razed in 1958. Some of the railroads of the past were the Rensselaer & Saratoga, Schenectady & Troy, Troy & Greenbush, Troy & Boston, and the Troy Union Railroad.

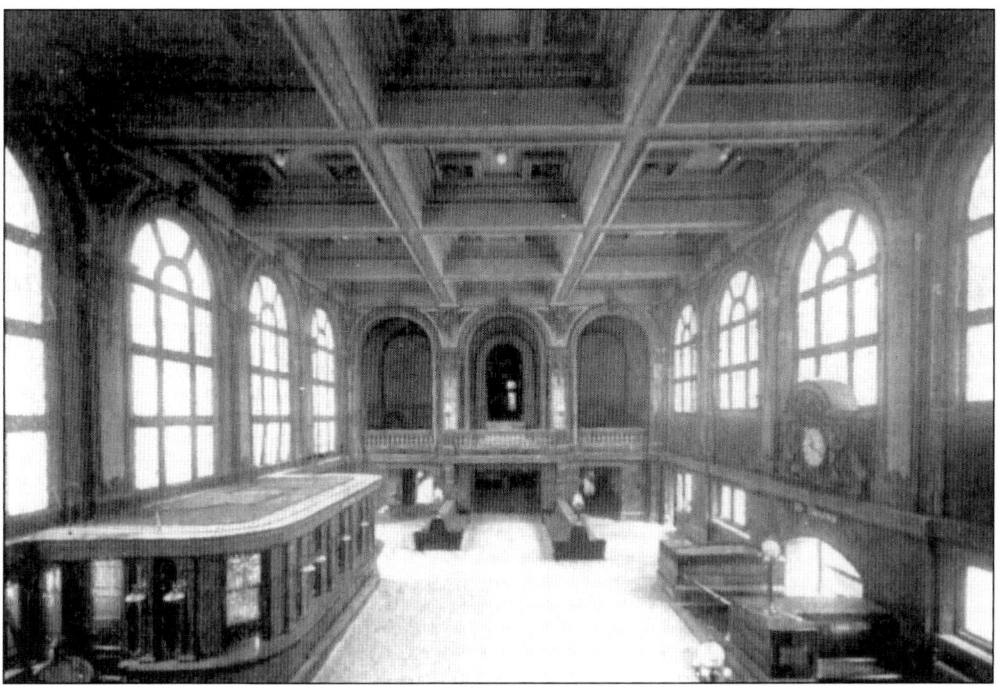

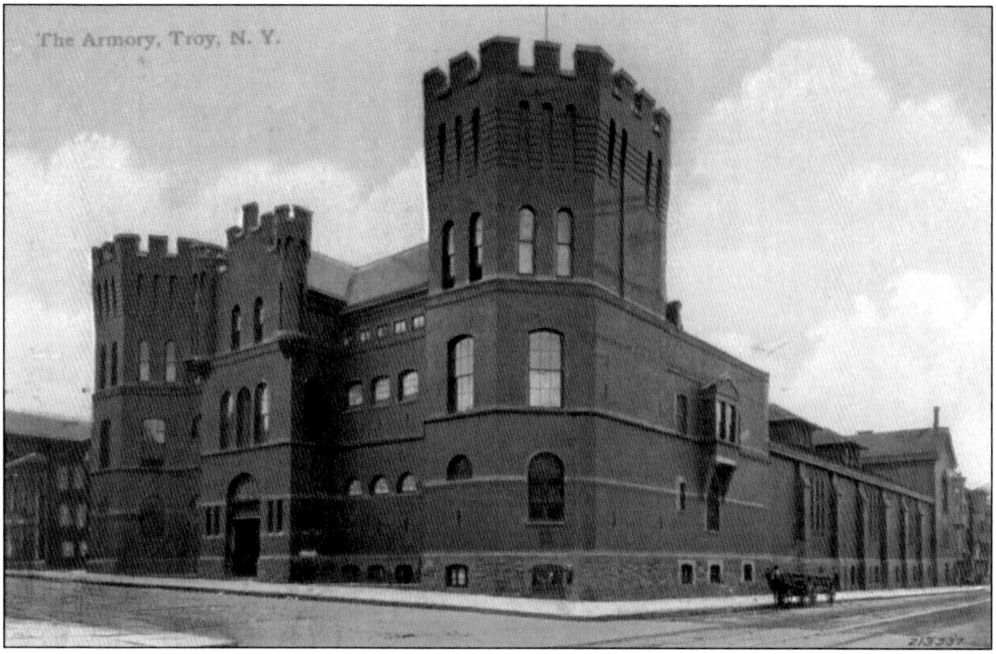

THE ARMORY. Located at Ferry and First Streets, the state armory was built in 1886 of brick and iron. The cost was a mere $240,000. It was destroyed by fire in 1917.

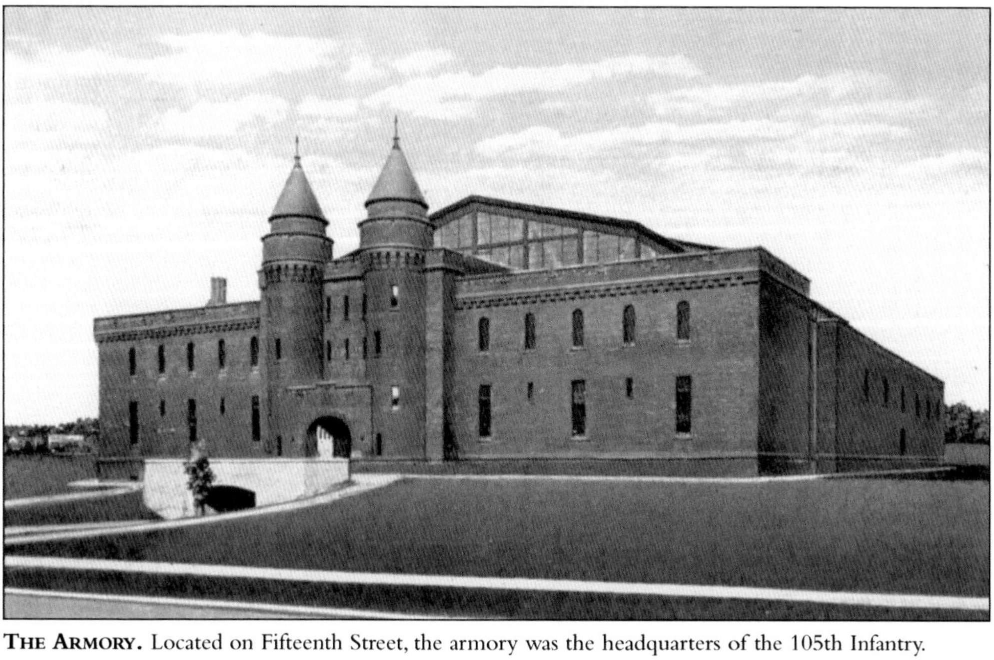

THE ARMORY. Located on Fifteenth Street, the armory was the headquarters of the 105th Infantry.

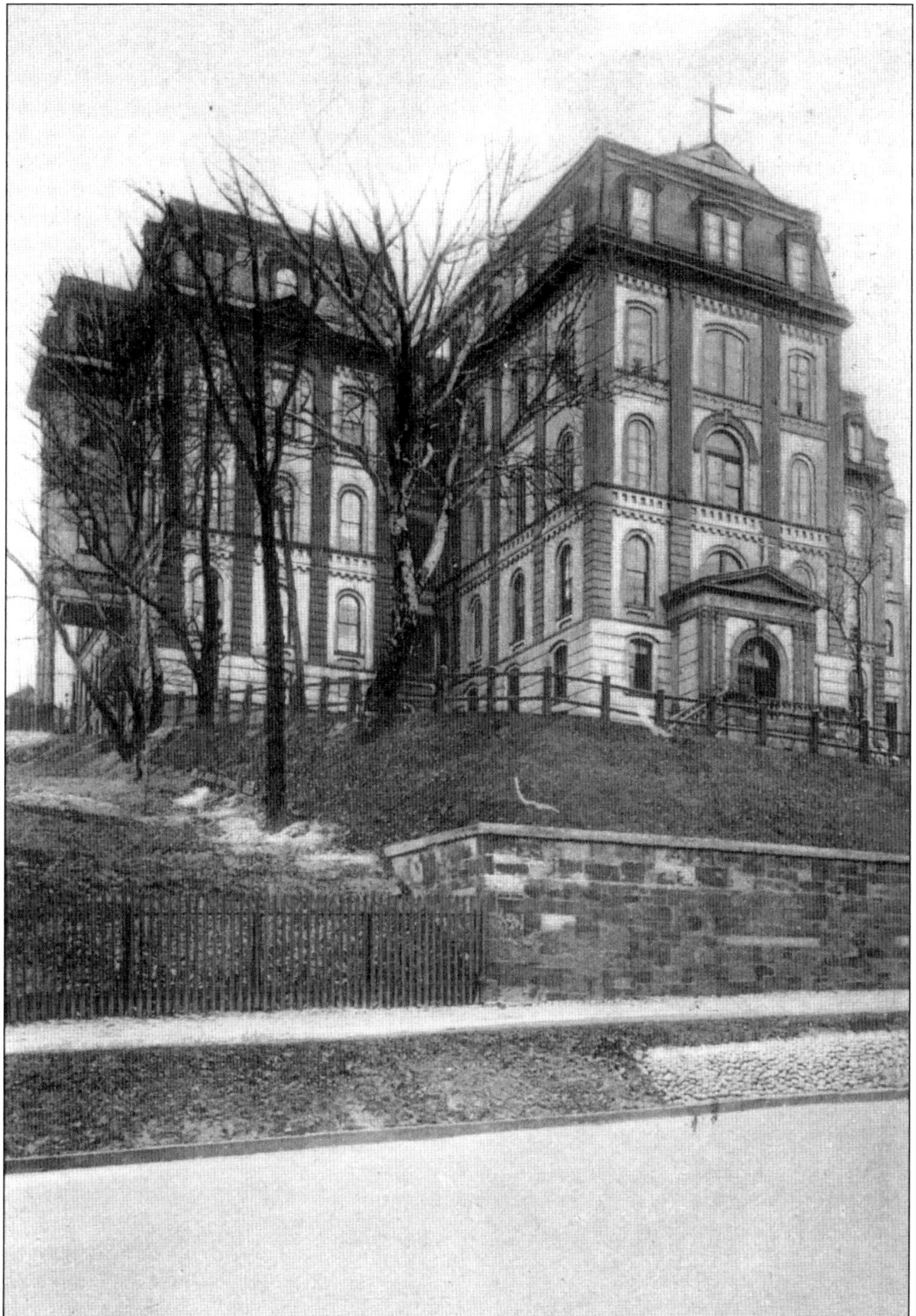

TROY HOSPITAL. In 1868, this three-story building was built on Eighth Street in the Second Empire style. Years later, the hospital moved. In 1923, Catholic Central High School started classes here. In 1953, the school moved to Lansingburgh. Today, the building is owned by Rensselaer Polytechnic Institute.

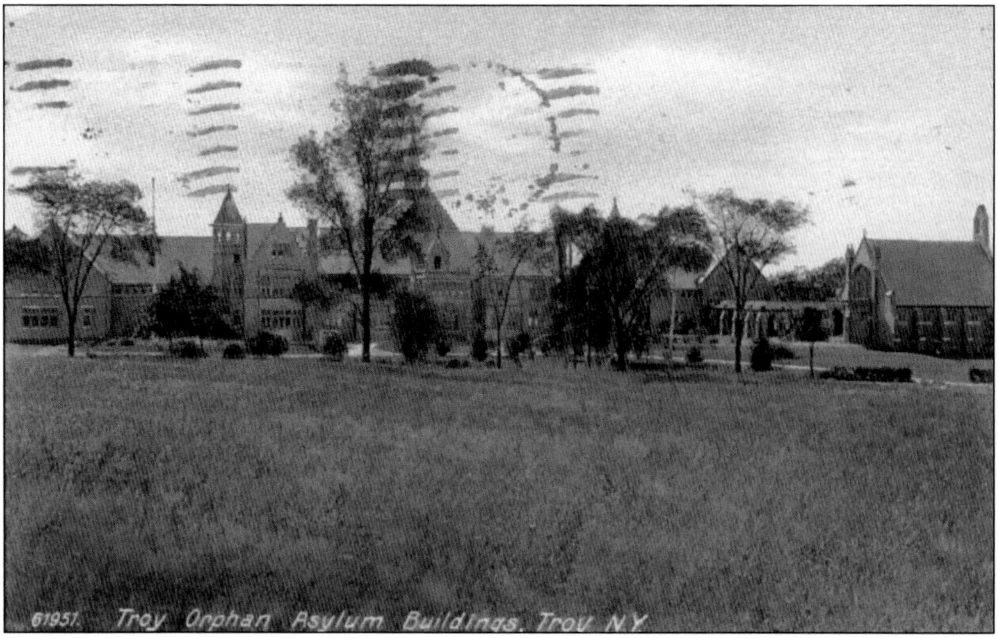

THE TROY ORPHAN ASYLUM. The Troy Orphan Asylum moved to Spring Avenue in 1893.

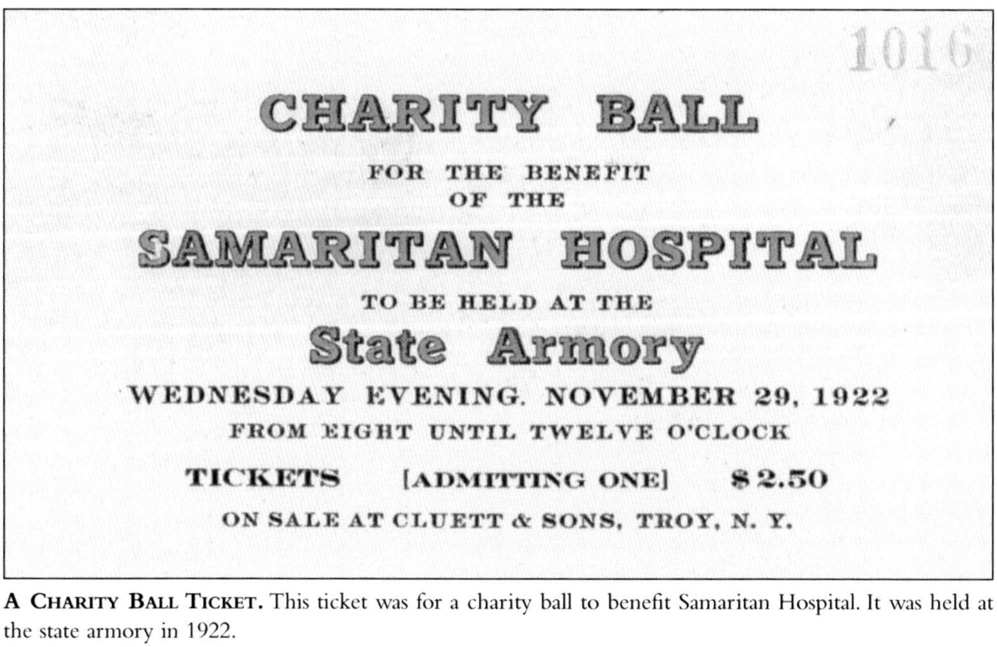

1016

CHARITY BALL

FOR THE BENEFIT
OF THE

SAMARITAN HOSPITAL

TO BE HELD AT THE

State Armory

WEDNESDAY EVENING, NOVEMBER 29, 1922

FROM EIGHT UNTIL TWELVE O'CLOCK

TICKETS [ADMITTING ONE] $2.50

ON SALE AT CLUETT & SONS, TROY, N. Y.

A CHARITY BALL TICKET. This ticket was for a charity ball to benefit Samaritan Hospital. It was held at the state armory in 1922.

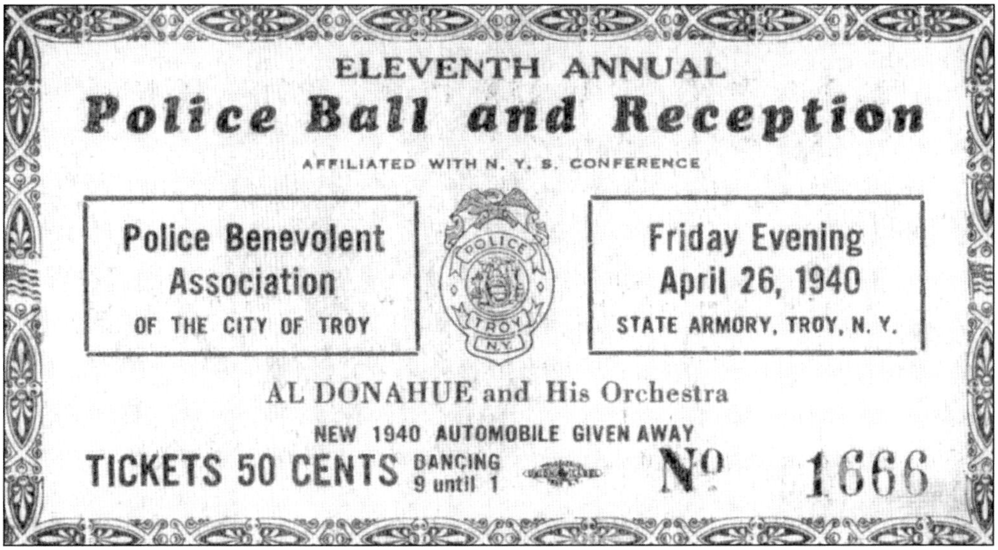

The Eleventh Annual Police Ball. This ticket is for the 1940 Police Ball and Reception, featuring Al Donahue and his orchestra. A new automobile was given away from Bart Motor Sales.

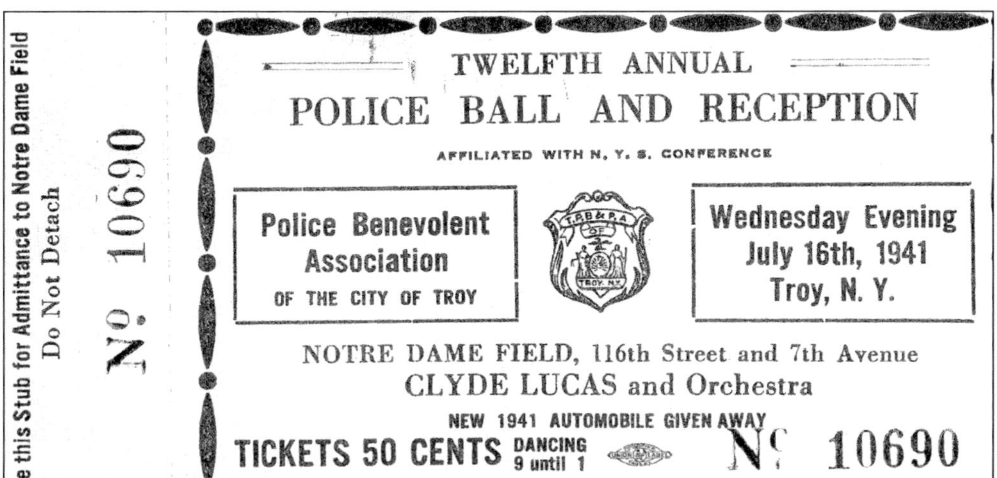

The Twelfth Annual Police Ball. The price of admission to the police ball never changed, but the band did. The 1941 ball featured Clyde Lucas and his orchestra with an automobile giveaway from Don Cowley Incorporated.

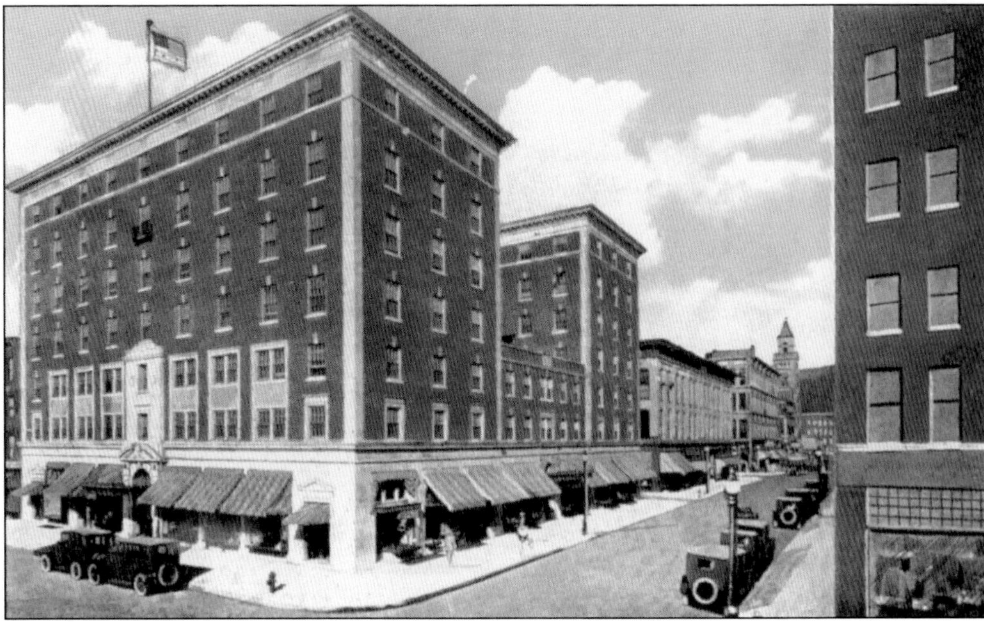

THE HENDRICK HUDSON HOTEL. The Hendrick Hudson Hotel opened in 1926 with 165 rooms, a dining and grill room, a ballroom, and various stores. Some of the stores were Allen's Bookstore, the Half Moon Café & Tea Room, and Ferguson's Men's Shop. The Troy Club was once located here after the original club burned down. Richard and Pat Nixon spent a night here in 1960.

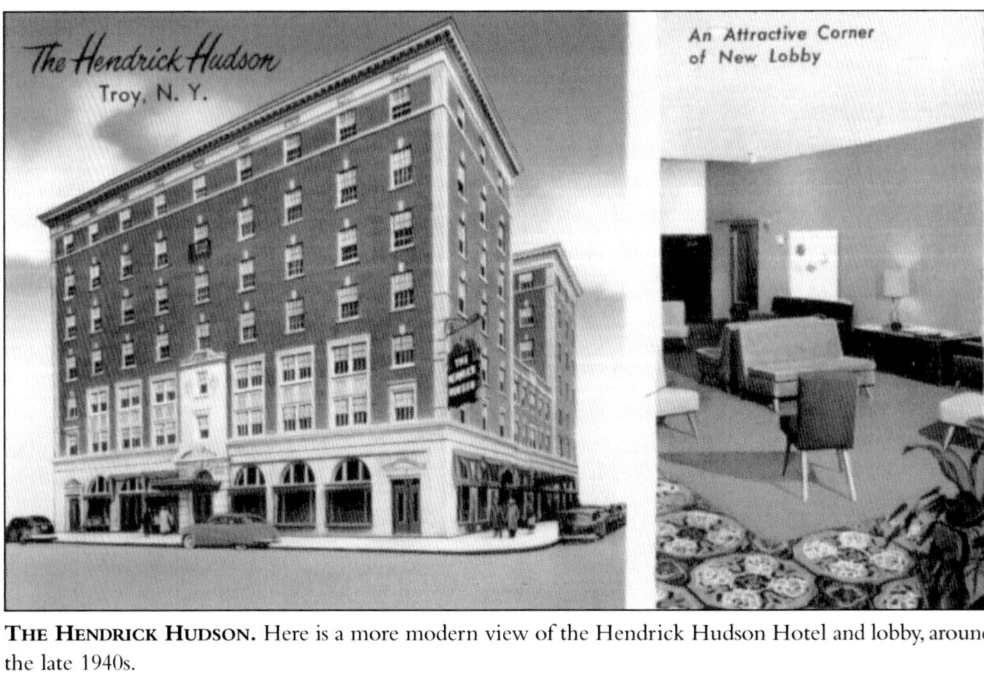

THE HENDRICK HUDSON. Here is a more modern view of the Hendrick Hudson Hotel and lobby, around the late 1940s.

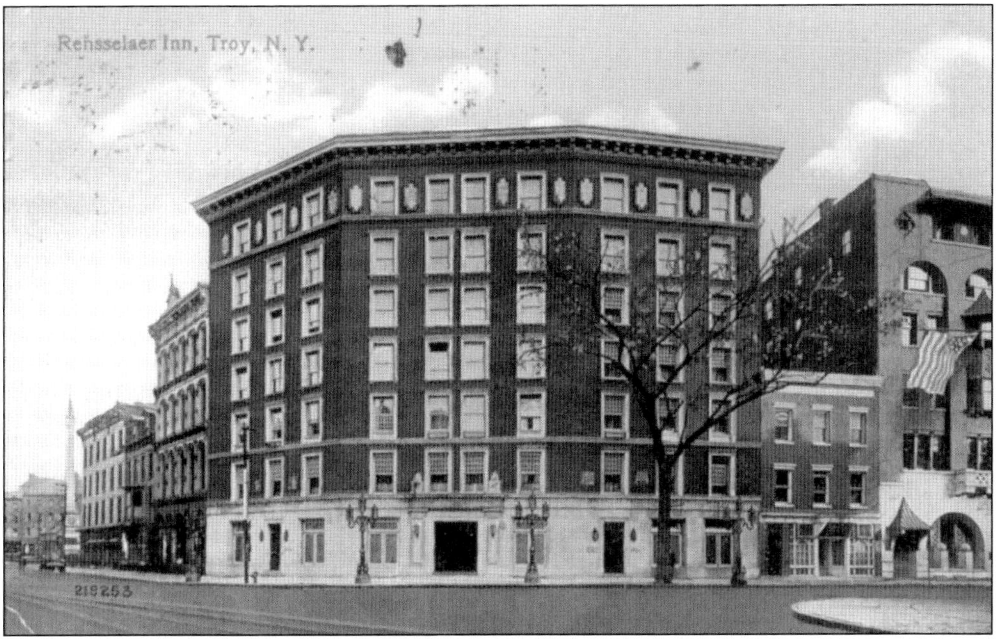

THE RENSSELAER INN. This inn was built on the site of the old Troy House. The cost of a room started at $1 and went up from there. The Rensselaer Inn had everything you could ask for in a hotel, including a dining room and a barbershop. Today, the building is an apartment complex.

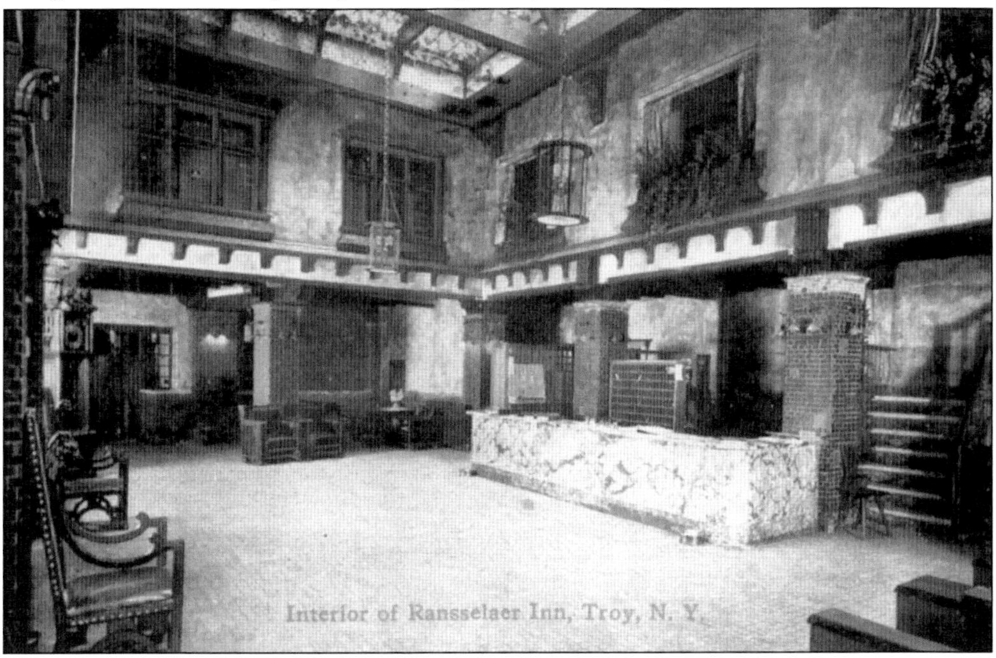

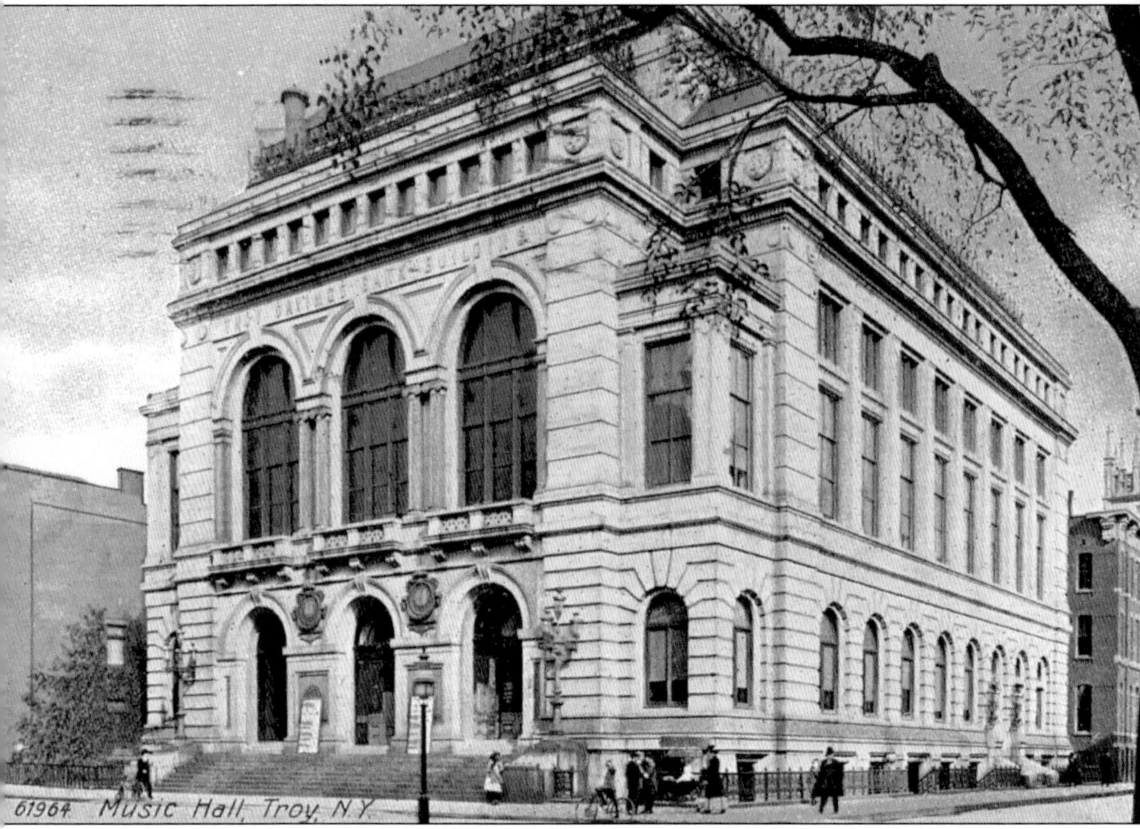

THE MUSIC HALL. The Troy Savings Bank Music Hall was designed by George Browne Post and was built between 1871 and 1875 in the Second Empire style with a French Renaissance interior. Many world-famous artists have performed here, from Vladimir Horowitz to Yo Yo Ma. It is one of Troy's most celebrated treasures.

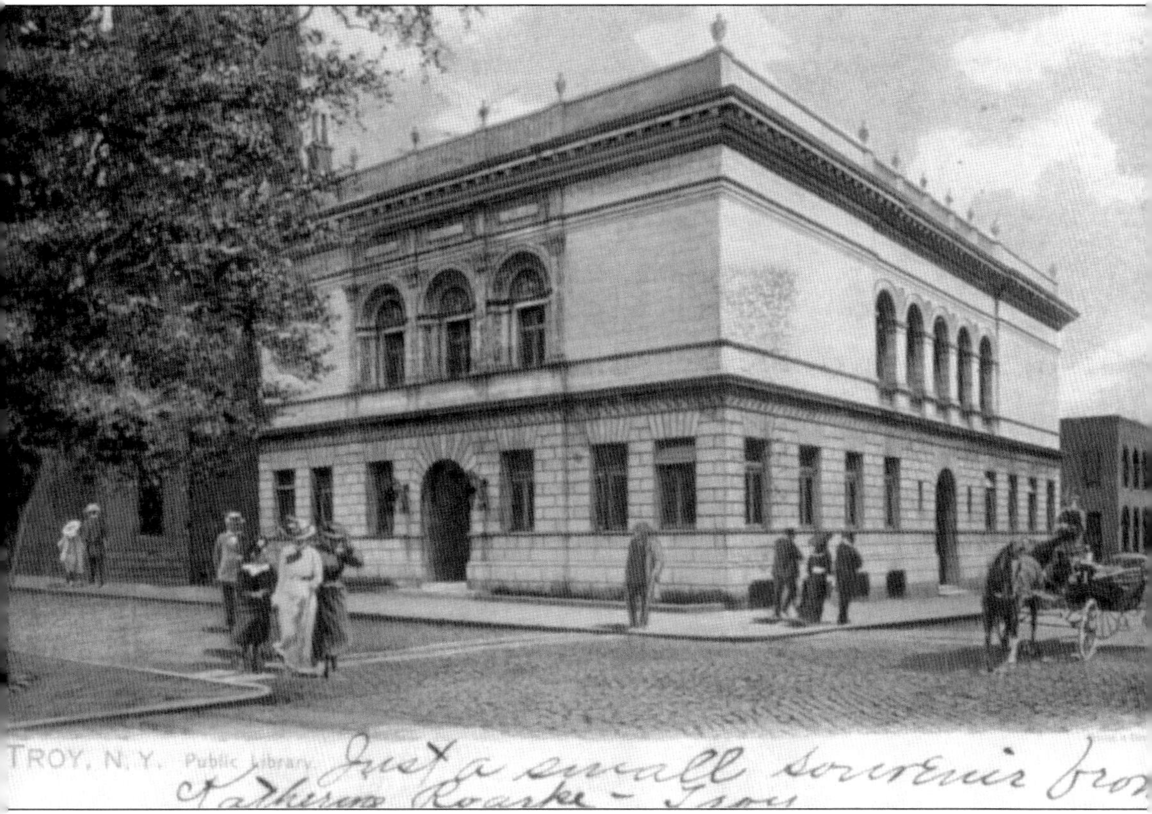

The Troy Public Library. The William Howard Hart Memorial Library is located at 100 Second Street, just across from Russell Sage College. Mary E. Hart made the gift of the library in the memory of her husband. Years later, the entrance to the Library was used in the film *Ironweed*. William Kennedy, an Albany local, won the Pulitzer Prize for the book. The building was designed by Barney & Chapman and was built between 1896 and 1897 in the Italian Renaissance style. Frederick Wilson designed a Tiffany window that sits above the circulation desk in the library.

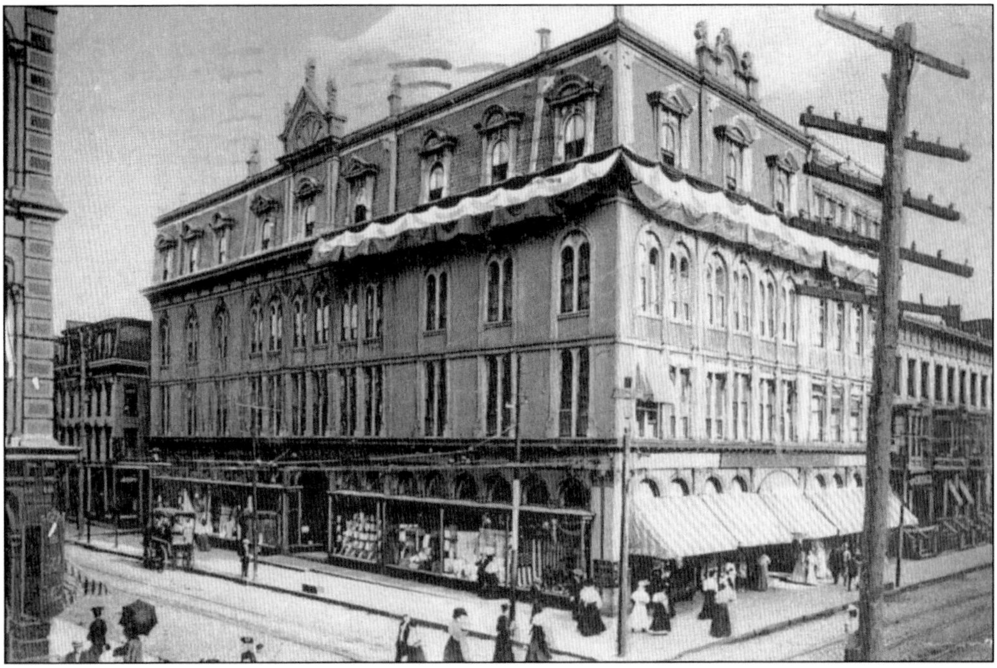

G.V.S. QUACKENBUSH & COMPANY. Gerrit Van Schaick Quackenbush went into the dry goods business in 1824 on River Street. Later the business was moved to Third and Broadway. In its advertising you would see "We give S&H Green Stamps." It went out of business and was replaced by W.T. Grant Company in 1937.

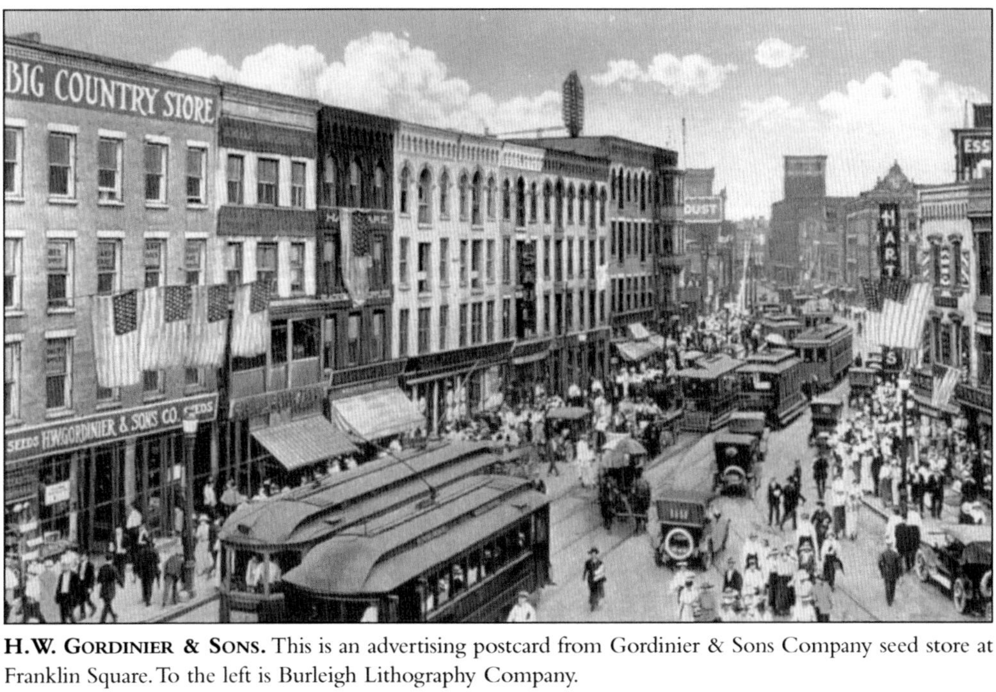

H.W. GORDINIER & SONS. This is an advertising postcard from Gordinier & Sons Company seed store at Franklin Square. To the left is Burleigh Lithography Company.

THE SIM PEIRSONS & COMPANY JEWELRY STORE. In this view we see the Sim Peirsons jewelry store, located in the Cannon Building, with its flag flying high above it. The store had silversmiths on staff. It also sold stationery and fountain pens. For the unusual in gifts, folks liked to shop in the store's dollar department.

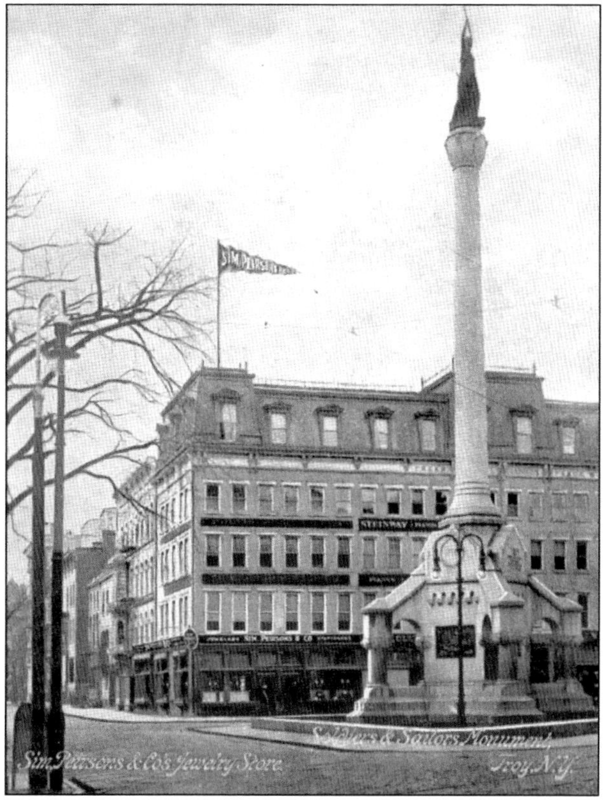

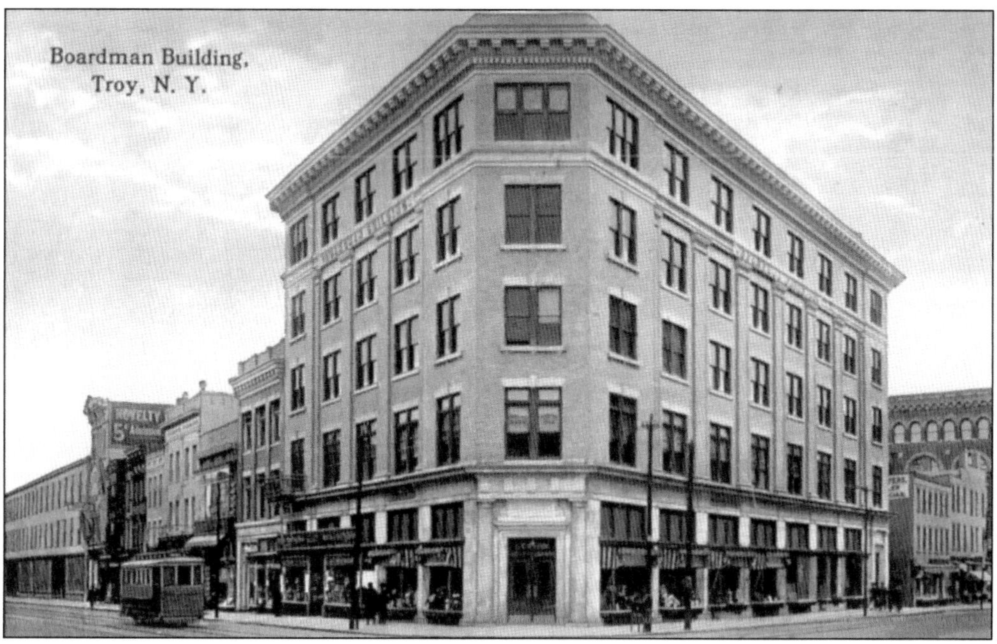

THE BOARDMAN BUILDING. The Boardman Building was located on the corner of River and Fulton Streets. It housed the Troy Business College and many fine shops.

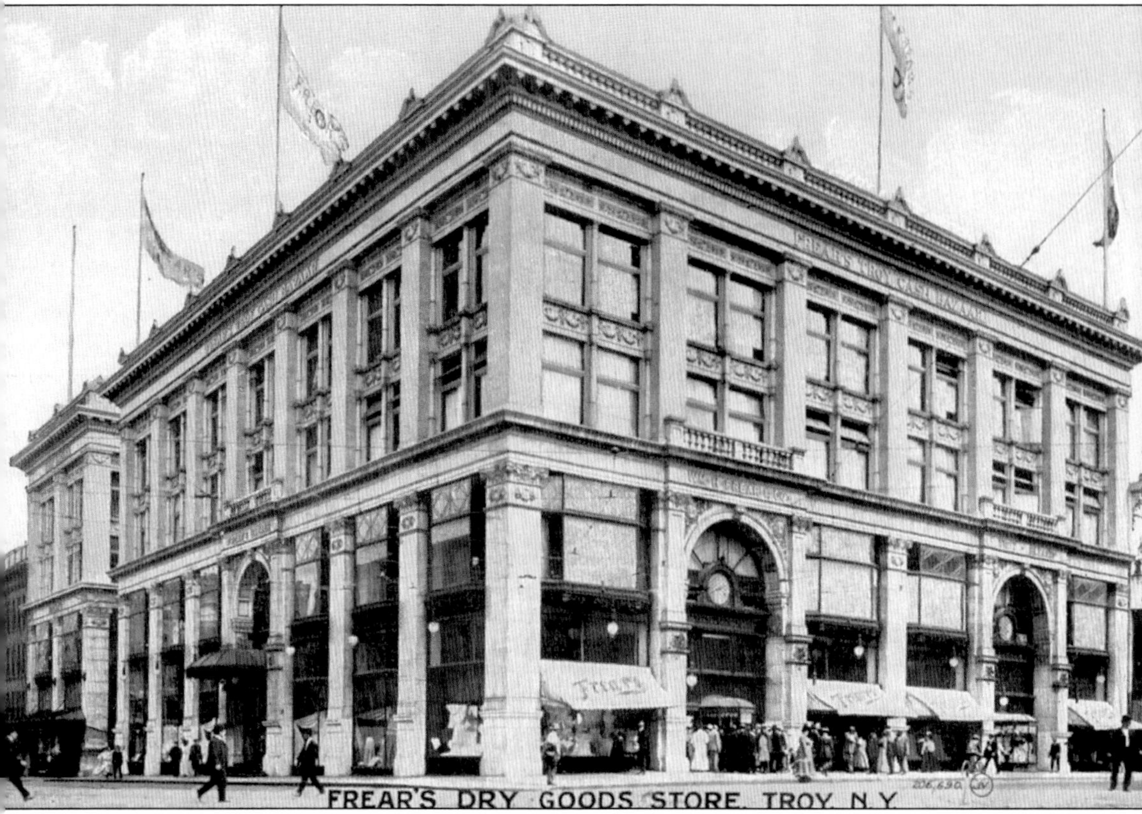

Frear's Dry Goods Store. This magnificent store on the corner of Third and Fulton carried everything you needed. Its first location was in the Cannon Building, just a few blocks away. Frear's claimed to have over 50 departments. Included were a glove, fur, lace, fan, dry goods, and a furniture department, just to name a few. A popular saying was "Meet me at Frear's."

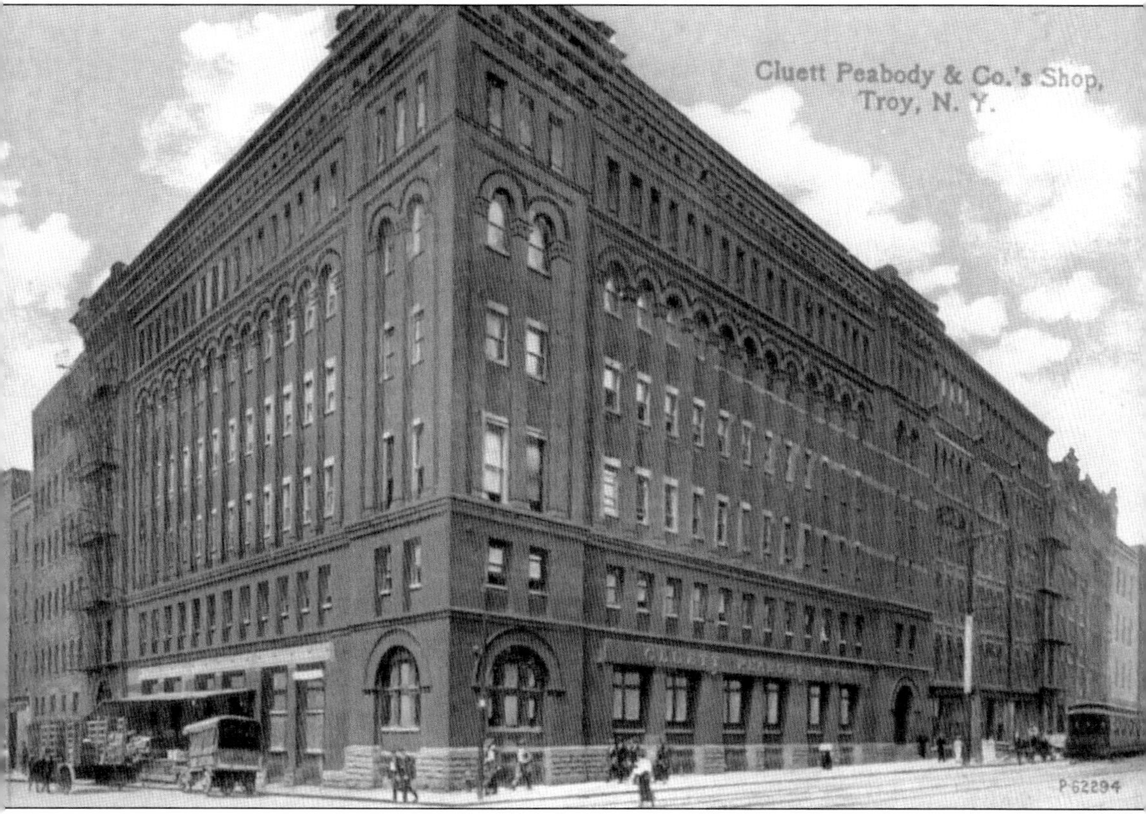

CLUETT PEABODY & COMPANY. Located on River Street, Cluett Peabody & Company made and distributed Arrow shirts and also made the Monarch and Crown collar. The business was started by George Cluett in the 1860s. Cluett Peabody & Company was called the largest manufacturer of its kind in the world. During the war years, they reached their peak with 3,000 employees.

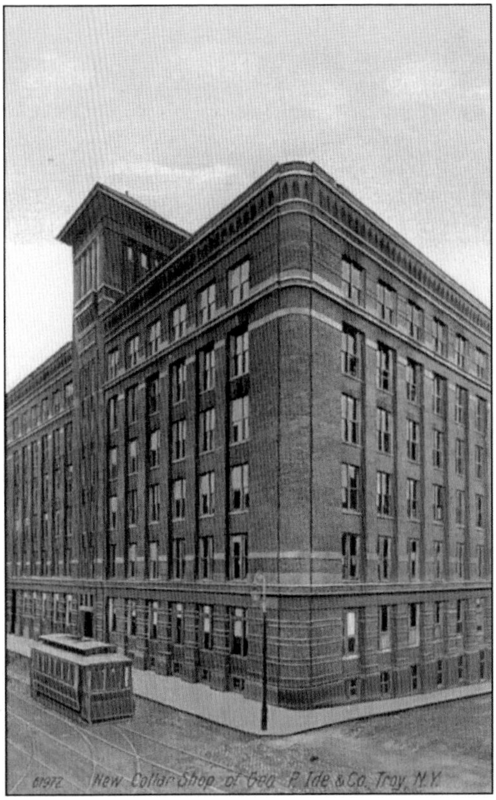

THE NEW COLLAR SHOP. The New Collar Shop of George P. Ide & Company had more than 1,000 employees during its heyday. They manufactured shirt collars, underwear, and pajamas.

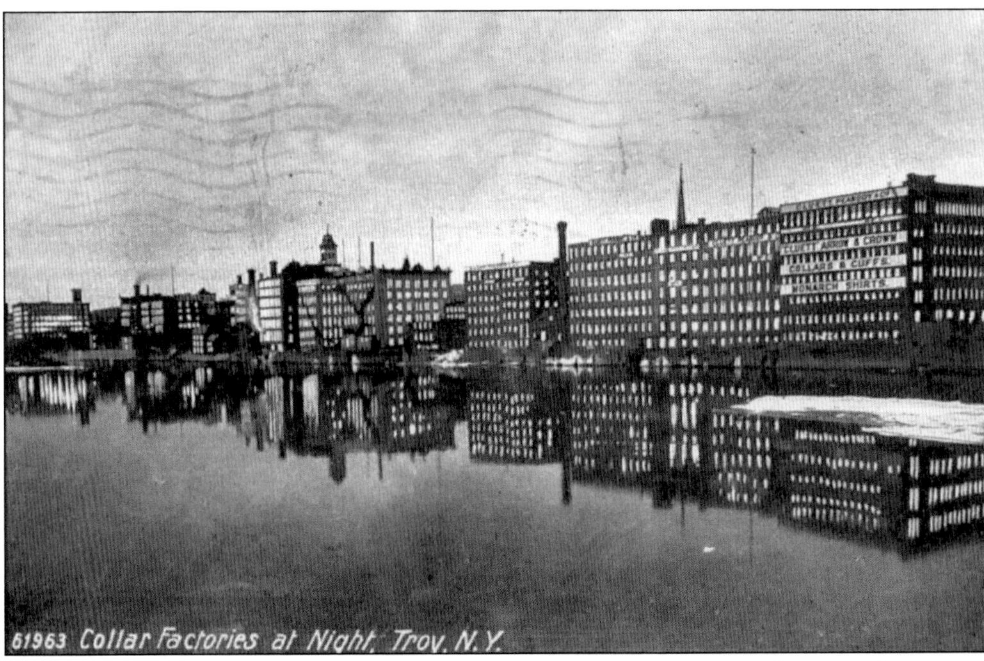

"COLLAR FACTORIES AT NIGHT." Here we see the Cluett Peabody buildings reflecting in the waters of the Hudson.

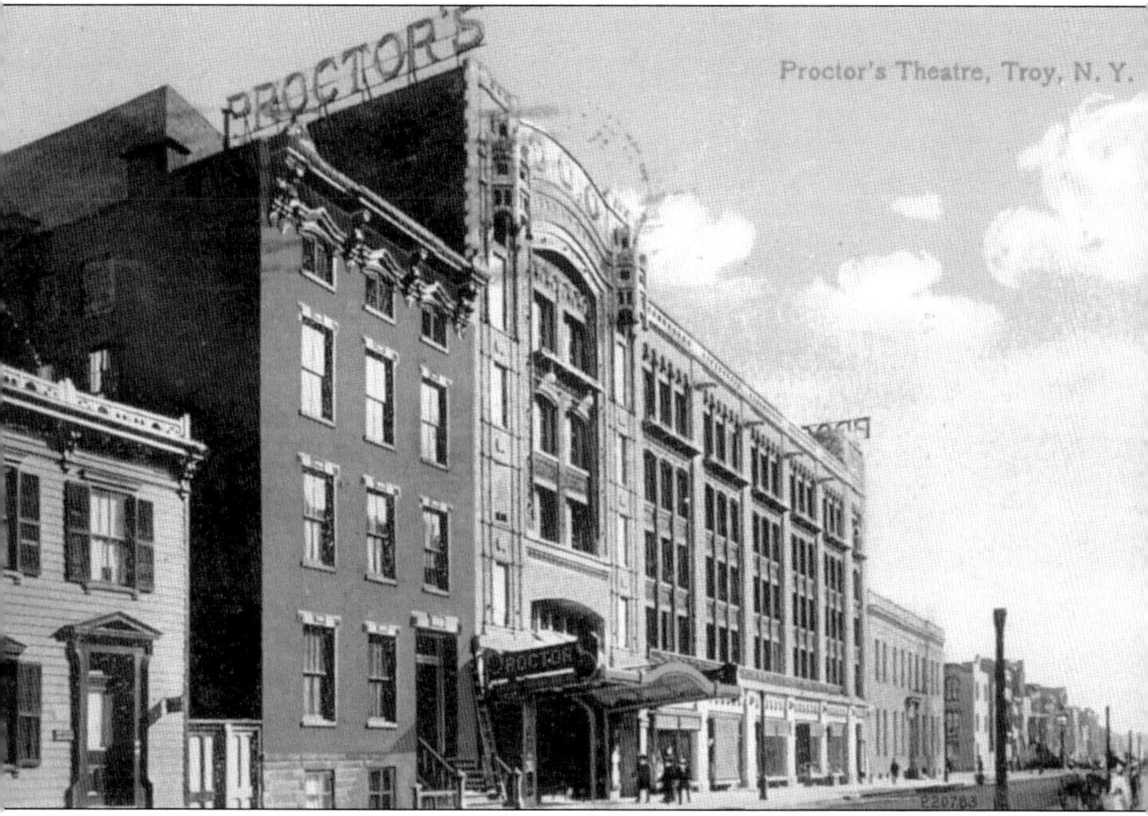

PROCTOR'S THEATRE. The movie theater played an important role in 20th-century Troy. Viewers watched their favorite stars, such as Tom Mix, or newsreels, such as *March of Time*. The theater was also a great place to take a date. This five-story building was built in Gothic style on Fourth Street. It first opened as a Vaudeville theater in 1914 and converted to movies in 1930. Proctor's was one of the many theaters and movie houses in Troy. Some of the others had great names like the Rivoli, the Palace, the American, and the Rose. The original building still stands. Today, Troy is the new Hollywood on the Hudson. In the 1980s, the films *The Bostonians,* with Christopher Reeve, and the Oscar-winning *Ironweed,* with Jack Nicholson and Meryl Streep, were filmed here. In the 1990s, *Scent of a Woman,* starring Al Pacino, and Martin Scorsese's *The Age of Innocence* were also filmed here.

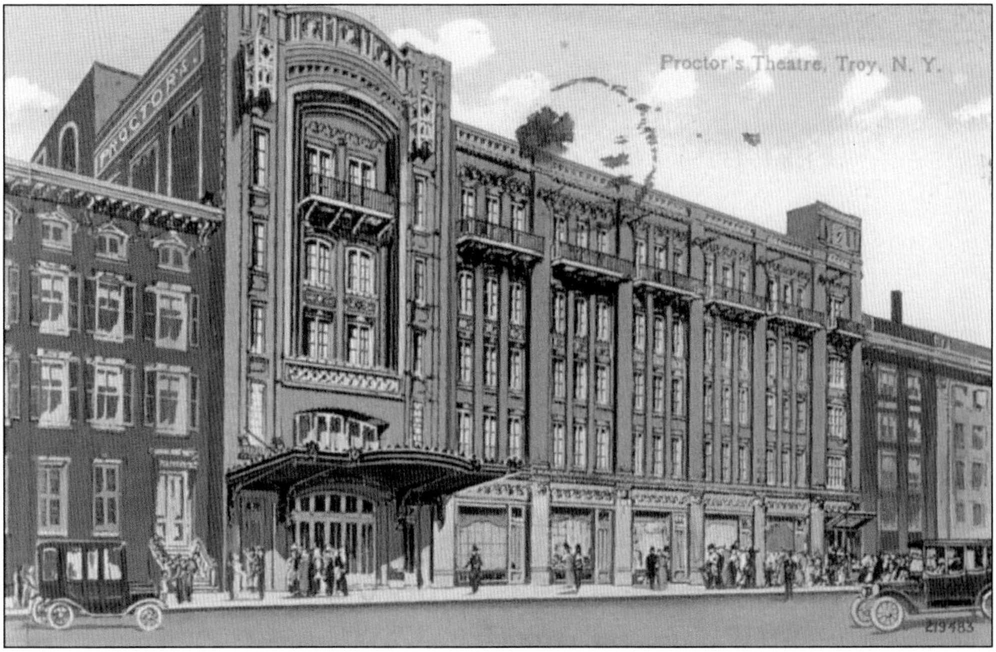

PROCTOR'S THEATRE. Lines are forming in front of Proctor's Theatre for the newest movie or Vaudeville show.

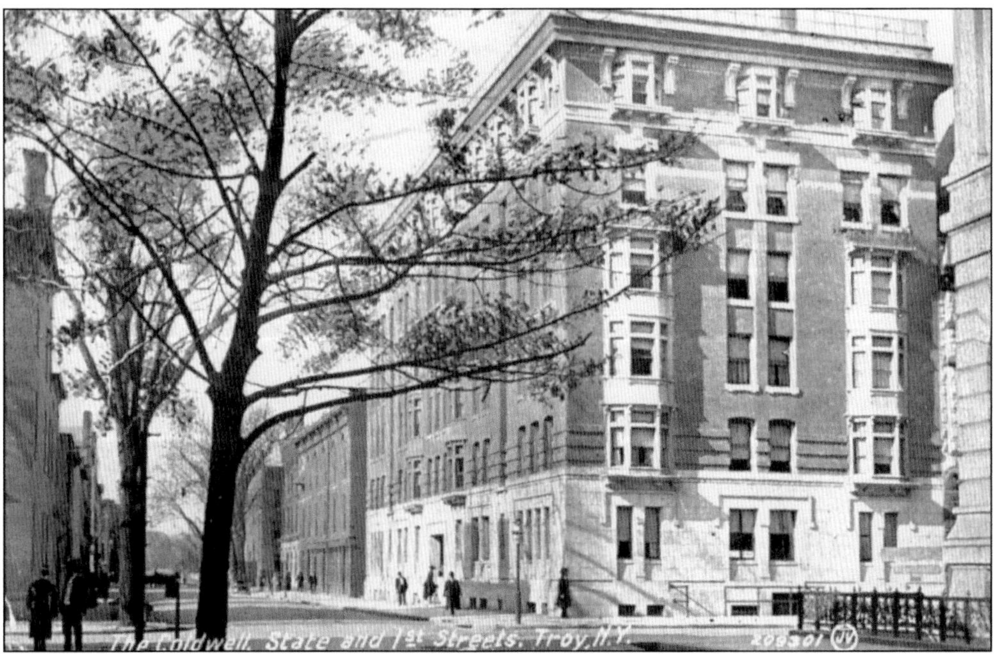

THE CALDWELL. This building, which dates to 1907, is located at State and Second Streets, directly across from the Troy Music Hall. It was named for James Caldwell, a local merchant and tailor. Its apartments are some of the most elegant in the city.

THE MASONIC TEMPLE. Located on Third Street, the Masonic Temple housed the Northern News Company on the first floor at the time of this card. Dedicated in 1872, it cost $100,000 to build, furnished.

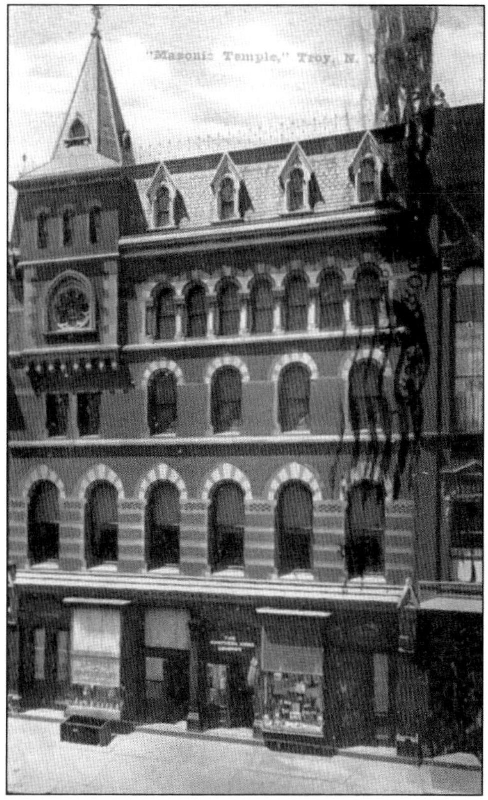

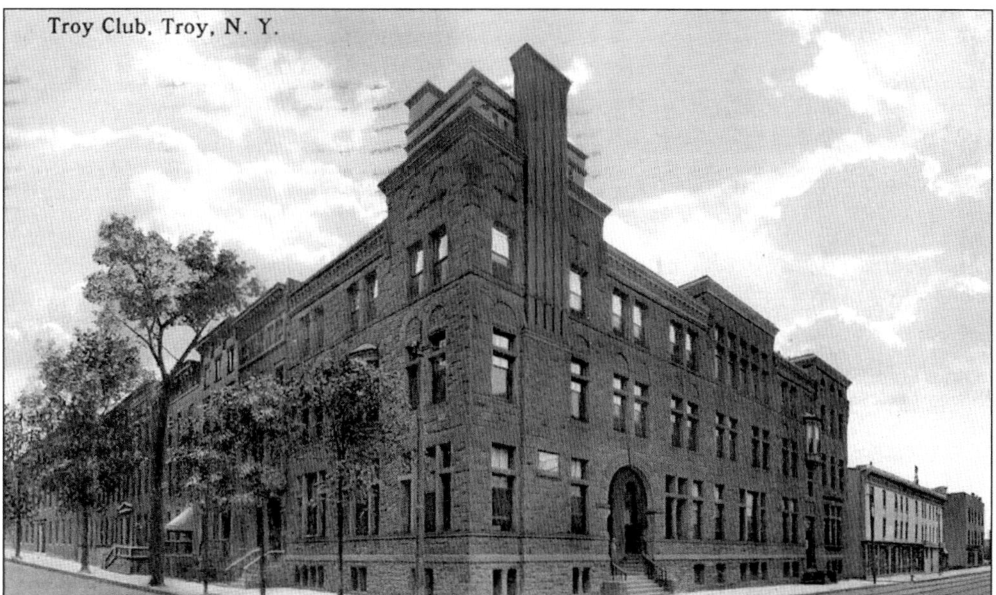

THE TROY CLUB. Built in 1888 in the Romanesque style and established in 1867, the Troy Club was a very prominent men's club on Congress and First Streets. Rumor has it that many good times were had behind these doors.

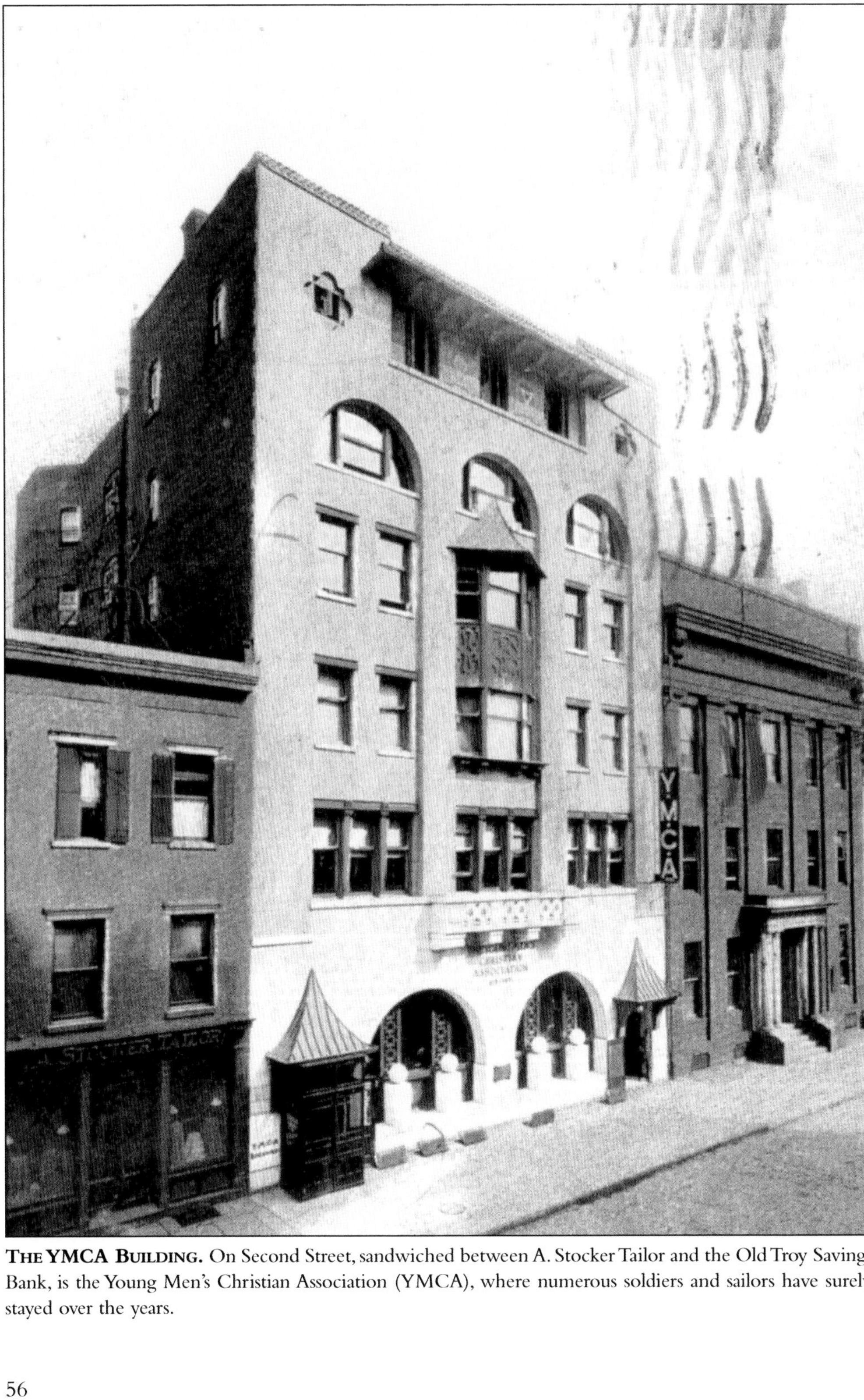

The YMCA Building. On Second Street, sandwiched between A. Stocker Tailor and the Old Troy Savings Bank, is the Young Men's Christian Association (YMCA), where numerous soldiers and sailors have surely stayed over the years.

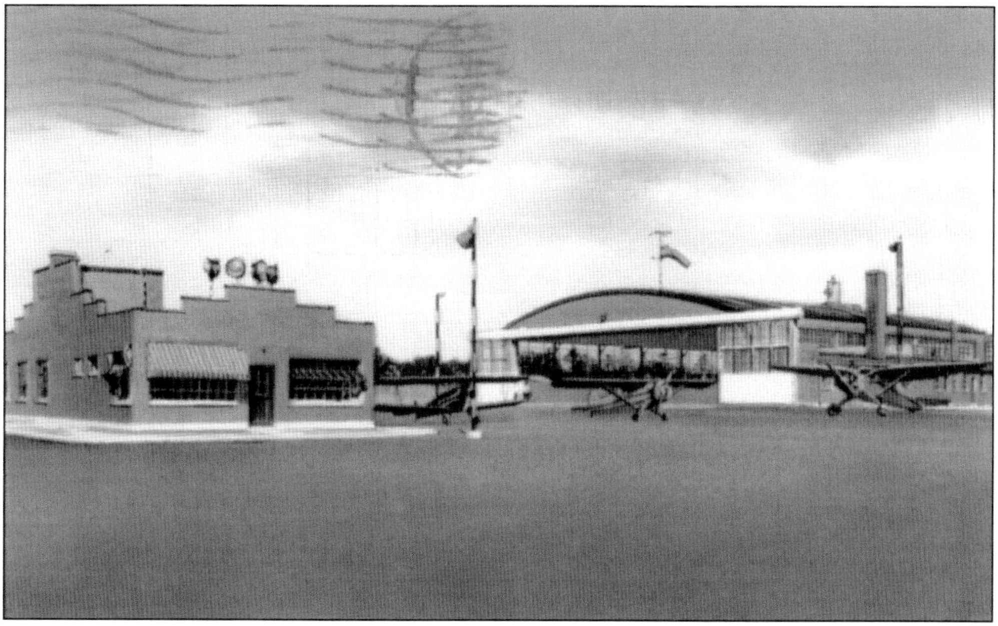

The Airport. The Troy Airport was located just south of Campbells Avenue. It was called "one of the finest fields for a private field in the East." It closed for good in June 1964.

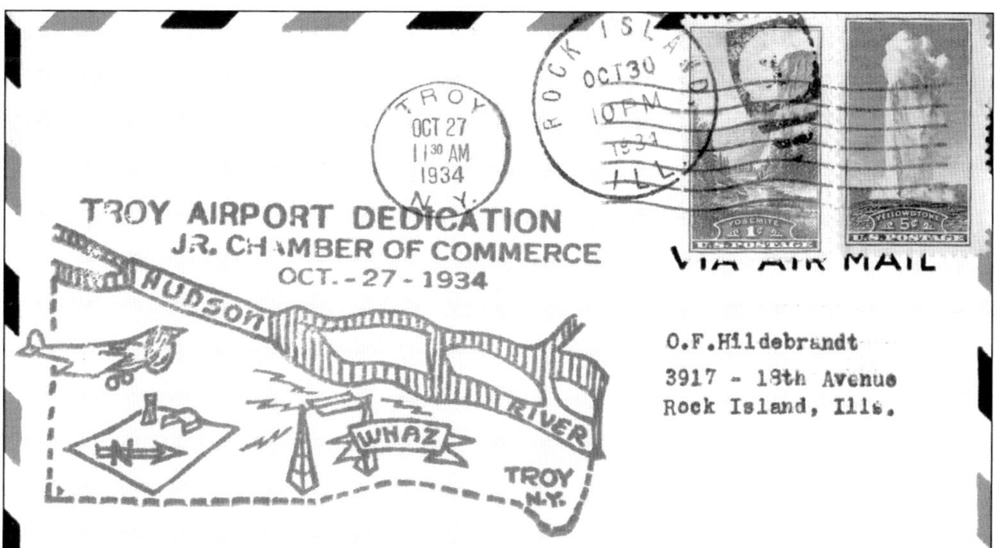

A First-Day Cover Dedication. This first-day cover is from the dedication of the Troy Airport on October 27, 1934. For 6¢, airmail from Troy to Rock Island, Illinois, took three days. Boy, have prices changed.

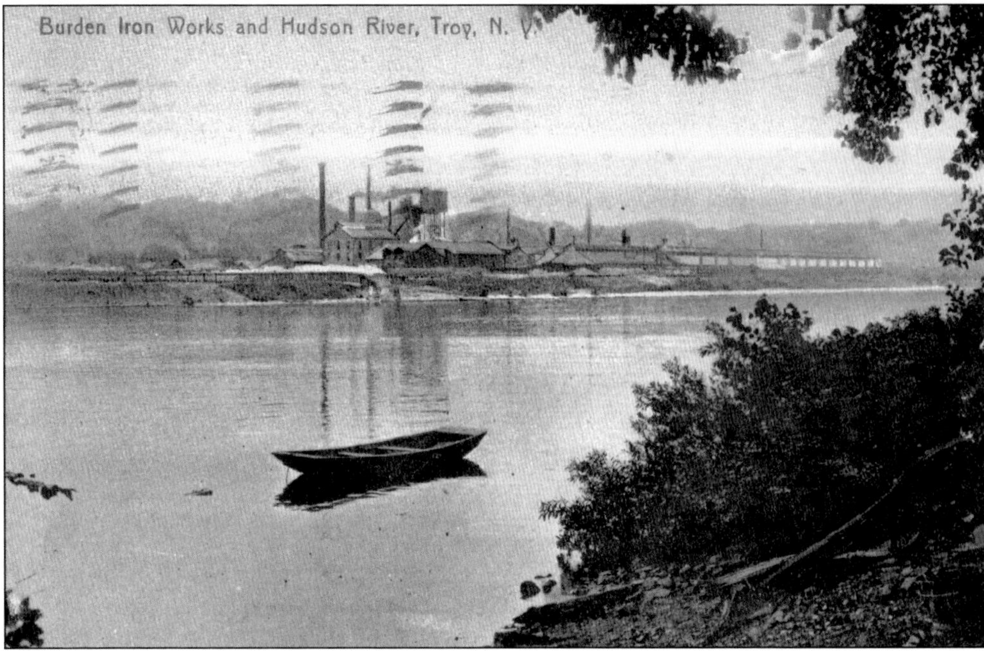

THE BURDEN MILL. The largest vertical waterwheel in the world was built by Henry Burden to power his horseshoe factory. Burden Iron Works was situated on the Hudson River. More than 50 million horseshoes were produced here each year. Some say George Ferris—a graduate from Rensselaer Polytechnic Institute—may have gotten the idea for his invention of the Ferris wheel from the Burden wheel. Burden Iron Works stopped operating in 1938. The waterwheel was dismantled for scrap during World War II.

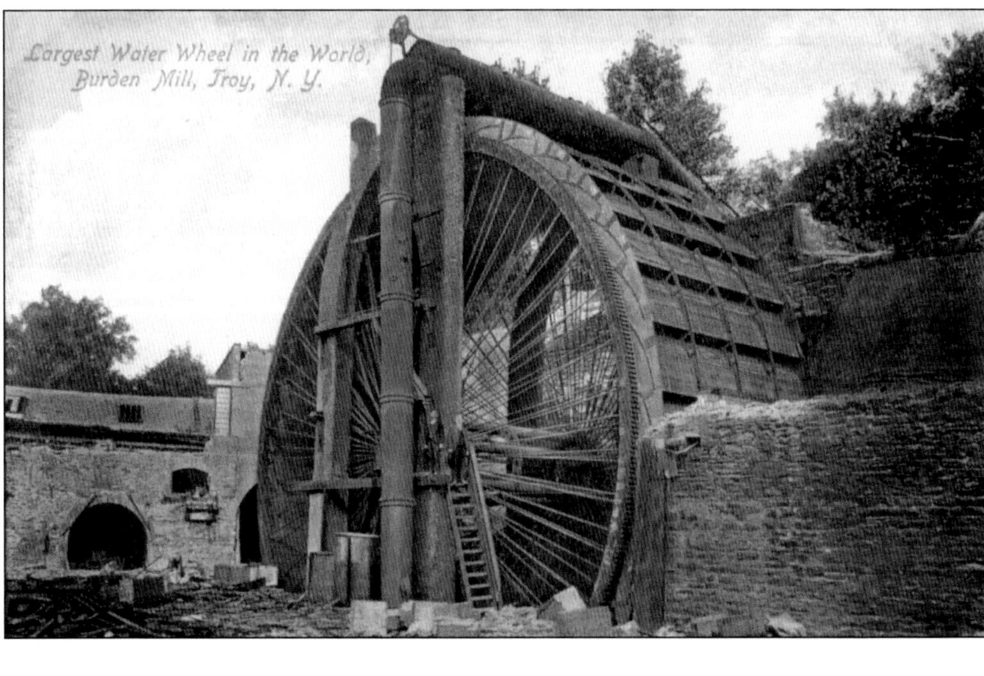

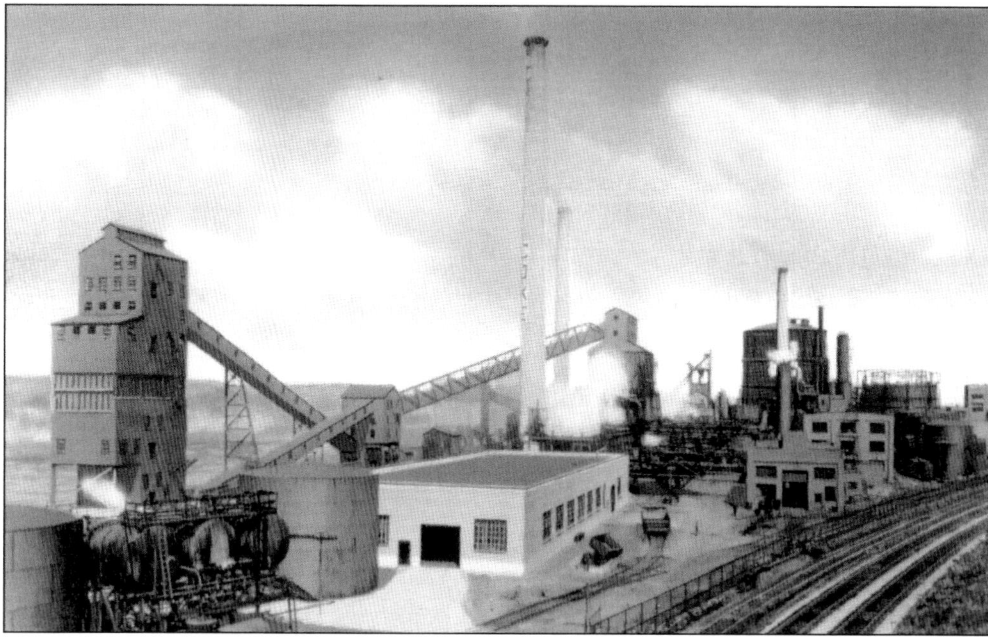

"HUDSON VALLEY FUEL CORP. COKE PLANT." Located in south Troy, it was once the site of the Republic Steel Plant and, before that, was home to the Burden Iron Company.

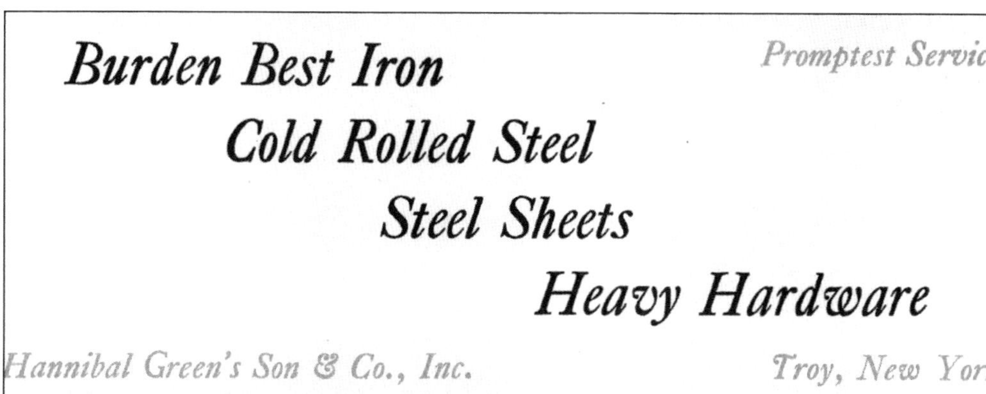

"BURDEN BEST IRON." Ink blotters were an excellent way to advertise your business, such as this one from Hannibal Green's Son & Company. You don't see a lot of blotters on a computer desk.

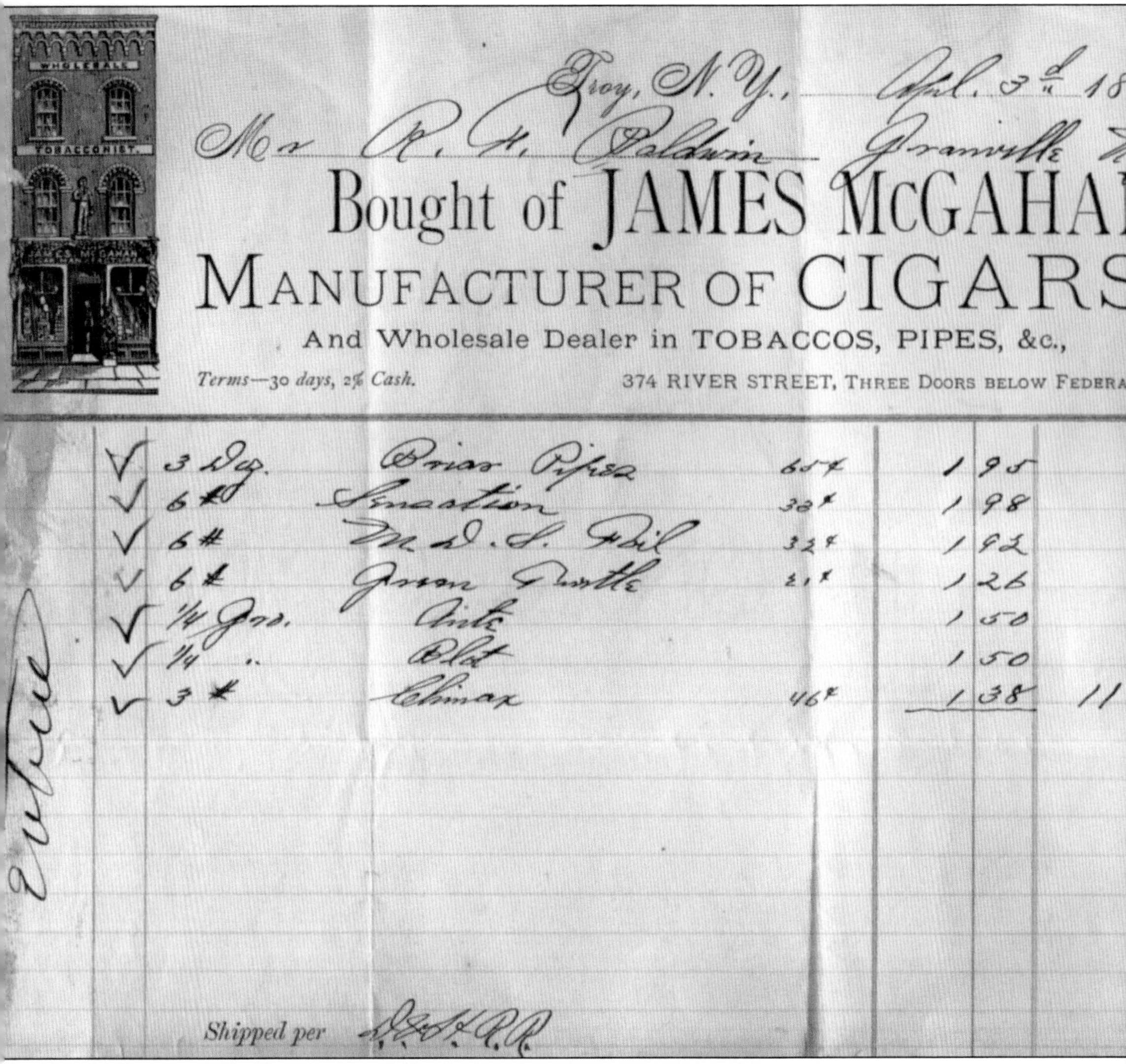

Troy, N.Y., Apl. 3d 18

Mr R. H. Baldwin Granville

Bought of JAMES McGAHAN

MANUFACTURER OF CIGARS

And Wholesale Dealer in TOBACCOS, PIPES, &c.,

Terms—30 days, 2% Cash. 374 RIVER STREET, THREE DOORS BELOW FEDERA

√	3 Doz.	Briar Pipes	65¢	1 95	
√	6#	Sensation	33¢	1 98	
√	6#	M.D.S. Foil	32¢	1 92	
√	6#	Green Turtle	21¢	1 26	
√	1/4 Gro.	Pinte		1 50	
√	1/4 ..	Blat		1 50	
√	3#	Climax	46¢	1 38	11

Entered

Shipped per D.&H.R.R.

A JAMES MCGAHAN BILL OF SALE. James McGahan was a manufacturer of cigars. His establishment was located at 374 River Street. This bill was made out in April 1888, a few weeks after the great blizzard. The items were shipped by the Delaware & Hudson Railroad to Granville. Hopefully, the snow had melted by then.

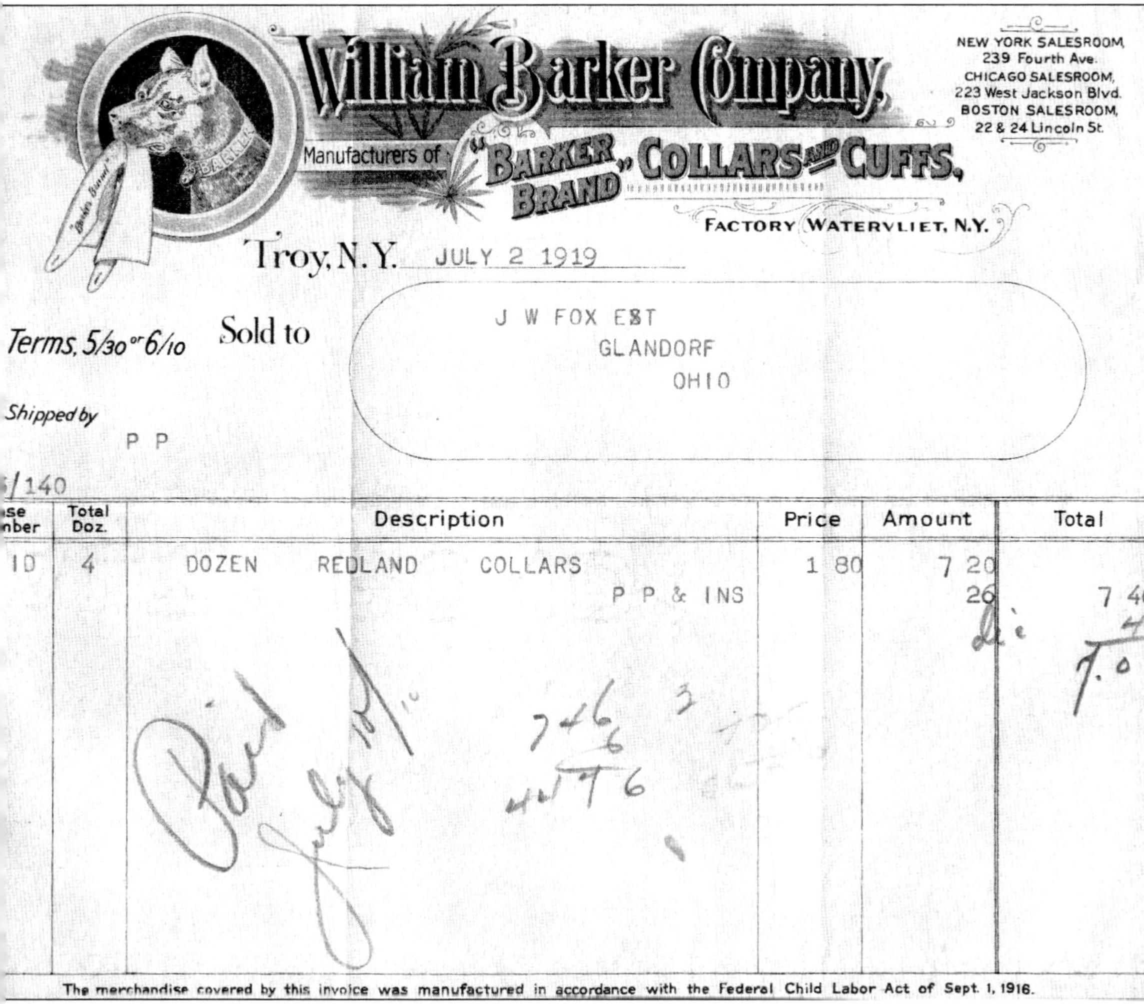

William Barker Company.

NEW YORK SALESROOM, 239 Fourth Ave.
CHICAGO SALESROOM, 223 West Jackson Blvd.
BOSTON SALESROOM, 22 & 24 Lincoln St.

Manufacturers of "BARKER BRAND" COLLARS AND CUFFS,

FACTORY WATERVLIET, N.Y.

Troy, N.Y. JULY 2 1919

Terms, 5/30 or 6/10

Sold to J W FOX EST
GLANDORF
OHIO

Shipped by
P P

/140

Case Number	Total Doz.	Description	Price	Amount	Total
10	4	DOZEN REDLAND COLLARS	1 80	7 20	
		P P & INS		26	7 46

Paid July 10

The merchandise covered by this invoice was manufactured in accordance with the Federal Child Labor Act of Sept. 1, 1916.

A William Barker Company Bill of Sale. William Barker became involved in the collar and cuff business in Troy in the 1880s. This bill shows the William Barker Company's sale of 48 Redland-brand collars to a shop in Ohio.

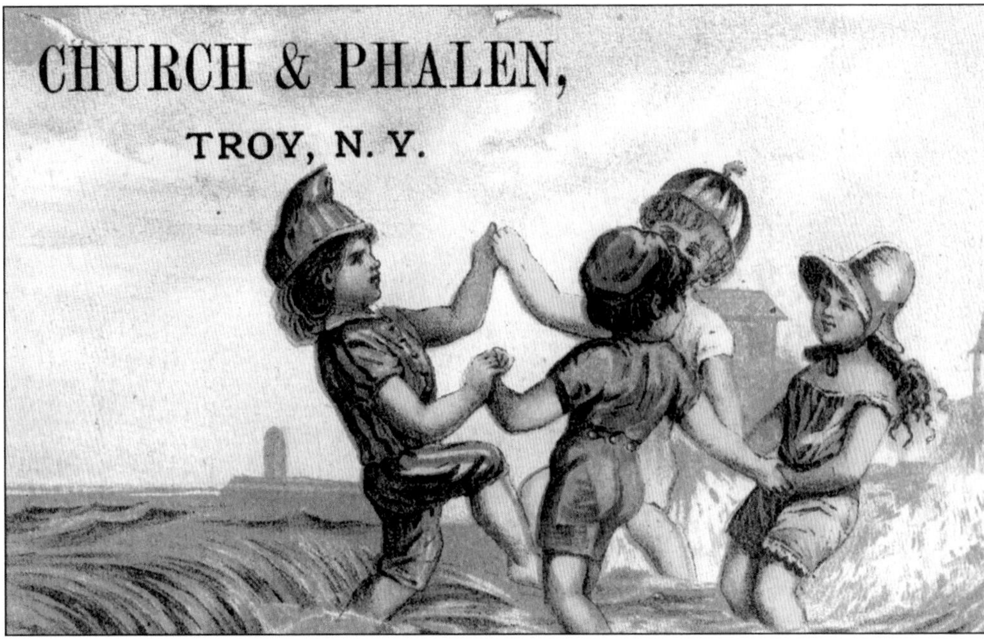

CHURCH & PHALEN'S. "Buy now and save money," states the advertisement on the back of this Church & Phalen's trade card.

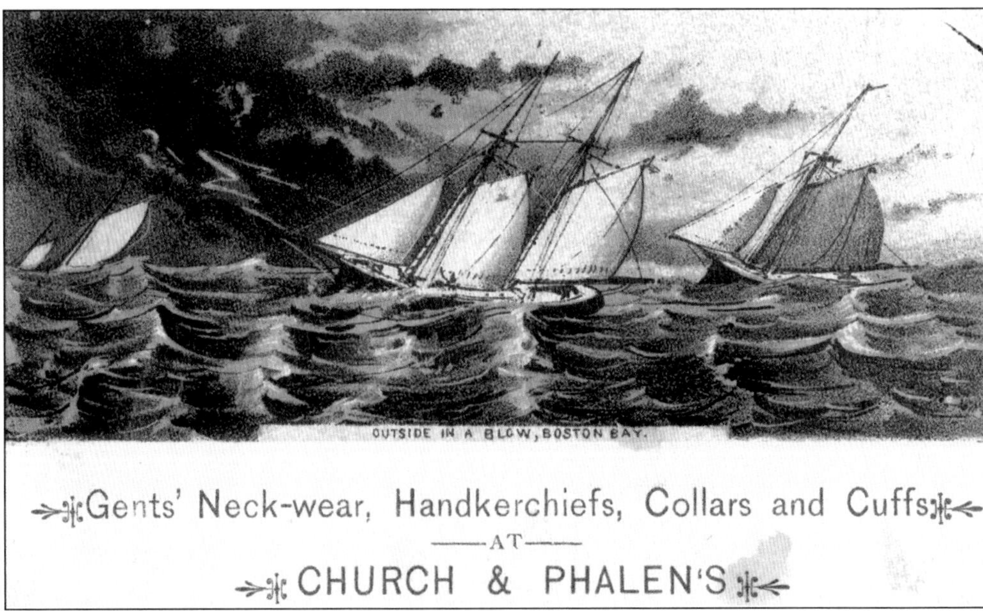

CHURCH & PHALEN'S. These dry goods merchants were located at two connecting buildings at Third and Congress Streets. They employed more than 100 workers. Church & Phalen's sold many goods, such as hosiery, silks, ribbon, and collars and cuffs, which are the usual items to be found in this type of establishment.

MORRIS GROSS CLOTHIER. Located at Marble Hall, Morris Gross Clothier & Merchant Tailor sold ready-made and made-to-order clothing for children, men, and boys.

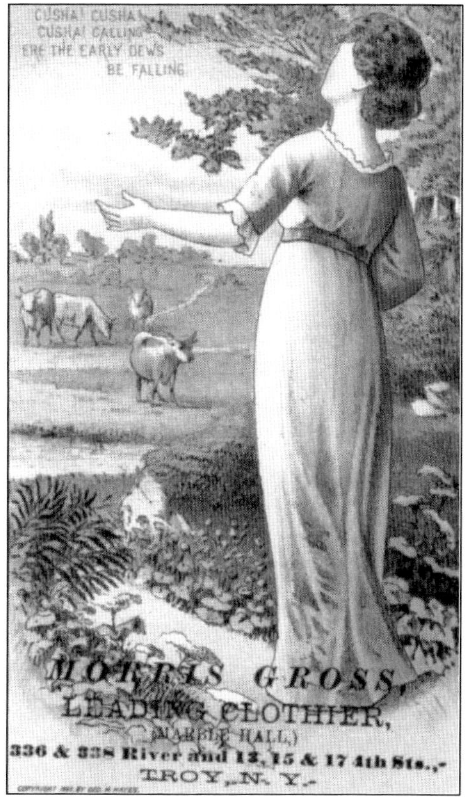

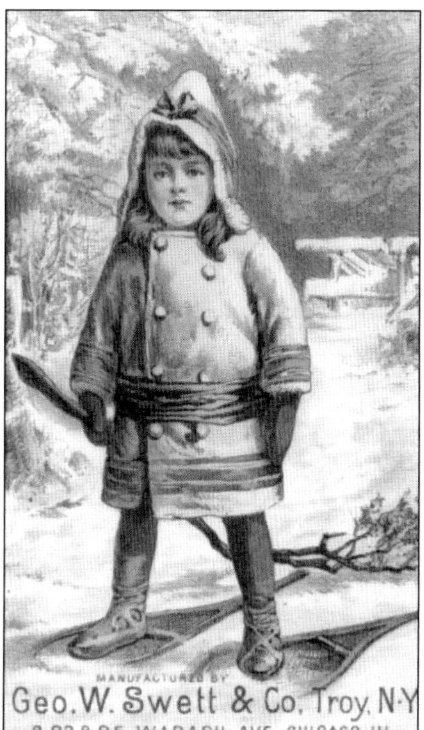

GEORGE W. SWETT & COMPANY. The George W. Swett Company showroom was located at 219 River Street. They sold very ornate parlor stoves.

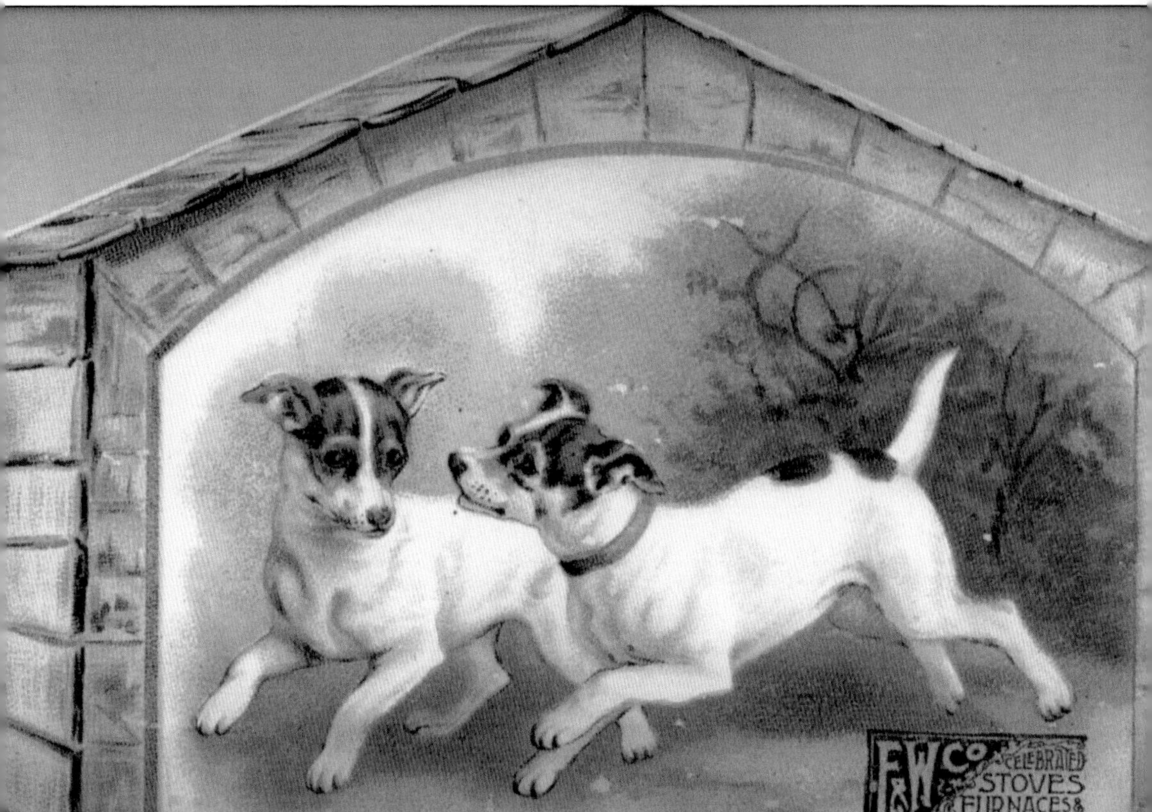

FULLER & WARREN. These two Jack Russell Terriers, known as Lucky and Lady, seem to be having fun advertising for the Fuller & Warren Stove Company. More than 60,000 ranges, stoves, and furnaces were made every year at the Clinton Stove Works. There were 1,200 workers on the payroll. It was located on six acres of land between Madison and Monroe Streets, and west of River Street.

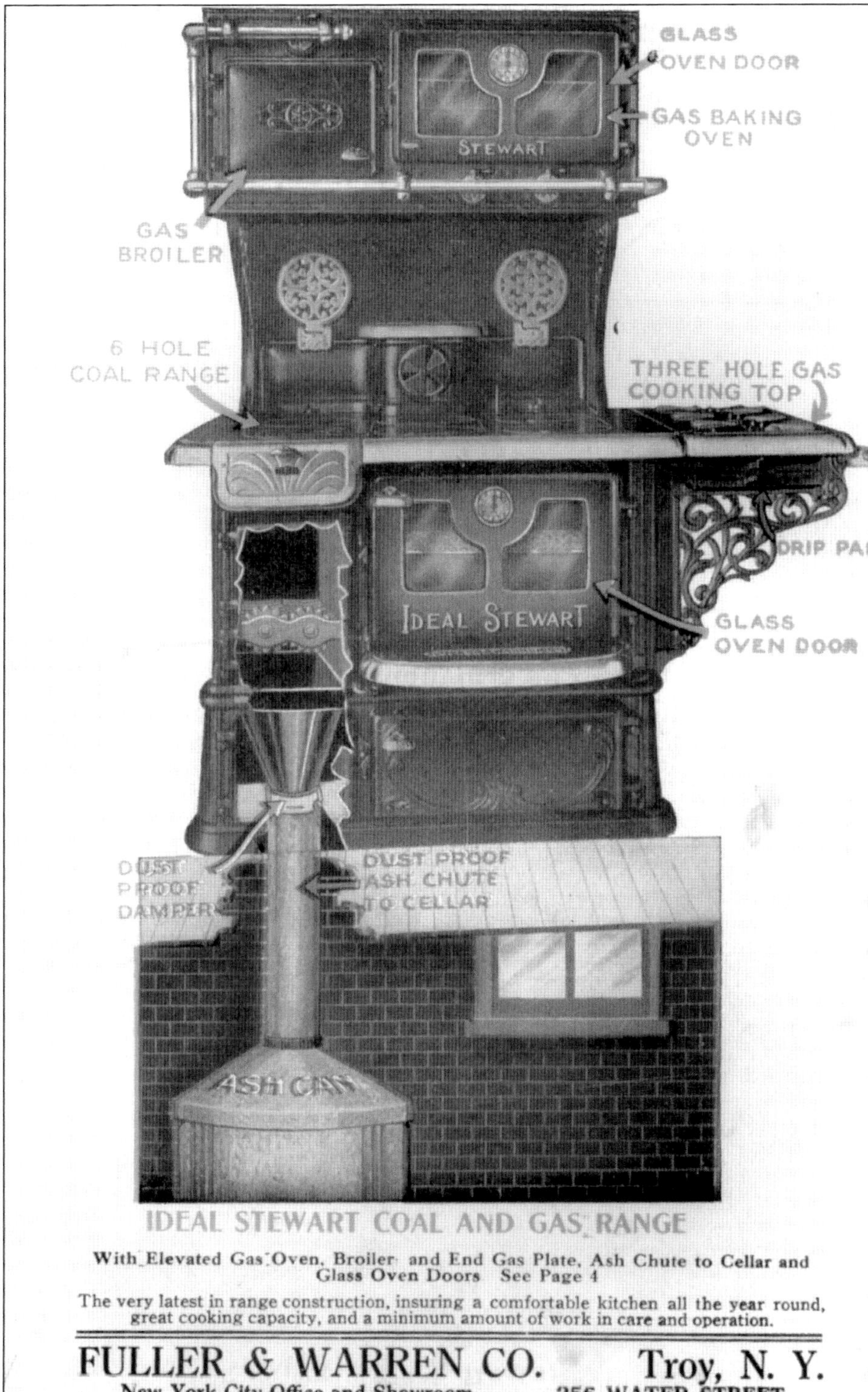

THE FULLER & WARREN TRADE CATALOG. Fuller & Warren Company was the manufacturer of the Stewart Range. This is a detailed version from one of their trade catalogs.

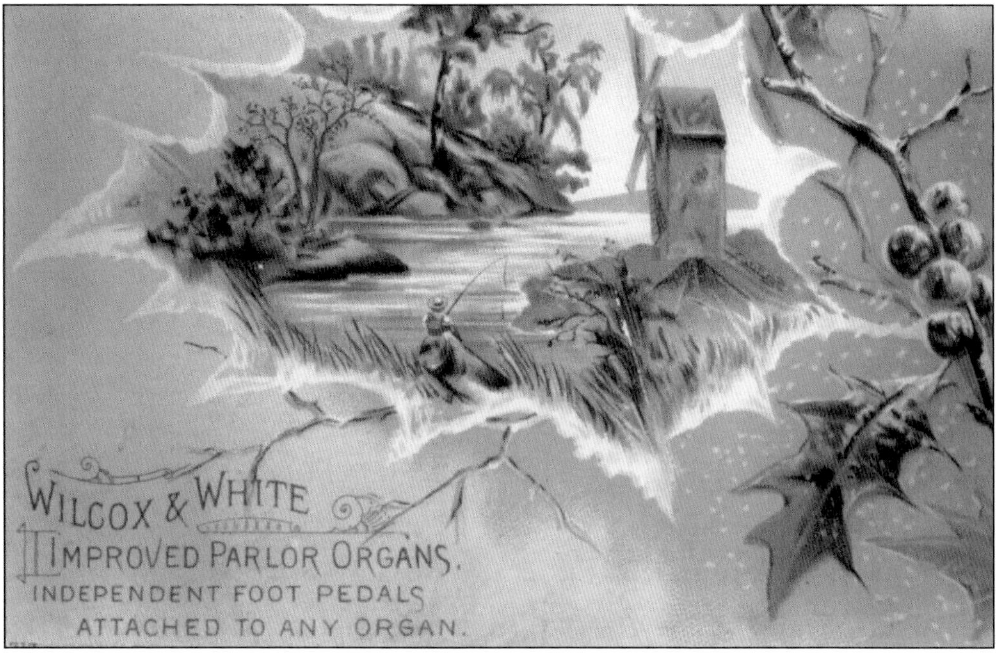

CLUETT & SONS. Wilcox & White was a brand of parlor organs sold by Cluett & Sons, which was located at 265 River Street in Troy, along with other locations around the Northeast. William Cluett and his son J.W.A. Cluett started the business in 1854. They would sell 1,000 to 2,000 pianos and organs yearly. Cluett & Sons was also a Steinway representative. In later years, they sold electrical appliances, Victor-Brunswick records, and Della & Bluebird records at three for a dollar. J.W.A. Cluett went on to the collar and cuff industry.

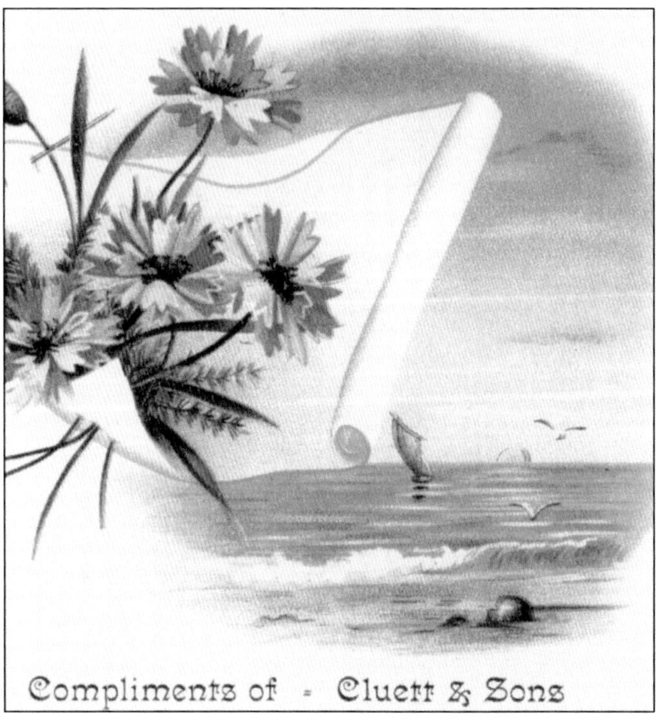

"COMPLIMENTS OF CLUETT & SONS." The Cluett & Sons piano company was located at the Cannon Place Block after Frear's moved to Third Street. They had skilled craftsmen on hand for repairing or restoring the entire piano.

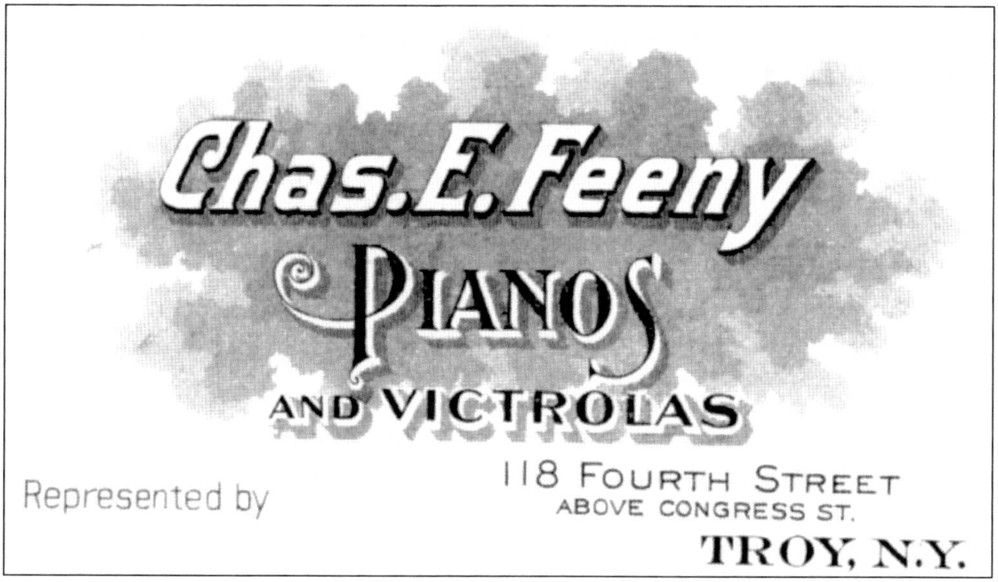

"CHAS. E. FEENY PIANOS." A little competition never hurt anybody. Charles E. Feeny also sold pianos and Victrolas in the Collar City.

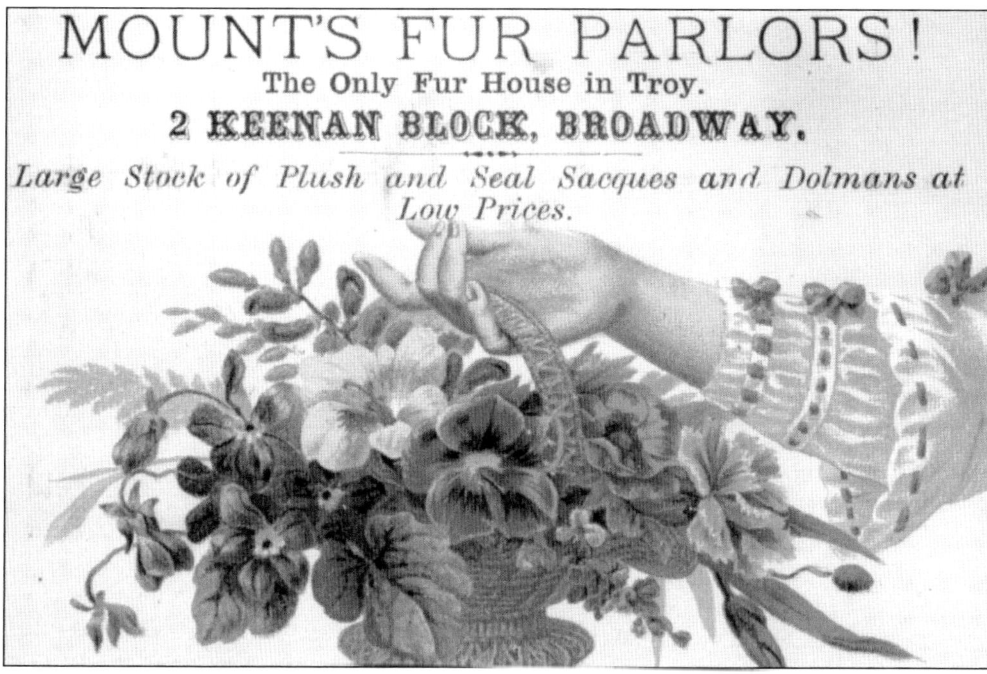

"MOUNT'S FUR PARLORS!" Established in 1863, Mount's claimed to be "the Only Fur House in Troy." It sold otter and seal furs starting at $100.

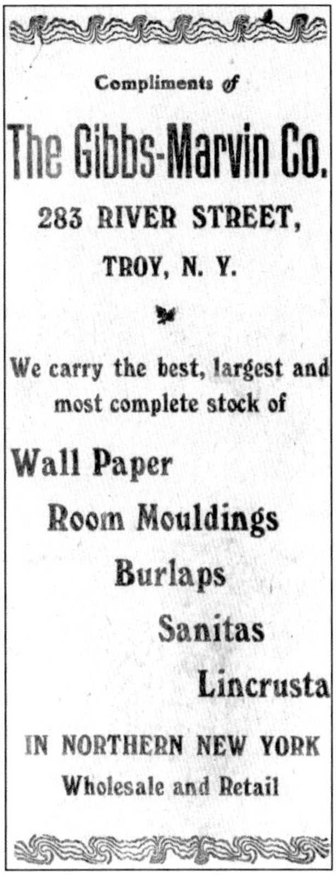

THE GIBBS-MARVIN COMPANY. This small notebook is "Compliments of the Gibbs-Marvin Company." This was the place to go if you were a paperhanger or just a customer in need of wallpaper. It was the largest wallpaper house in Upstate New York *c.* 1910.

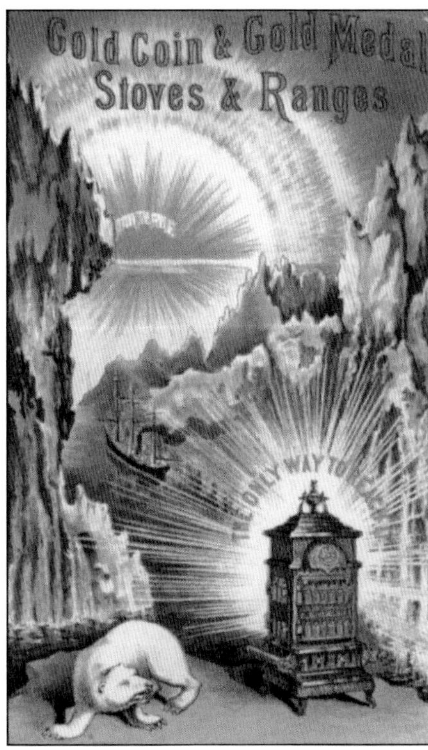

THE BUSSEY & MCLEOD STOVE COMPANY. The Bussey & McLeod Stove Company employed 350 workers and cast 20,000 stoves a year at its Oakwood Avenue foundry. The business began in 1863.

M.P. GOLD. This 1927 calendar from M.P. Gold, is promoting its line of Iron Sox.

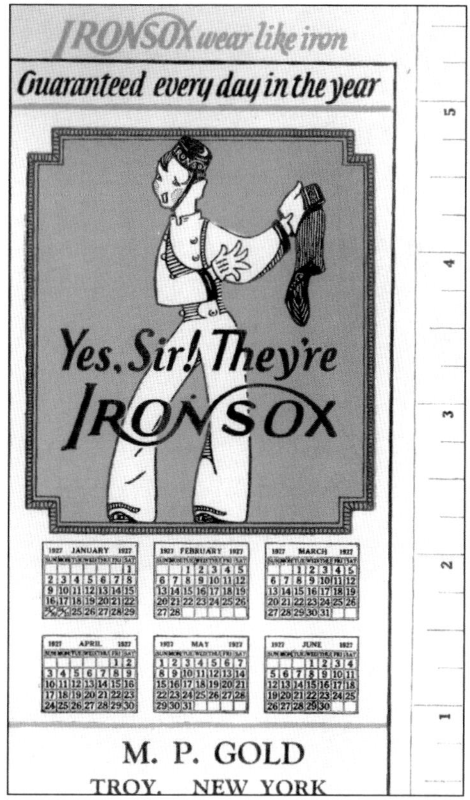

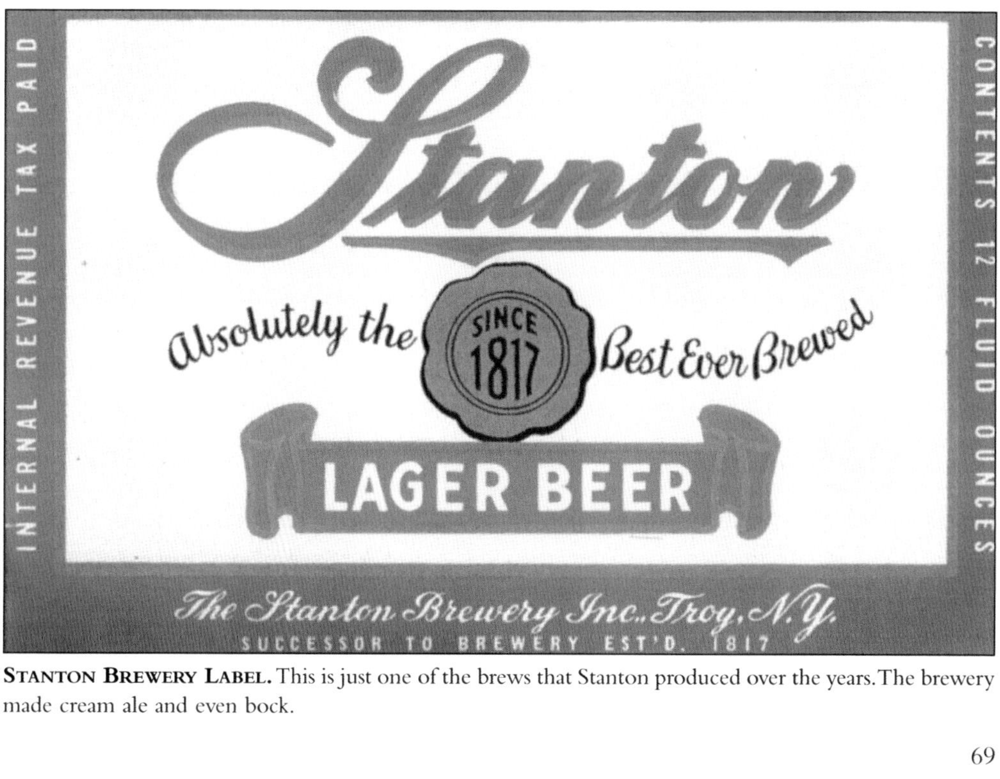

STANTON BREWERY LABEL. This is just one of the brews that Stanton produced over the years. The brewery made cream ale and even bock.

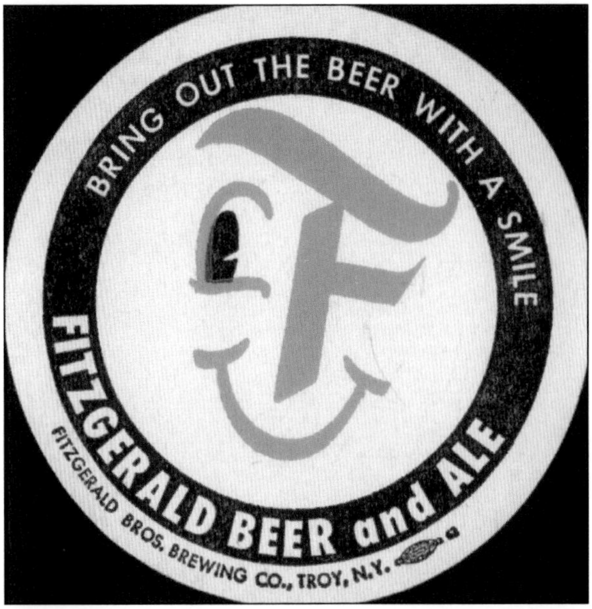

BEER COASTERS. This is just a sampling of some of the many coasters that a bartender might have placed under your mug or bottle of locally brewed beer.

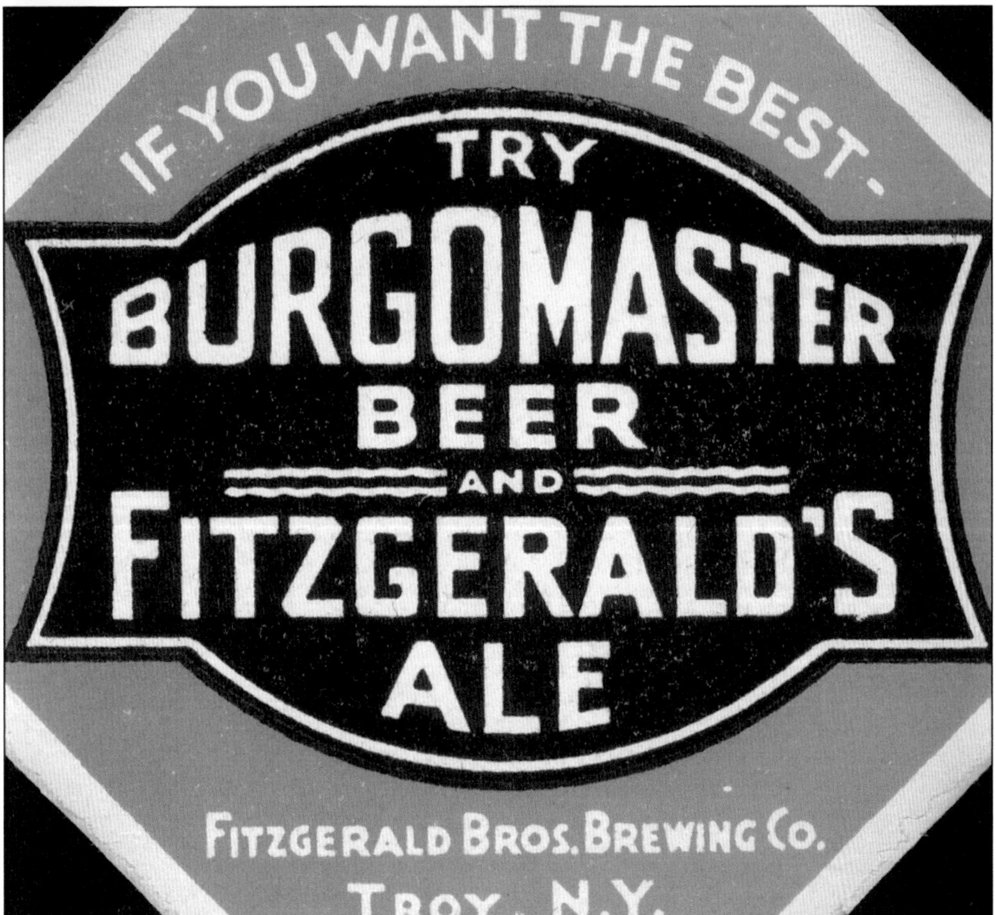

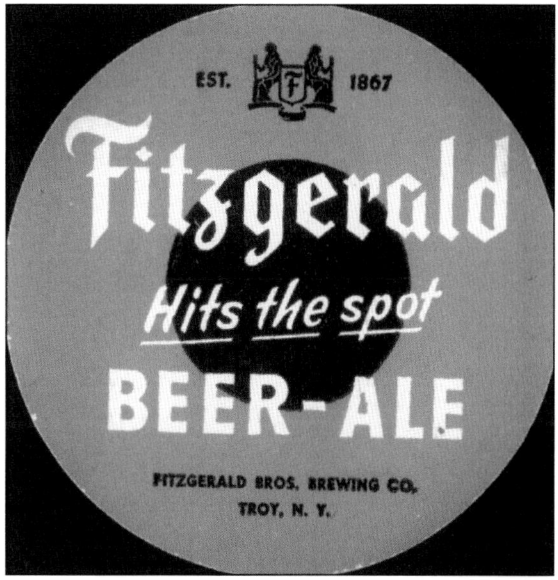

FITZGERALD AND QUANDT'S COASTERS. These coasters are from just two of the many breweries that used to flourish in Troy.

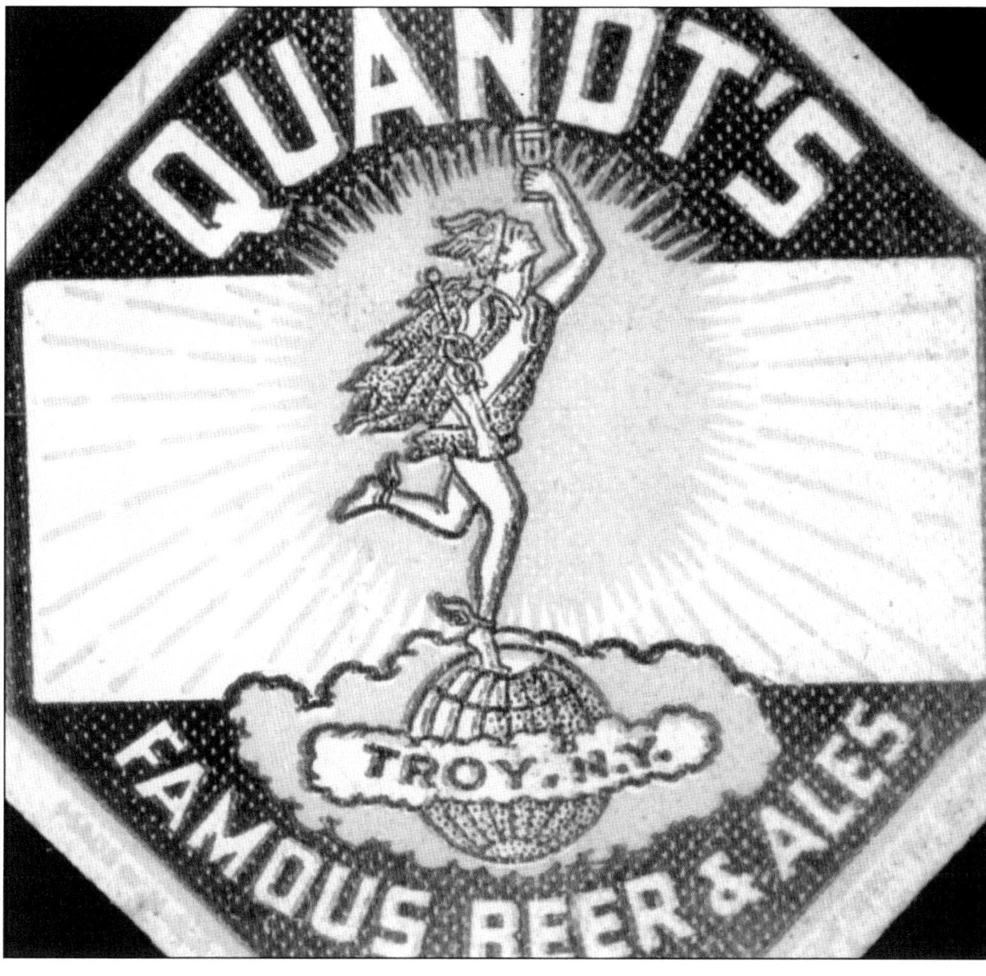

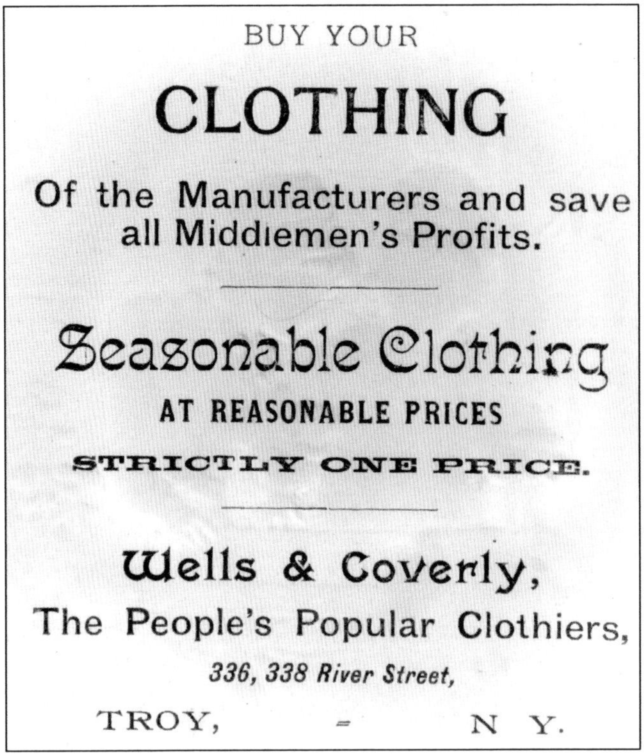

WELLS & COVERLY. Wells & Coverly, known as "the People's Popular Clothiers," was located on River Street. This was a great place to buy clothes right into the 1970s.

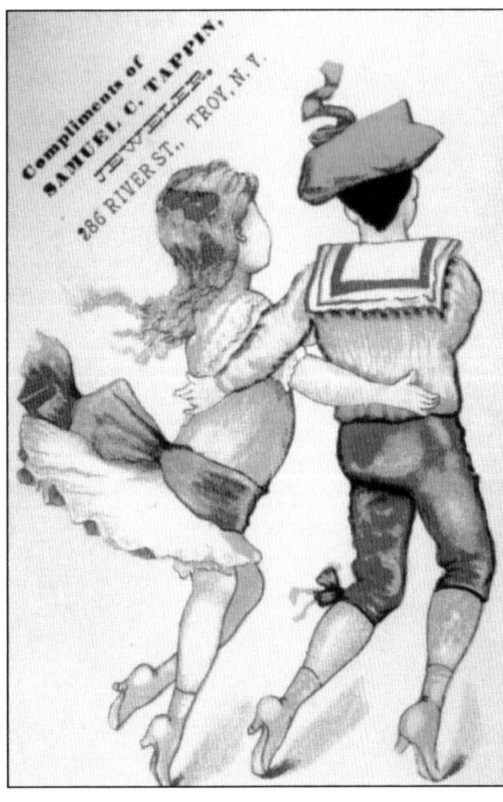

SAMUEL C. TAPPIN. Samuel C. Tappin opened his jewelry business on River Street in 1877.

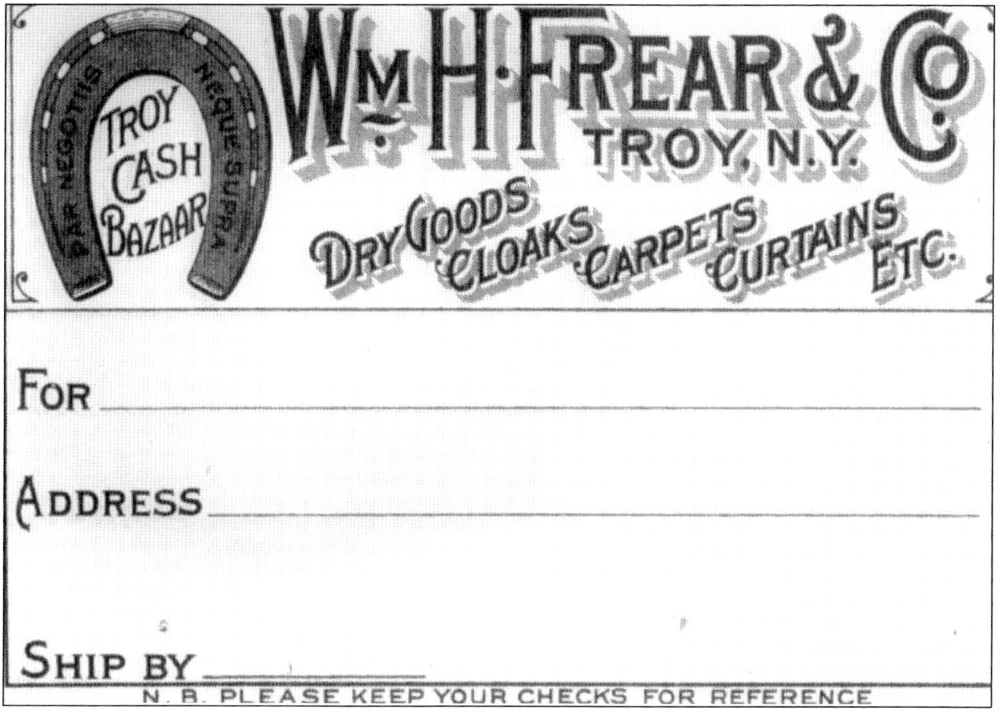

William H. Frear & Company. When you received your package in the mail from Frear's, this is what the shipping label looked like. Mail-order business dates back to long before the computer.

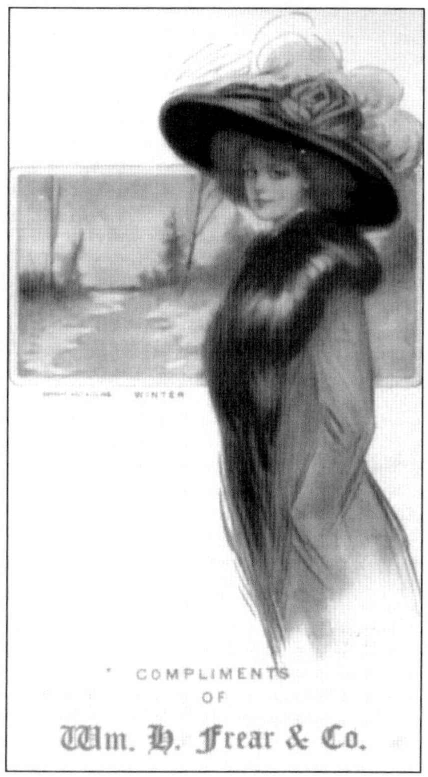

"Compliments of Wm. H. Frear & Co." This is the cover of a sewing kit given away when you went to Frear's Cash Bazaar. They were the largest dealer in millinery.

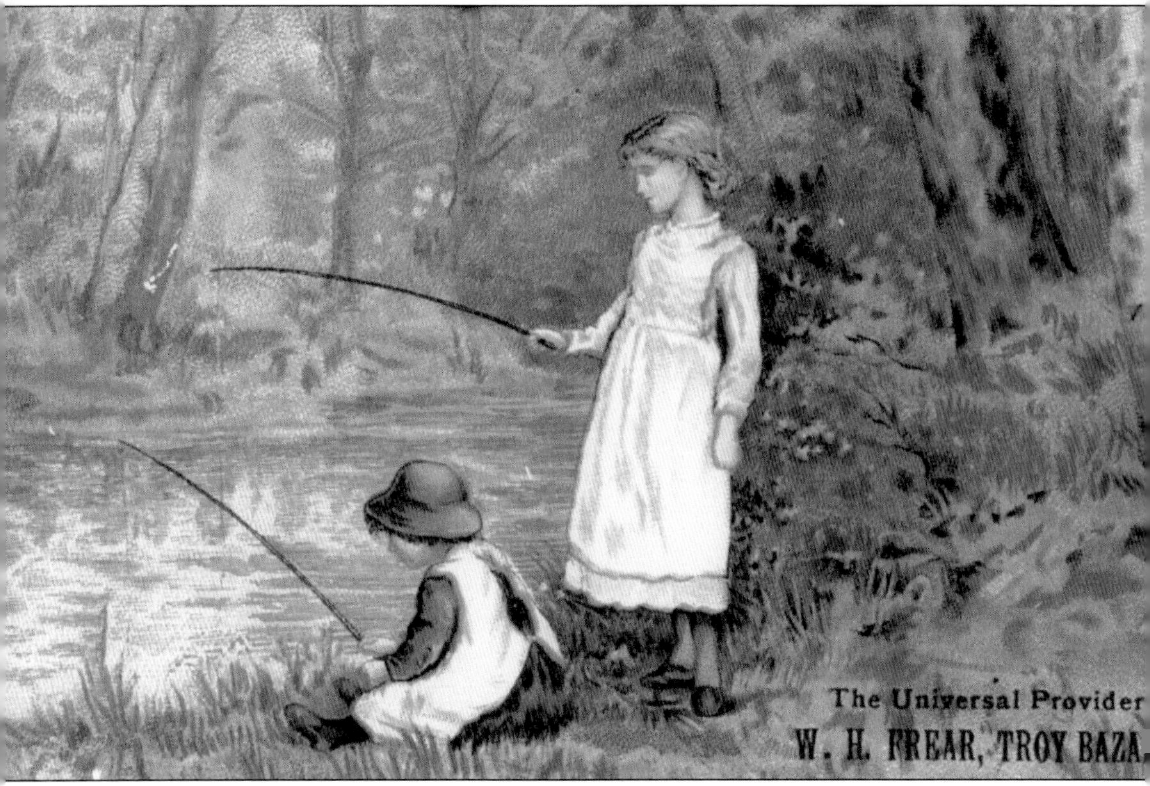

"The Universal Provider." This is one of the many trade cards from W.H. Frear, Troy Bazaar.

FREAR'S BAZAAR. On this card, Frear's Bazaar boasts that it is "the Place to Save Money!" Frear's advertised its 30 departments teeming with bargains. People came from miles around to shop at Frear's.

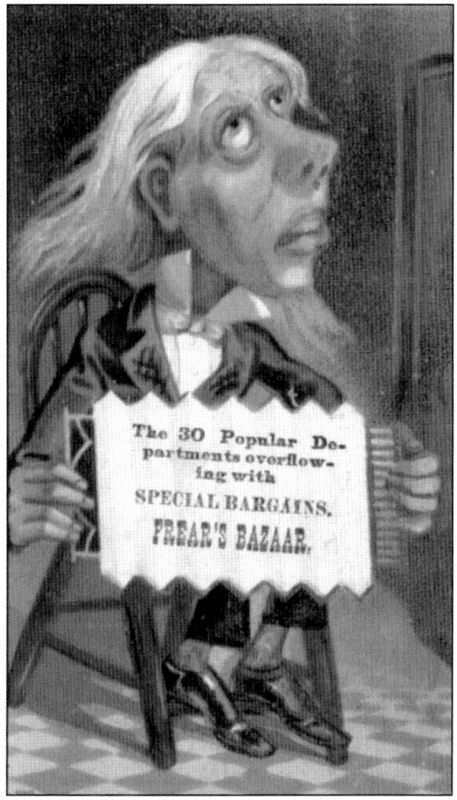

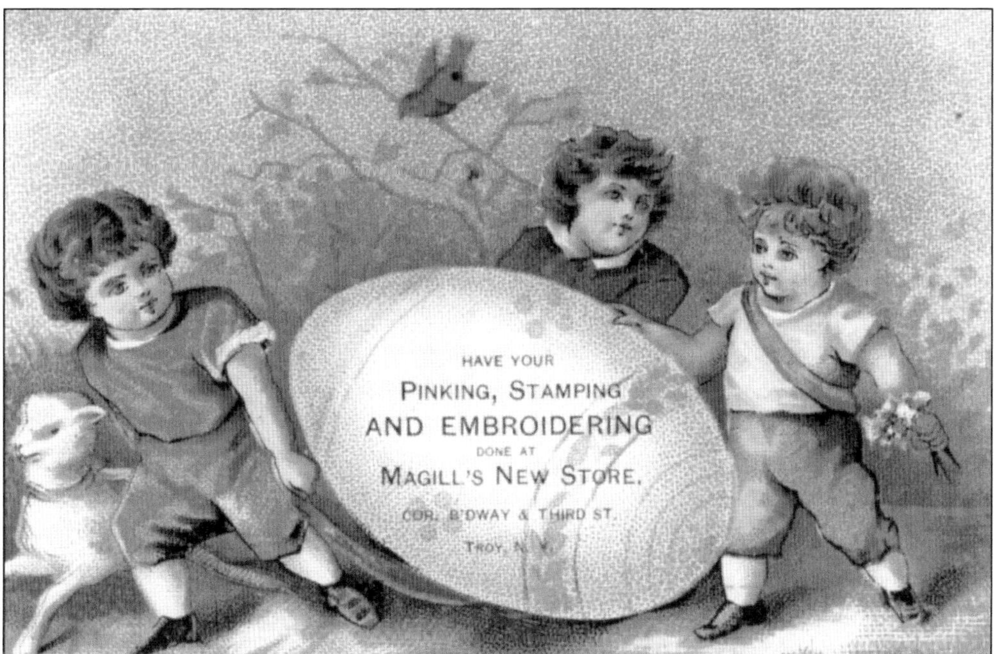

MAGILL'S NEW STORE. Magill's was located at Broadway and Third in the Keenan Building. It sold woman's clothing, parasols, jewelry, and silks.

J. M. WARREN & CO.,

IMPORTERS AND DEALERS IN

Hardware, Iron, Steel, Nails,

TIN, COPPER,

Sheet & Boiler Iron,

TROY, N. Y.

We keep at all times a Large Stock of AMERICAN REFINED, BURDEN'S, H. B. & S., and BURDEN'S BEST IRON, also SHEET and BOILER IRON, HOBSON'S CHOICE and SANDERSON'S BEST CAST STEEL, and BESSEMER STEEL, rounds flats and squares, and are able to fill orders for Special Sizes and Lengths at short notice and at the Lowest Market Rates.

VALUE OF IRON PER TON

AT FROM 2 TO 12 1-2 CENTS PER POUND.

2	44	80	4 1/8	92	40	6 1/4	140	00	8 3/8	187	60	10 1/2	235	20
2 1/8	47	60	4 1/4	95	20	6 3/8	142	80	8 1/2	190	40	10 5/8	238	00
2 1/4	50	40	4 3/8	98	00	6 1/2	145	60	8 5/8	193	20	10 3/4	240	80
2 3/8	53	20	4 1/2	100	80	6 5/8	148	40	8 3/4	196	00	10 7/8	243	60
2 1/2	56	00	4 5/8	103	60	6 3/4	151	20	8 7/8	198	80	11	246	40
2 5/8	58	80	4 3/4	106	40	6 7/8	154	00	9	201	60	11 1/8	249	20
2 3/4	61	60	4 7/8	109	20	7	156	80	9 1/8	204	40	11 1/4	252	00
2 7/8	64	40	5	112	00	7 1/8	159	60	9 1/4	207	20	11 3/8	254	80
3	67	20	5 1/8	114	80	7 1/4	162	40	9 3/8	210	00	11 1/2	257	60
3 1/8	70	00	5 1/4	117	60	7 3/8	165	20	9 1/2	212	80	11 5/8	260	40
3 1/4	72	80	5 3/8	120	40	7 1/2	168	00	9 5/8	215	60	11 3/4	263	20
3 3/8	75	60	5 1/2	123	20	7 5/8	170	80	9 3/4	218	40	11 7/8	266	00
3 1/2	78	40	5 5/8	126	00	7 3/4	173	60	9 7/8	221	20	12	268	80
3 5/8	81	20	5 3/4	128	80	7 7/8	176	40	10	224	00	12 1/8	271	60
3 3/4	84	00	5 7/8	131	60	8	179	20	10 1/8	226	80	12 1/4	274	40
3 7/8	86	80	6	134	40	8 1/8	182	00	10 1/4	229	60	12 3/8	277	20
4	89	60	6 1/8	137	20	8 1/4	184	80	10 3/8	232	40	12 1/2	280	00

J.M. WARREN & COMPANY. Located at 245–247 River Street, J.M. Warren & Company was the largest hardware business at the time. You could find anything from bicycles to boat motors at J.M. Warren.

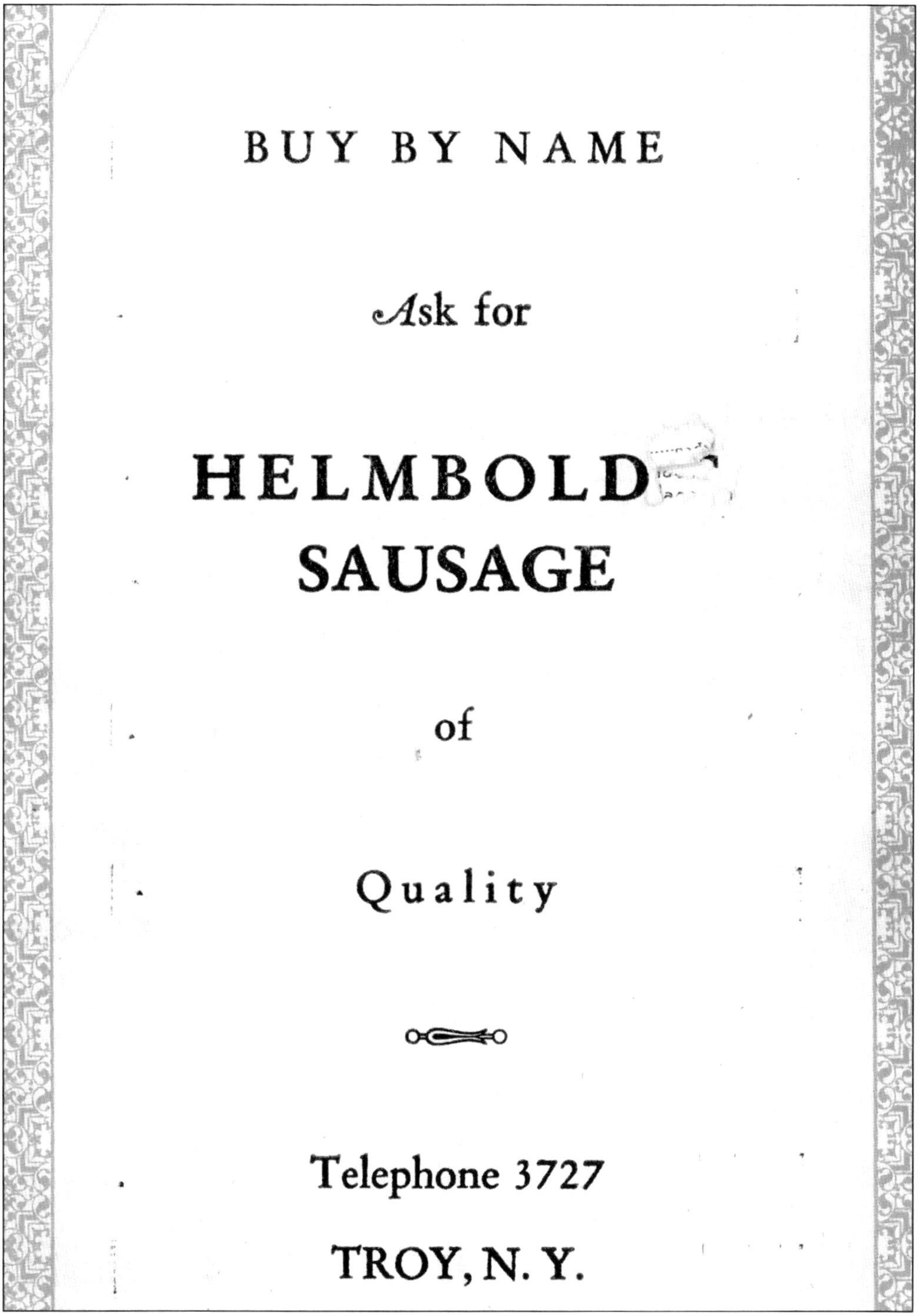

Helmbold's Sausage. "Ask for Helmbold's Sausage" is suggested on the back of this sausage cookbook. Fritz Helmbold, known as "Troy's sanitary pork store," was located at 120 Fourth Street. They were manufacturers of bolognas, frankfurters, and sausage—a specialty. They are still in business today at another location in the city.

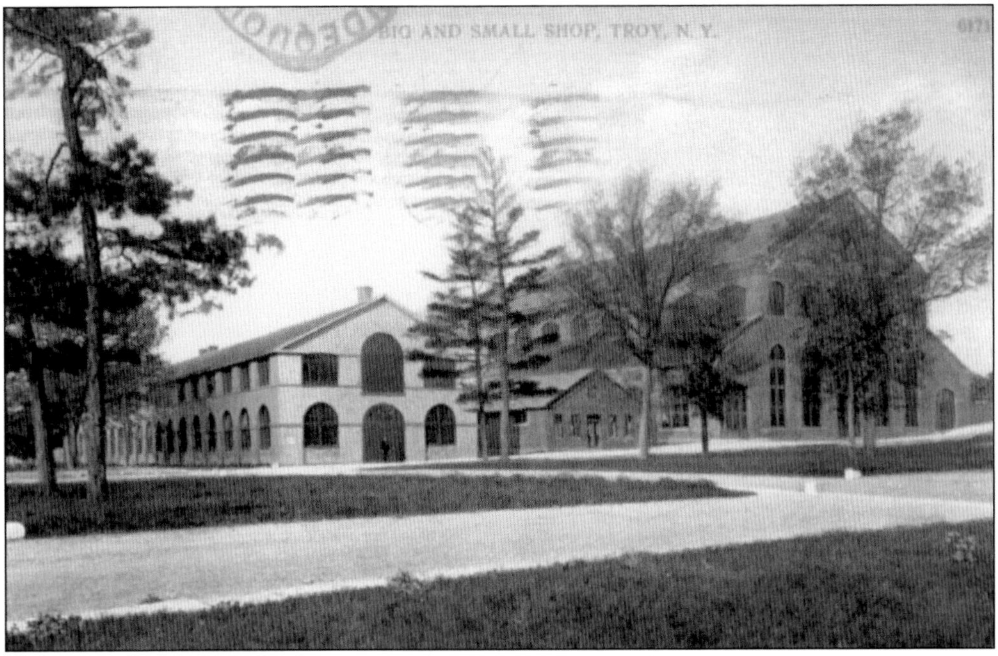

"BIG AND SMALL SHOP." No, this is not the big and small clothing shop. This is the Watervliet Arsenal, which is located just across the river. Established in 1813, it is the oldest arsenal in the United States. These postcards show where the big guns were made and also show the men who made them. The arsenal is still in operation today. There is also a museum here, which began in 1968.

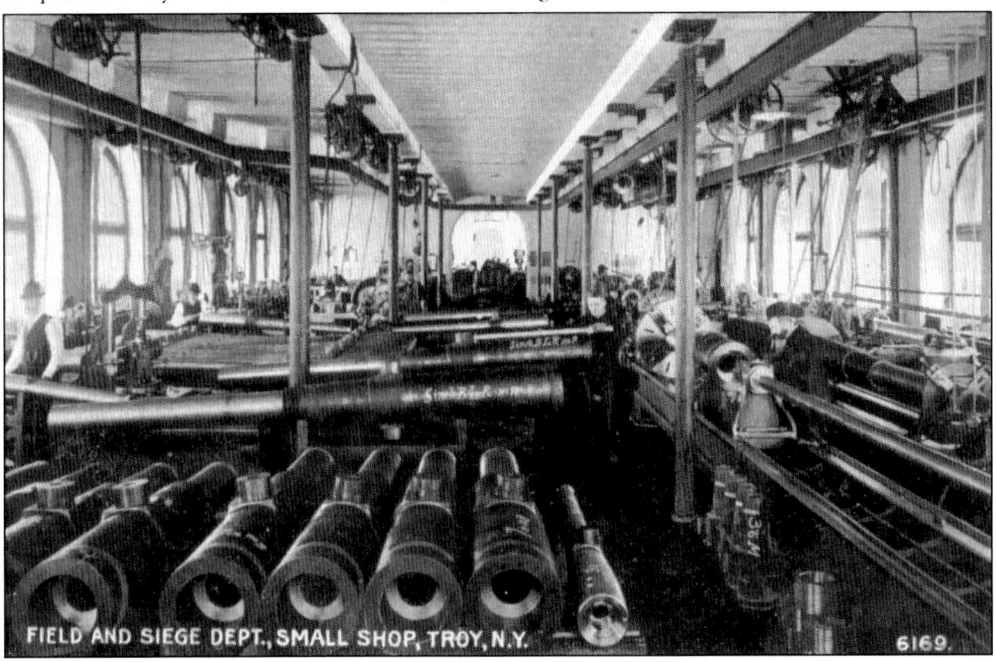

Five

School Days

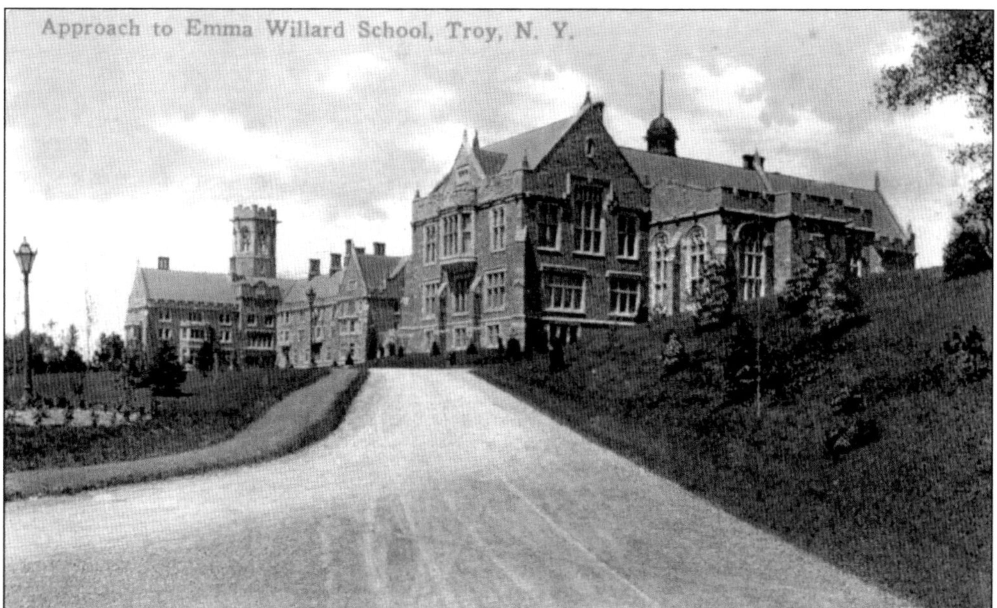

"Approach to Emma Willard School." This is the entrance to the Emma Willard School, with its castlelike buildings and finely trimmed lawn. Many years later, it was the scene of the movie *Scent of a Woman,* with Al Pacino. Pacino won an Oscar for his role in the 1992 film.

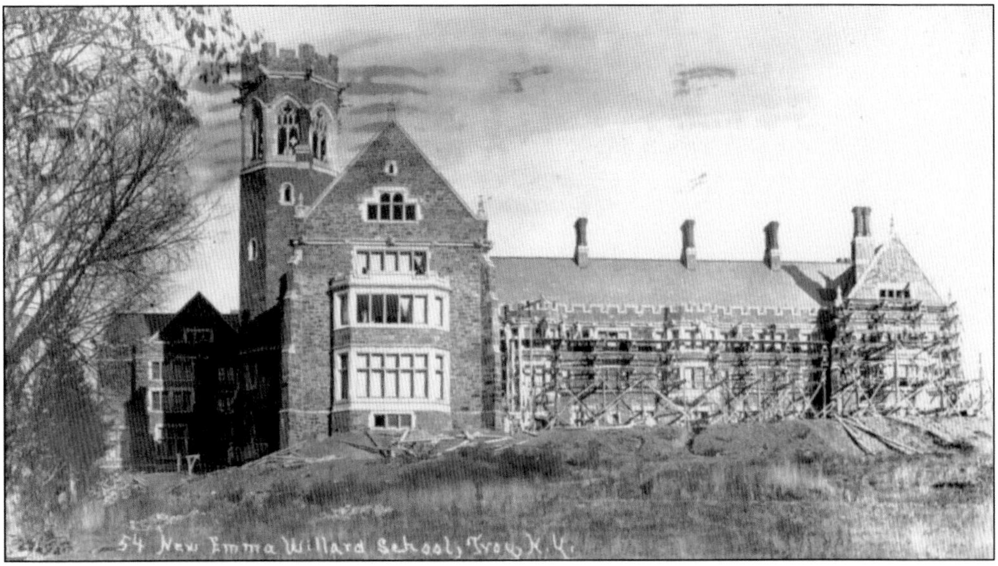

"NEW EMMA WILLARD SCHOOL." Construction of the new Emma Willard School residence hall began in 1910. Emma Willard School sits on a 55-acre campus on Pawling and Elm Grove Avenues. The first three original buildings are Jacobean in style and were designed by M.F. Cummings. Today, there are 18 buildings on campus.

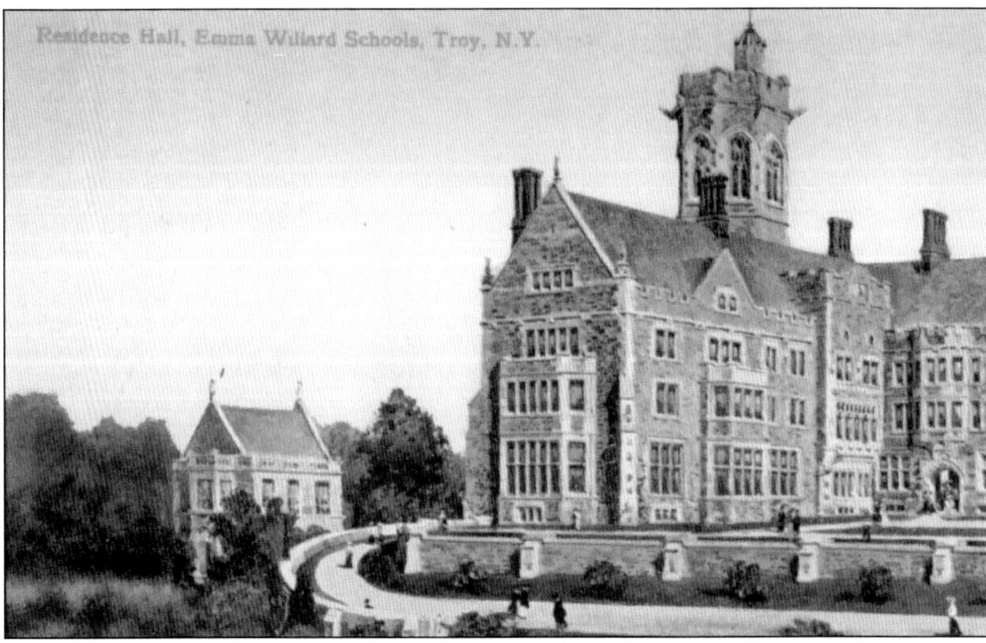

A RESIDENCE HALL. The Emma Willard School is the longest-existing girls' school in the United States.

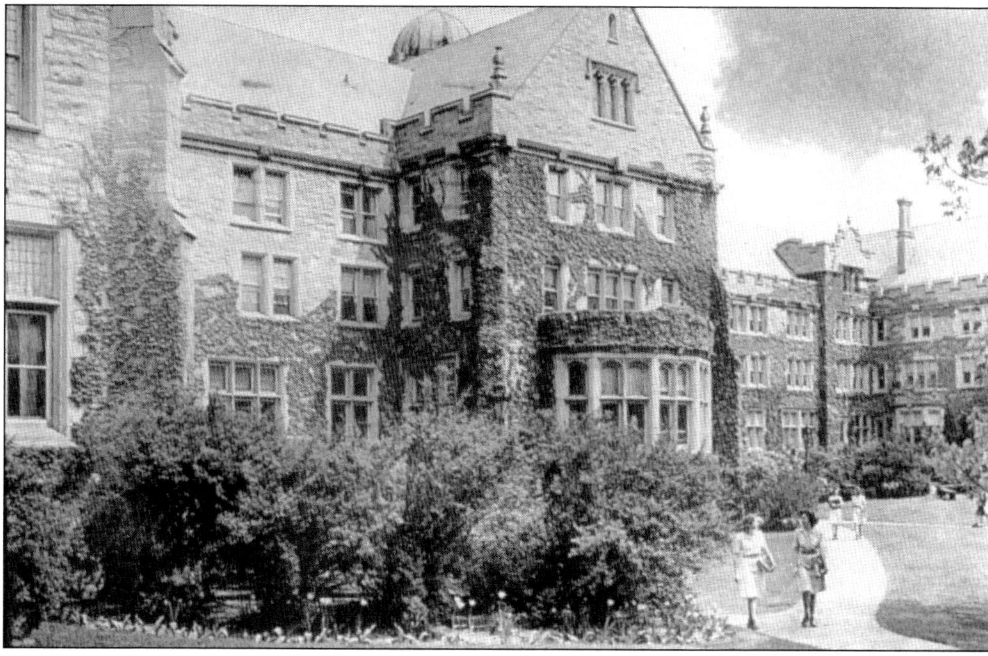

KELLAS HALL. Spring has arrived at Emma Willard's Kellas Hall. The tulips are in bloom, and the female students are thinking about final exams. Eliza Kellas was the principal at Emma Willard from 1910 to 1942.

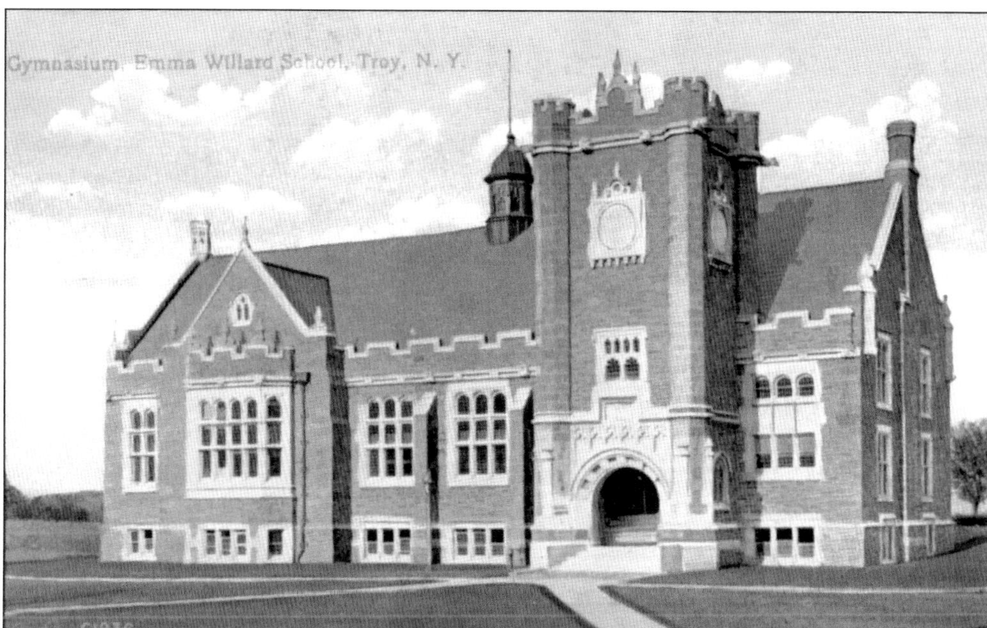

THE GYMNASIUM. This postcard shows a view of the gymnasium at Emma Willard.

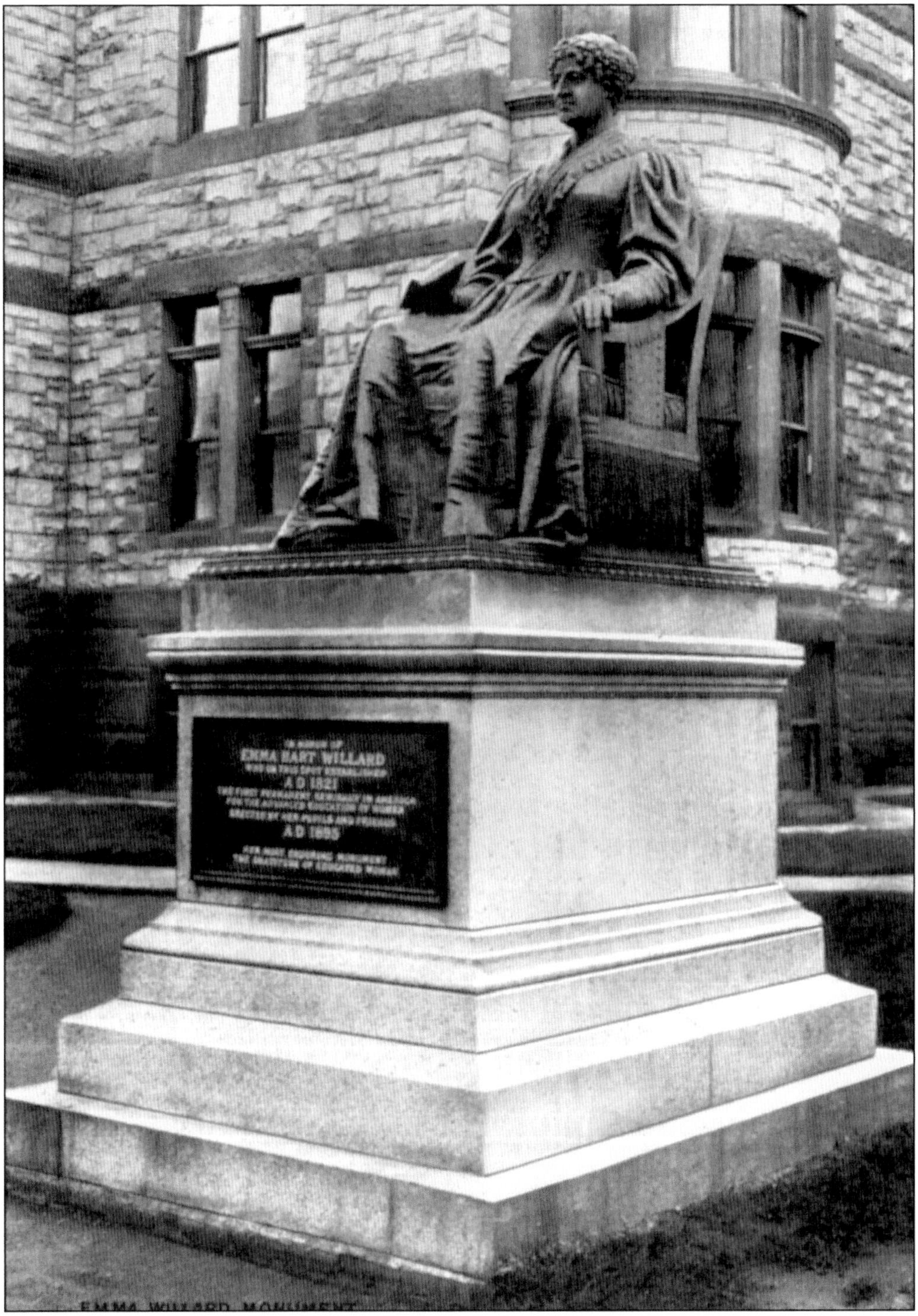

THE EMMA WILLARD MONUMENT. This monument is located in Seminary Park at Russell Sage College. The plaque reads: "In honor of Emma Hart Willard who on this spot established A D 1821 the first permanent Seminary in America for the advanced education of woman erected by her pupils and friend A D 1895 her most enduring monument the gratitude of educated woman."

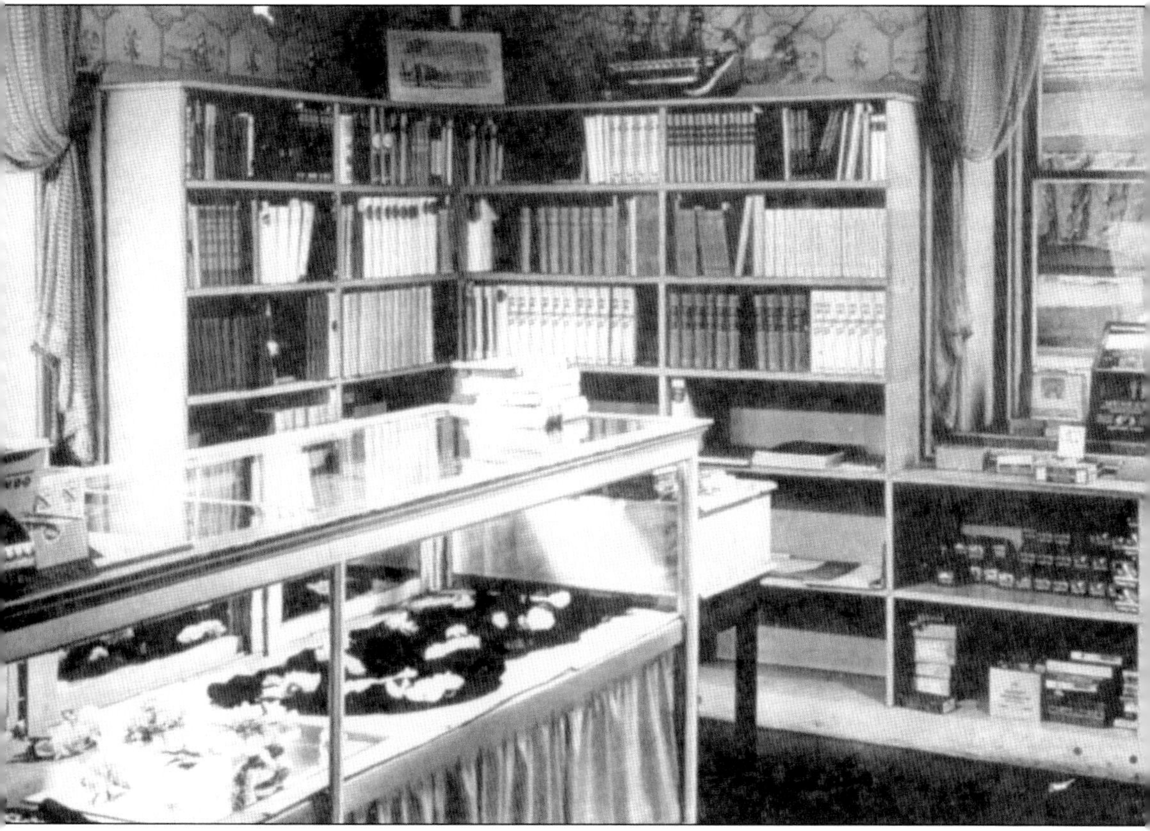

THE RUSSELL SAGE BOOKSTORE. This view shows the interior of the Russell Sage Bookstore. The store sold not only books and school supplies but also (as seen in the showcase) corsages for special events and dances.

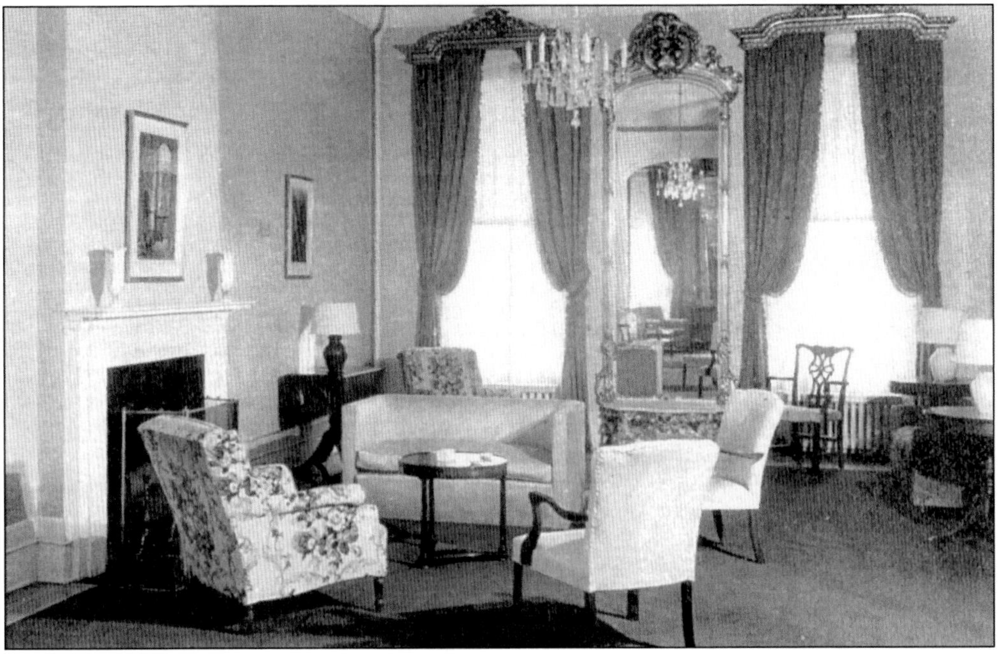

A Living Room at Russell Sage. This interior view shows the living room of the Eliza Kellas House at Russell Sage.

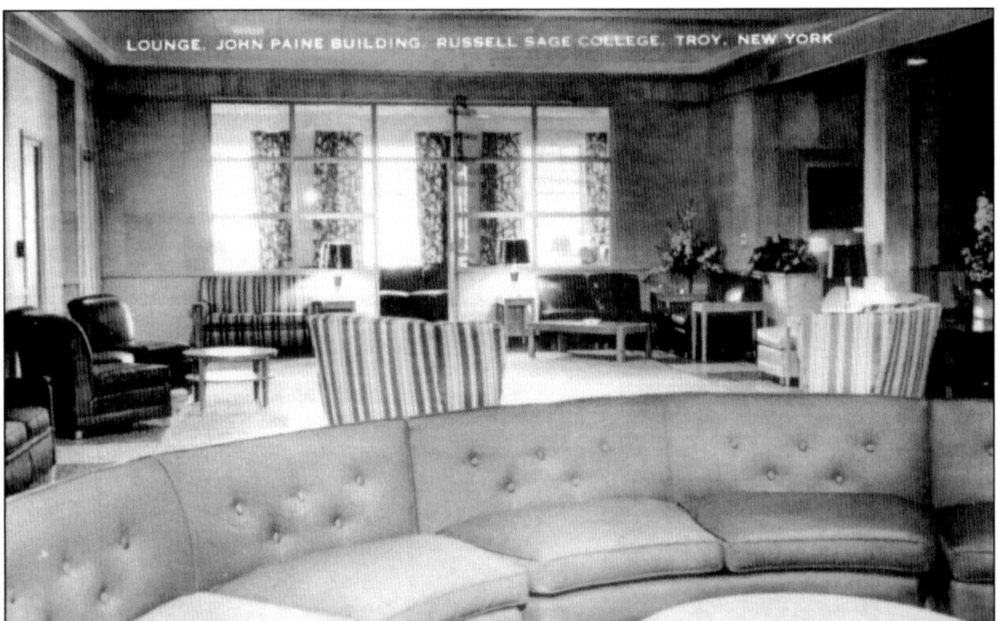

A Lounge at Russell Sage. This card shows a view of the lounge in the John Paine Building at Russell Sage College.

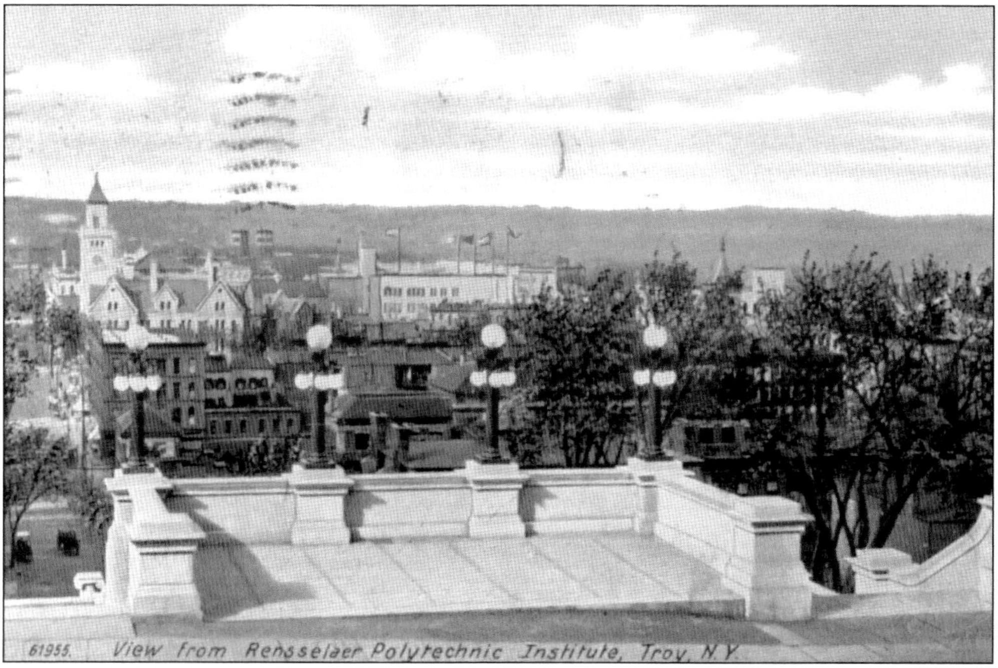

THE BROADWAY APPROACH. The Louis Rubin Memorial Approach at Broadway connects the city of Troy with Rensselaer Polytechnic Institute. The approach was built after two buildings burned down on campus. At a cost of $40,000, the city built this link to keep the institute from relocating. In the last few years, it has been restored.

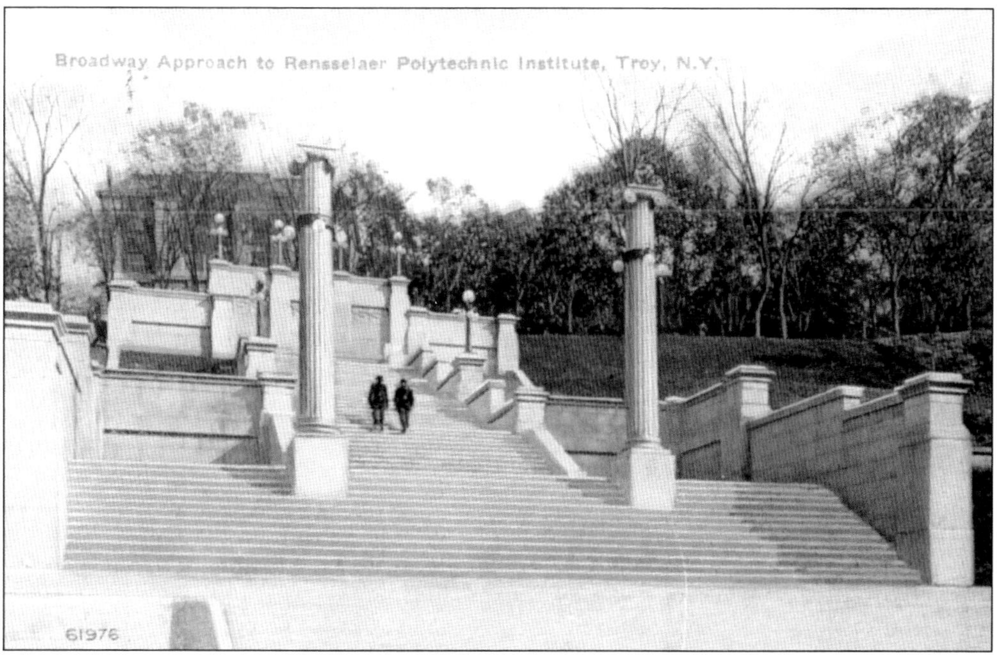

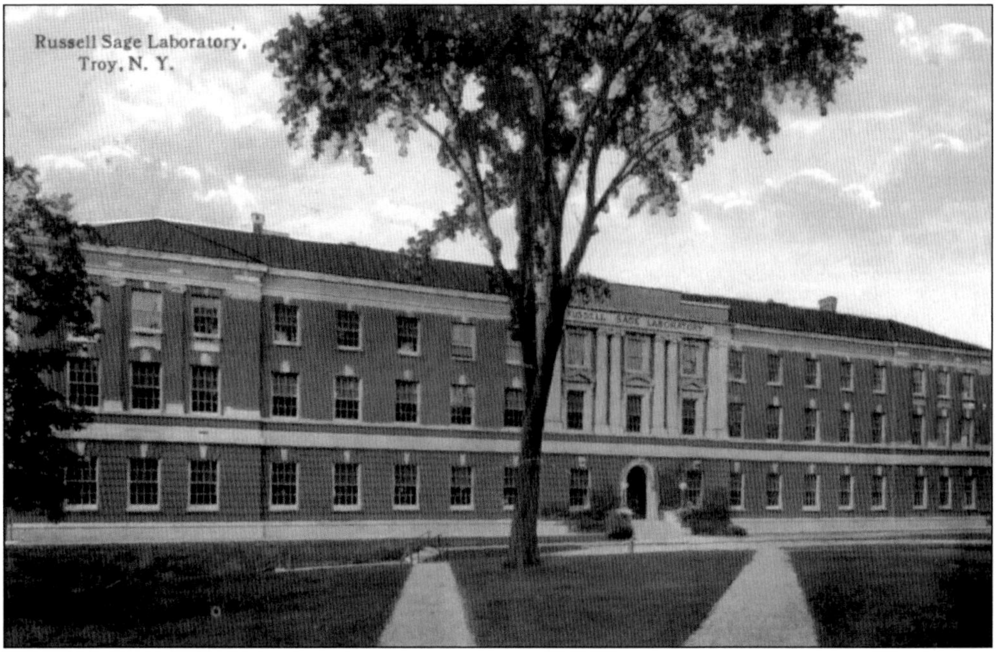

THE RUSSELL SAGE LABORATORY. Russell Sage was a trustee from 1896 to 1906. The four-story building was completed in 1909 at a cost of $425,000.

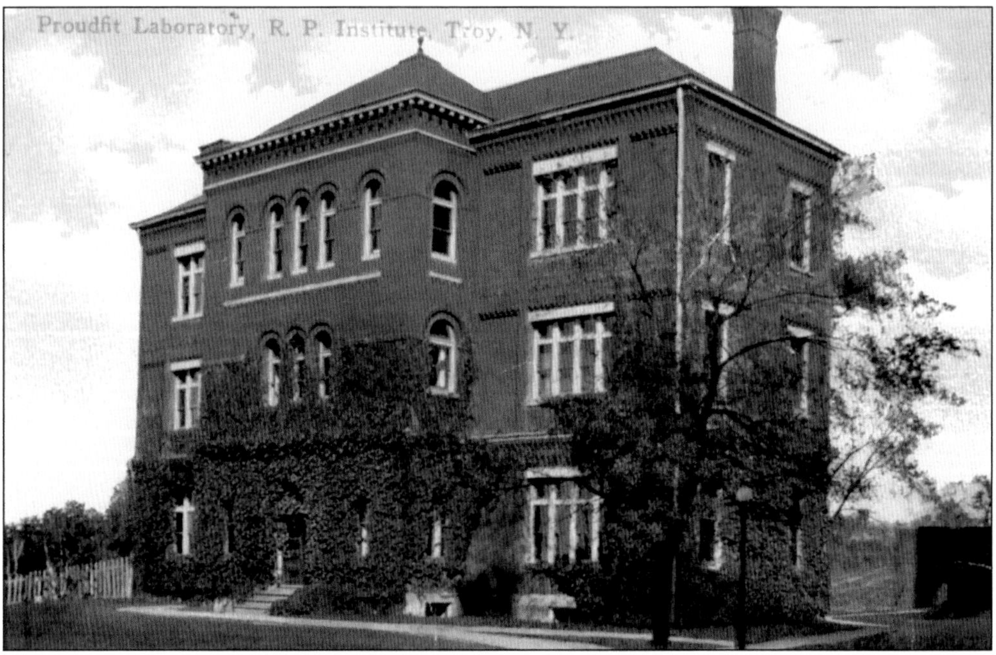

THE PROUDFIT LABORATORY. This laboratory was given by Mr. and Mrs. Ebenezer Proudfit of Troy as a memorial to their son William. William was in the Class of 1877, but he died tragically after being thrown from his horse and carriage in 1875.

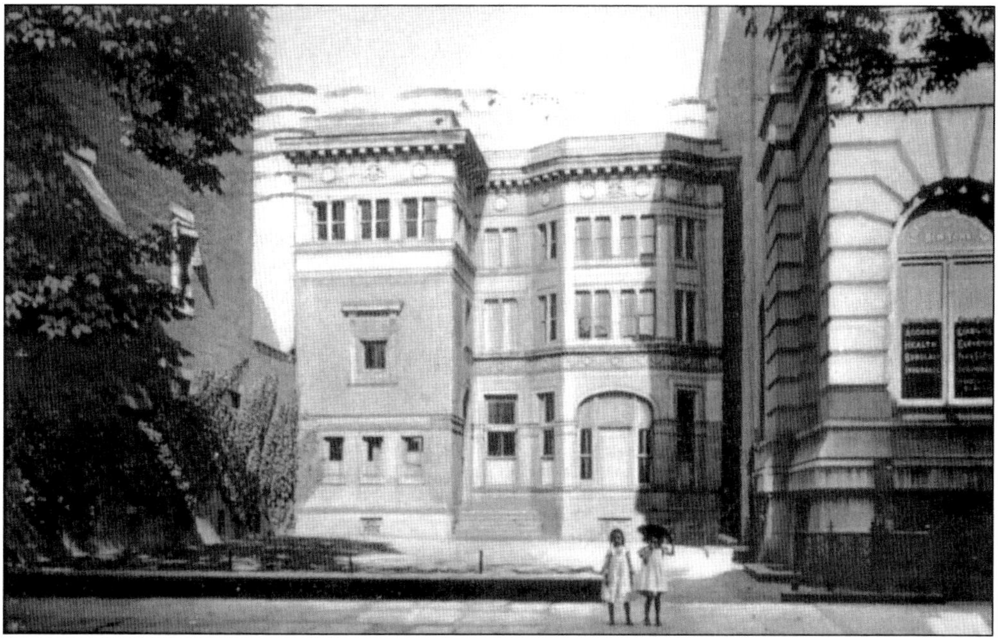

The Alumni Building. This card, mailed in 1907, shows a view of Rensselaer Polytechnic Institute's alumni building. The building was built in 1893.

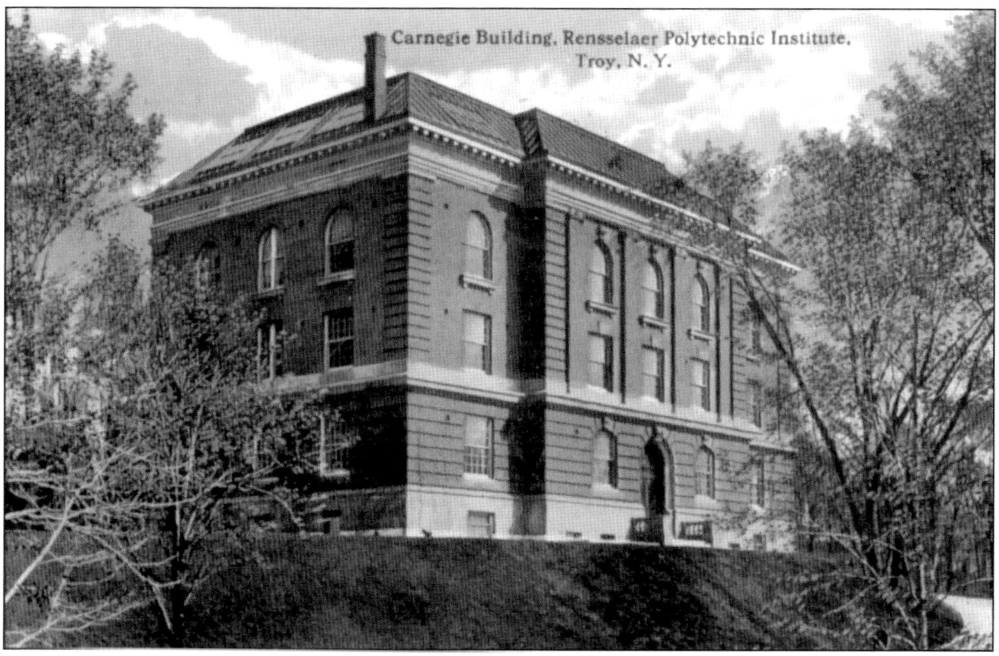

The Carnegie Building. The Carnegie Building at Rensselaer Polytechnic Institute was named after Andrew Carnegie. Construction began in 1905. Carnegie contributed $125,000 of the $133,000 it cost to finish the building.

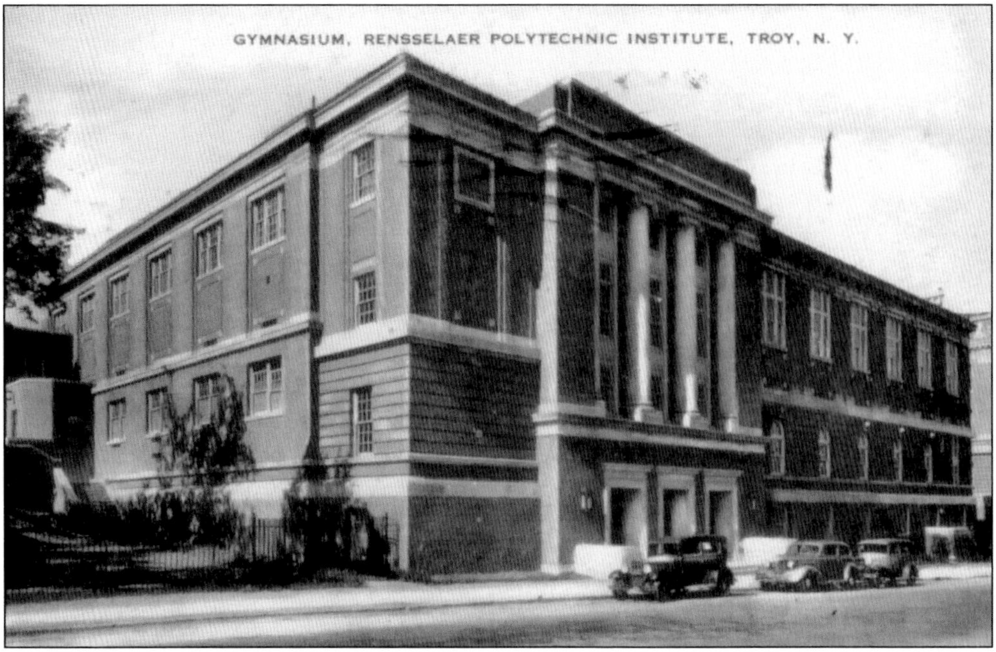

THE GYMNASIUM. This gymnasium at the institute was built with money from the Class of 1887 at a cost of $163,000. It was equipped with the finest equipment of the time.

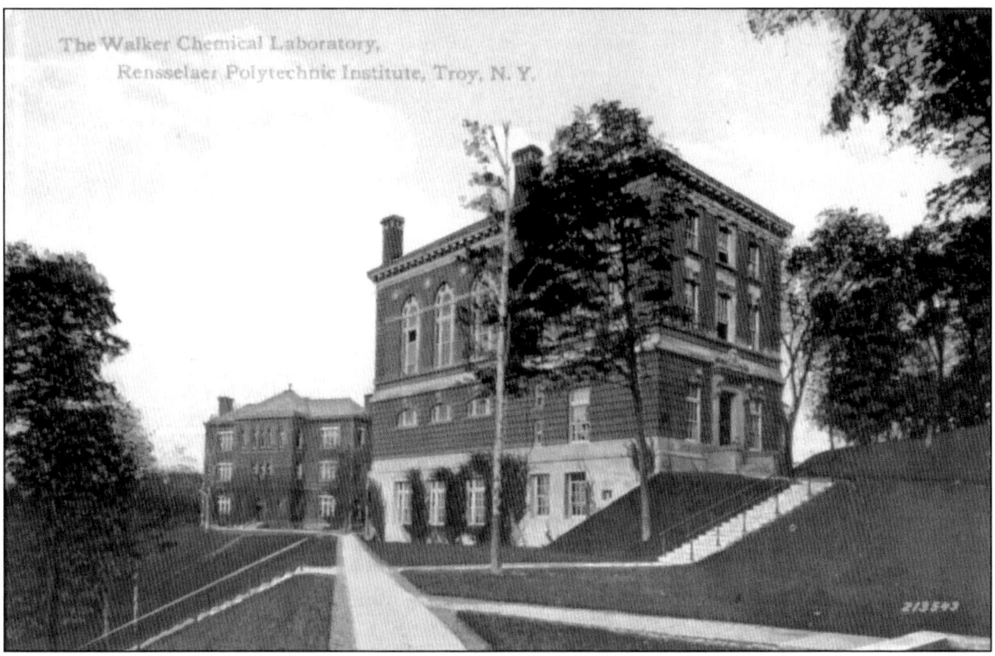

THE WALKER CHEMICAL LABORATORY. The Walker Chemical Building at Rensselaer Polytechnic Institute was under construction at the same time as the Carnegie Building. It was built as a memorial for Dr. William Weightman Walker, who graduated in 1886.

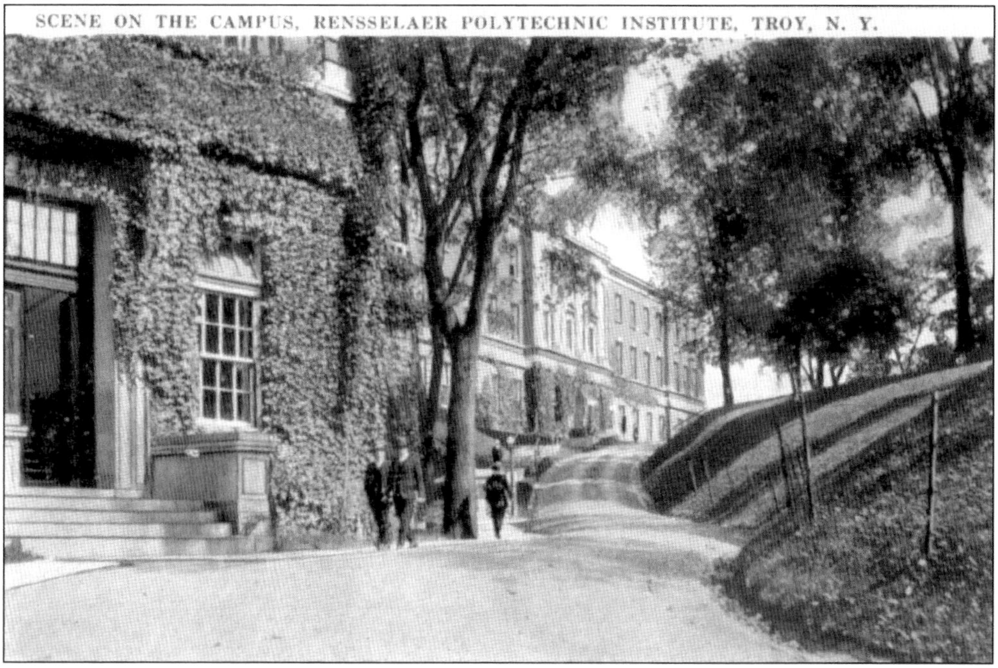

RENSSELAER POLYTECHNIC INSTITUTE. The institute was first known as the Rensselaer School when it was opened in 1824 by Stephen Van Rensselaer. Its name changed two more times from the Rensselaer Institute in 1833 to today's Rensselaer Polytechnic Institute, which it changed to in 1861.

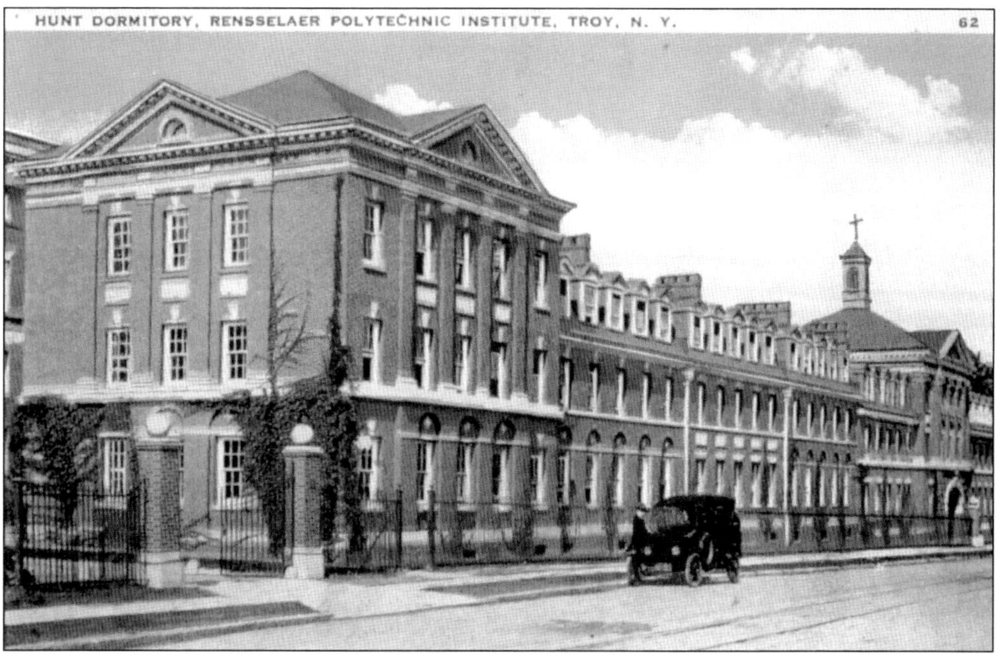

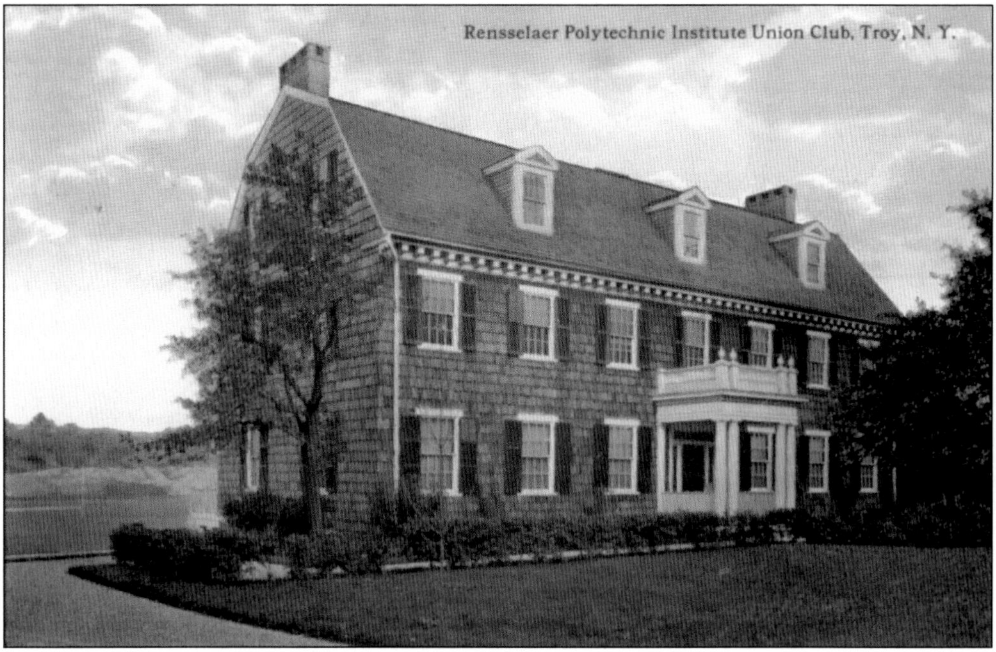

THE UNION CLUB AT RENSSELAER POLYTECHNIC INSTITUTE. The student clubhouse, called the Union Club, was built in 1908. The cost to build it was $19,000.

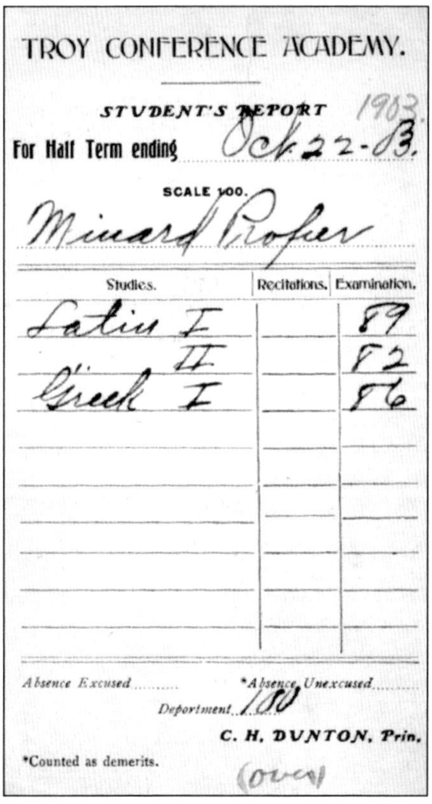

TROY CONFERENCE ACADEMY.

STUDENT'S REPORT 1903

For Half Term ending Oct 22-03.

SCALE 100.

Minard [illegible]

Studies.	Recitations.	Examination.
Latin I		89
" II		82
Greek I		86

Absence Excused .... *Absence Unexcused ....

Deportment 100

C. H. DUNTON, Prin.

*Counted as demerits.

(over)

TROY CONFERENCE ACADEMY STUDENT'S REPORT. Here is a report card dated 1903 from the Troy Conference Academy. The academy was incorporated in 1834. It was a prep school for Rensselaer Polytechnic Institute. The school closed in 1917 and was torn down in 1923.

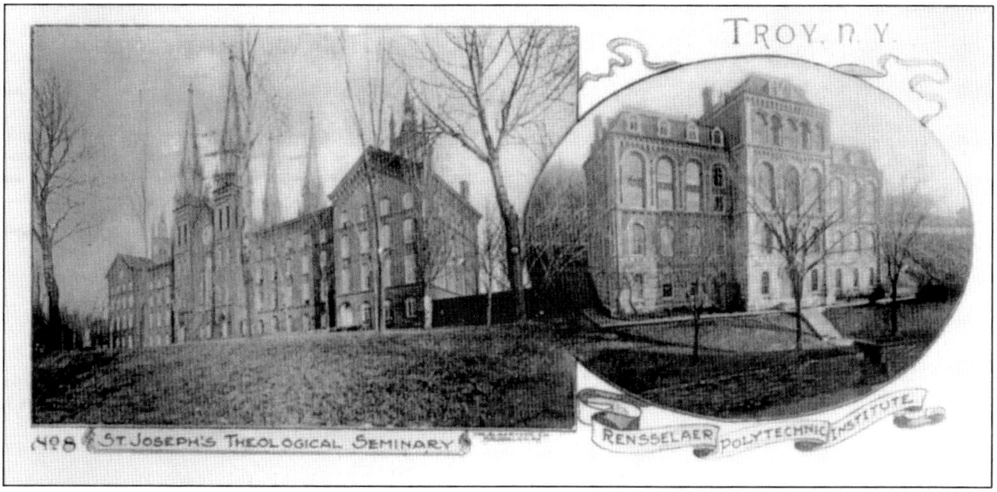

ST. JOSEPH'S THEOLOGICAL SEMINARY. In 1858, the building was originally constructed as Troy University, which only lasted for four years. The Catholic church purchased it for a seminary. It then became the seminary for Sisters of St. Joseph. The Rensselaer Polytechnic Institute acquired it in the 1950s.

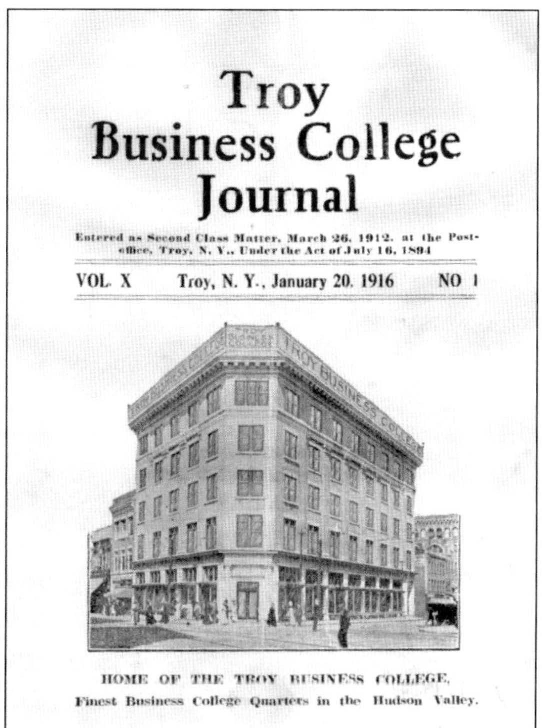

Troy Business College Journal

Entered as Second Class Matter, March 26, 1912, at the Post-office, Troy, N. Y., Under the Act of July 16, 1894

VOL. X Troy, N. Y., January 20, 1916 NO 1

HOME OF THE TROY BUSINESS COLLEGE,
Finest Business College Quarters in the Hudson Valley.

TROY BUSINESS COLLEGE JOURNAL. Established in 1858, the Troy Business College was located in the Boardman Building, at the corner of River and Fulton Streets. The college boasted that it was "the finest business college quarters in the Hudson Valley."

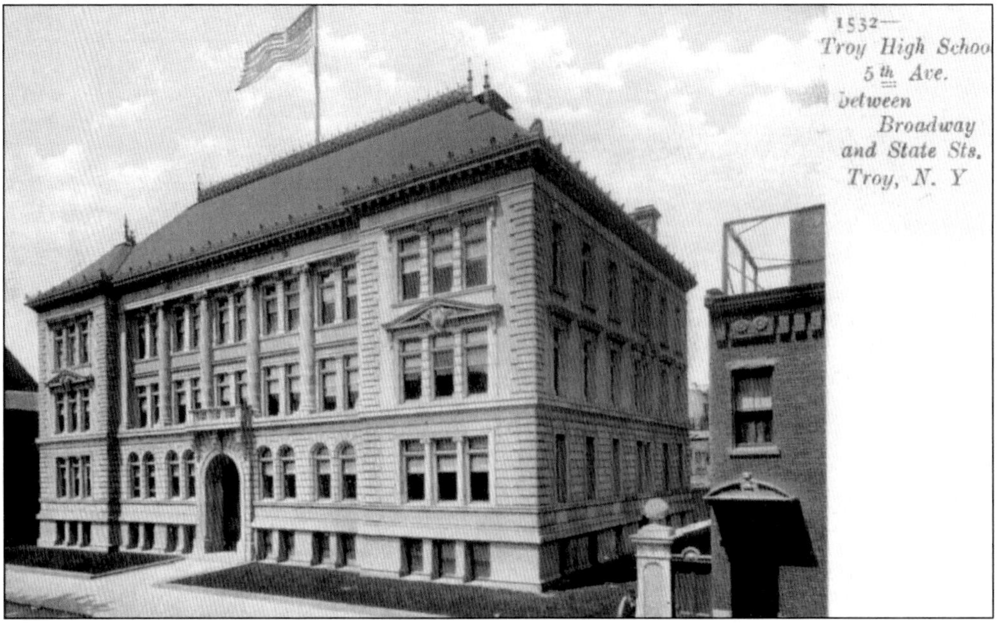

Troy High School. Located on Fifth Avenue between Broadway and State Streets, it almost became city hall, but it never went through. The building was torn down in the 1960s.

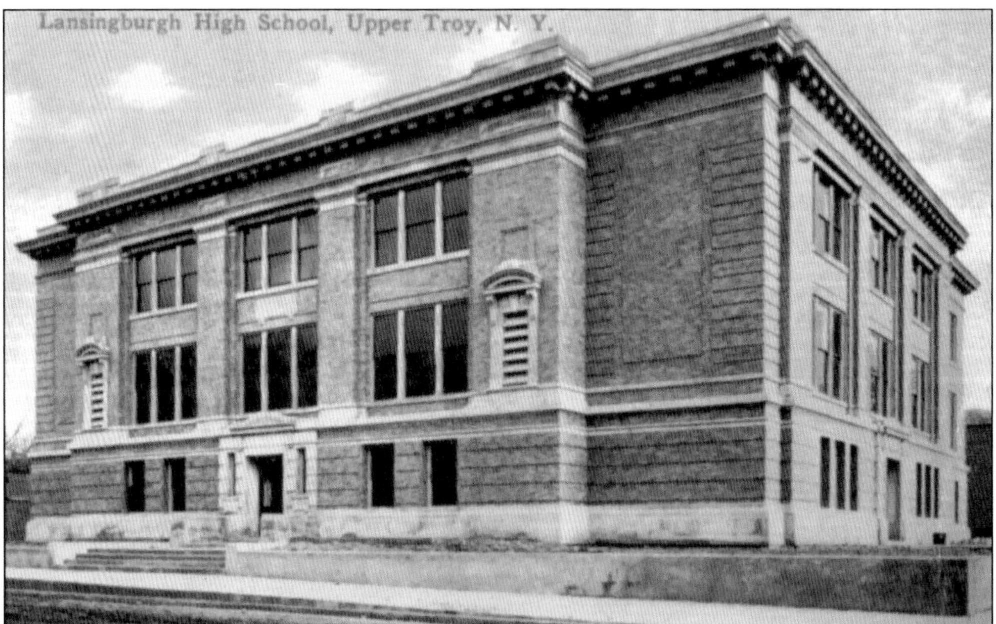

Lansingburgh High School. This card shows the Lansingburgh High School *c.* 1912. The high school is located north of Troy in the village of Lansingburgh. It is still in use today.

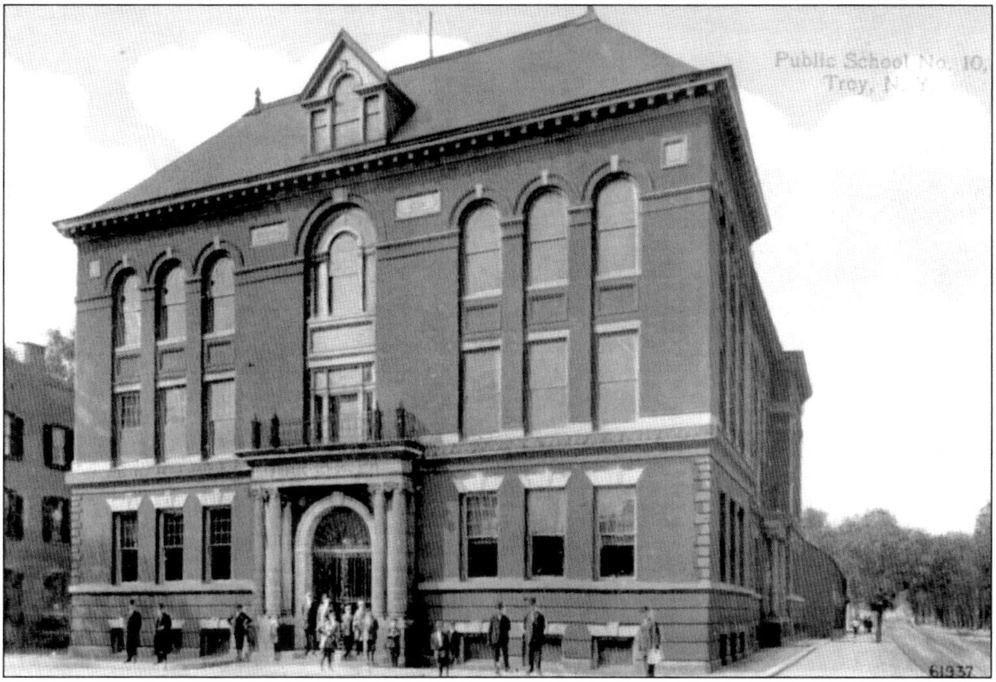

PUBLIC SCHOOL NO. 10. This school was built in 1898 on Adams and Third Streets.

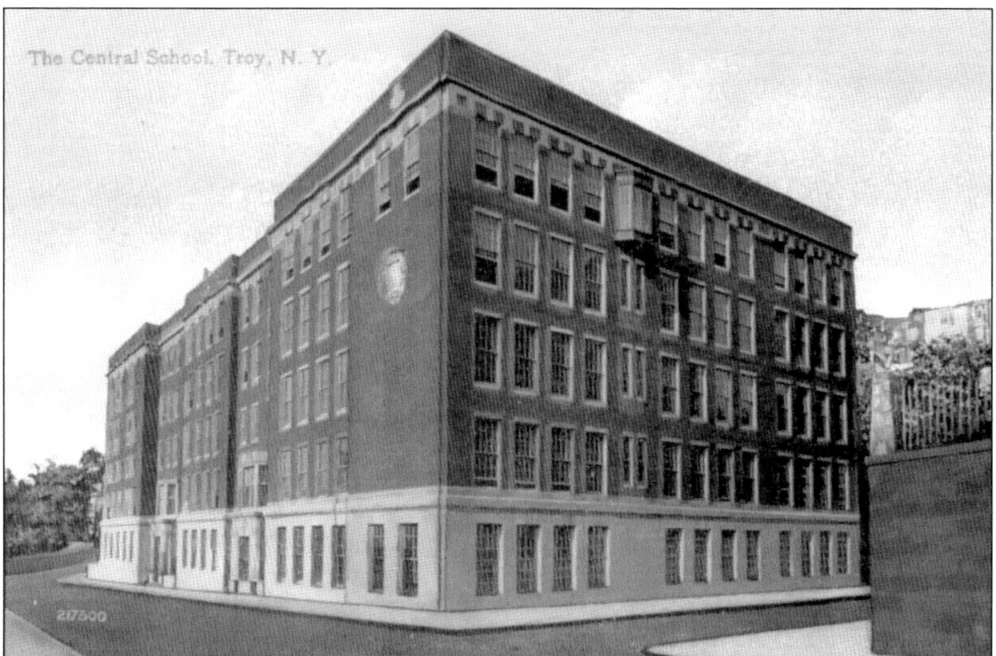

THE CENTRAL SCHOOL. Located on the east side of Seventh Avenue and south of State Street was the former Troy High School, then called the Central School.

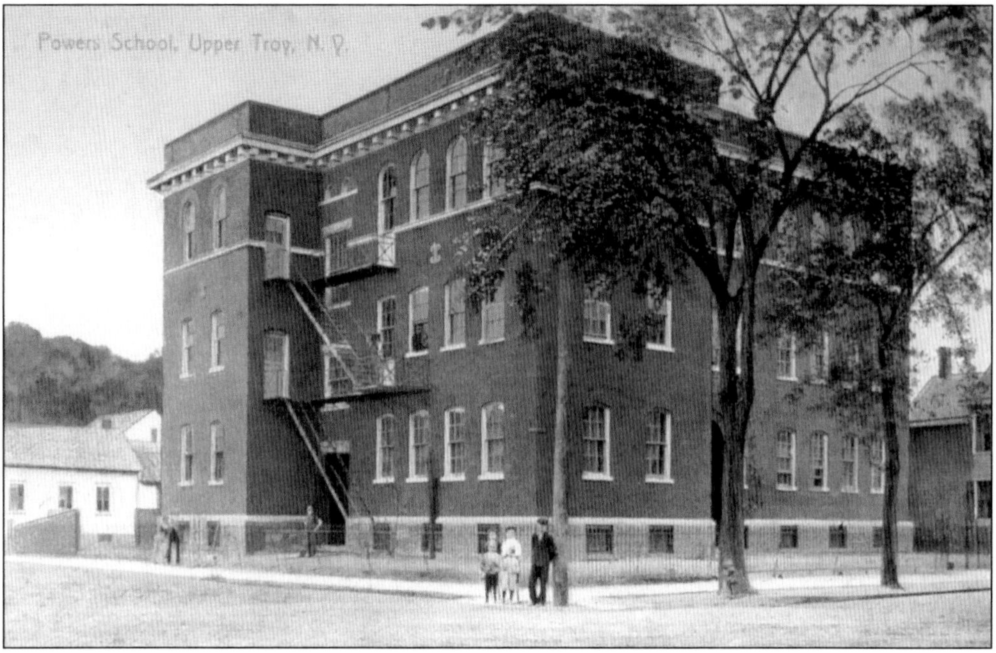

THE POWERS SCHOOL. The Powers School was located at Fourth Avenue and 111th Street in Lansingburgh.

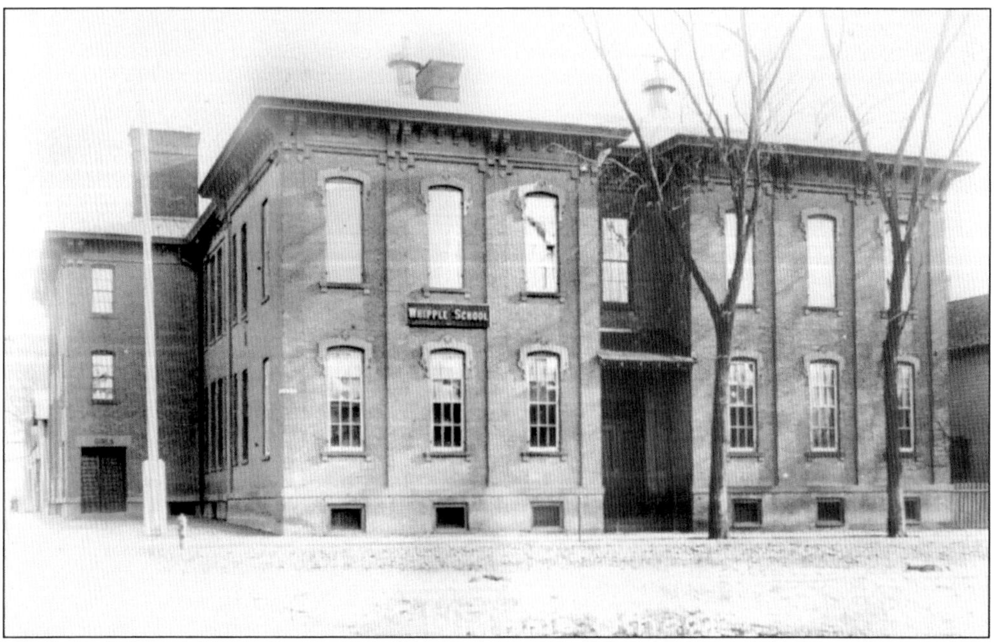

WHIPPLE SCHOOL. This school was located at 121st Street and Fourth Avenue in Lansingburgh.

Six

Fire and Water

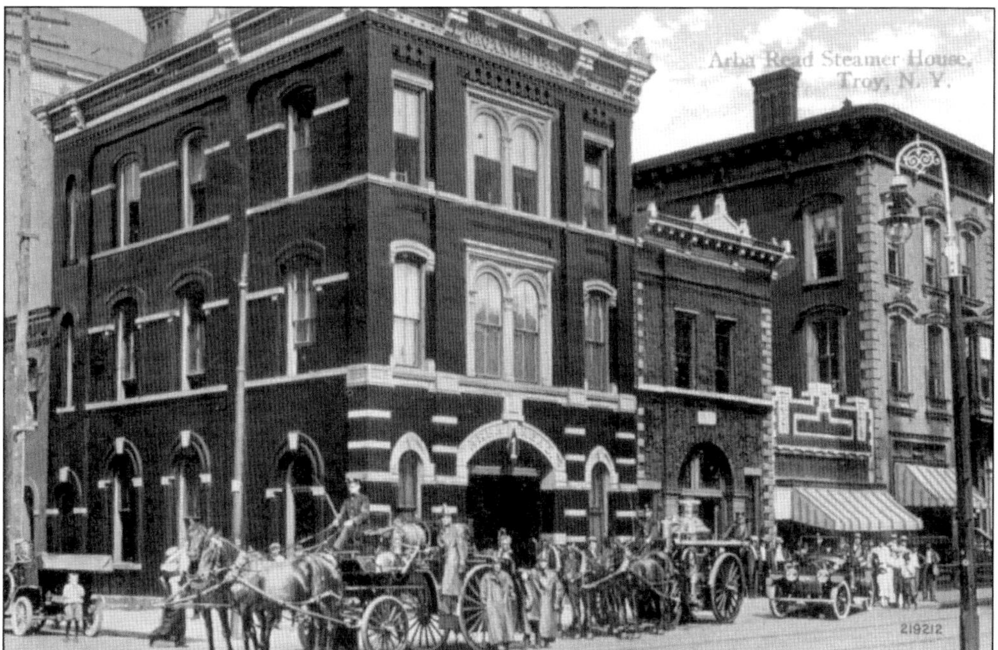

The Arba Read Steamer House. Arba Read was a Troy brewer from the Excelsior Brewing family. The steamer company, which originated in 1859, was located on State and Third Streets. This was one of the companies that fought the fire of 1862. This view shows a very proud group of firemen.

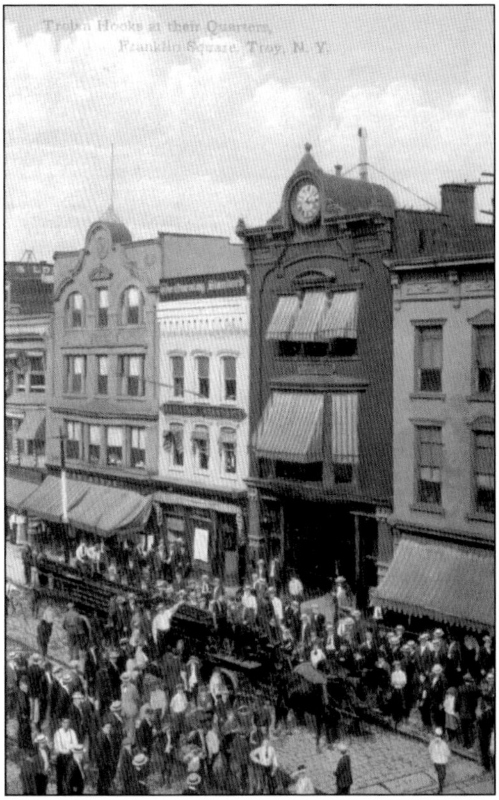

"TROJAN HOOKS AT THEIR QUARTERS, FRANKLIN SQUARE." In this view, folks are gathered on the cobblestone street and are posing for pictures in front of the Trojan Hooks Firehouse. To the left is the old Evening Standard newspaper. Men were proud to become volunteer firemen, and their lives revolved around their department. It is the same around the country today with volunteer firefighters. In the 1920s, when firemen began to be paid, the horse-drawn engine became a thing of the past and fire trucks replaced them.

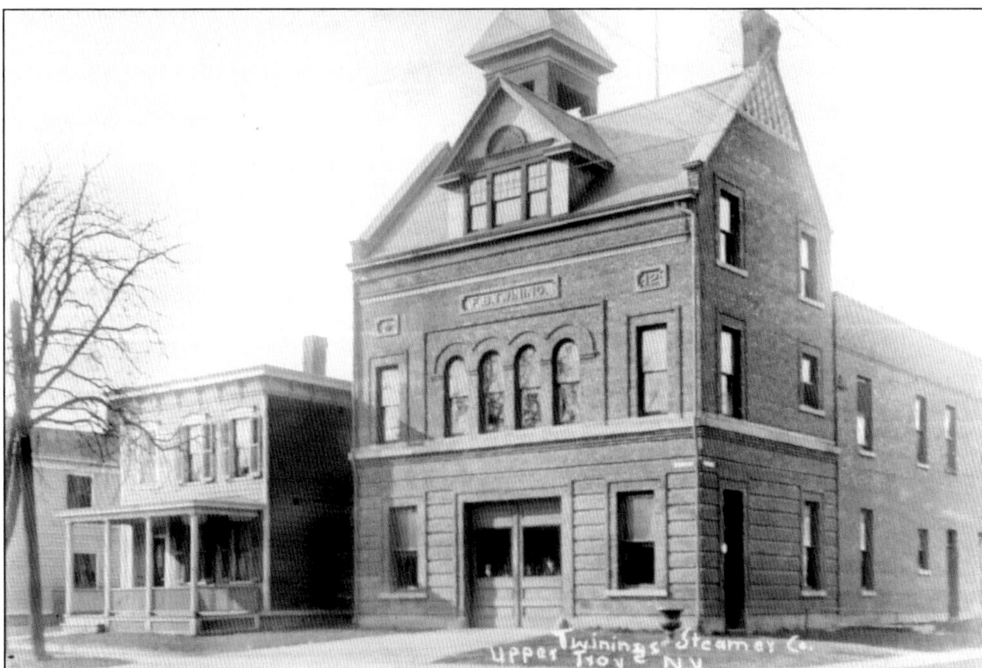

THE TWININGS STEAMER COMPANY. The Frank B. Twinings Steamer Company was a manufacturer of collars and cuffs. The firehouse was located at 122nd and Second Avenue in Lansingburgh.

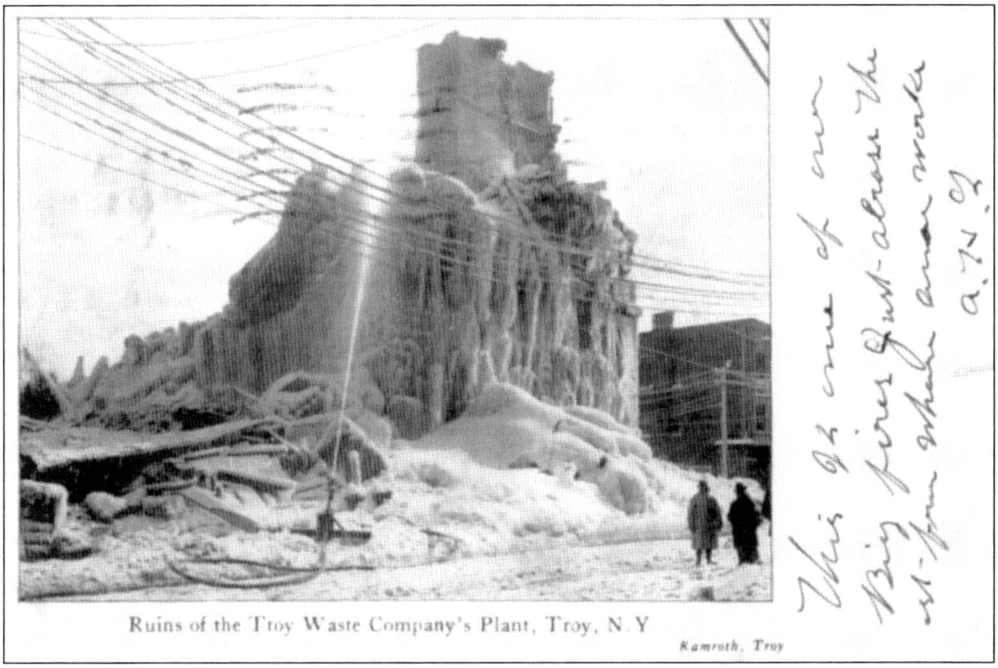

"RUINS OF THE TROY WASTE COMPANY'S PLANT." This building, located at the corner of River and King Streets, was destroyed by fire in February 1907. The trolley schedule was interrupted because the tracks were frozen over.

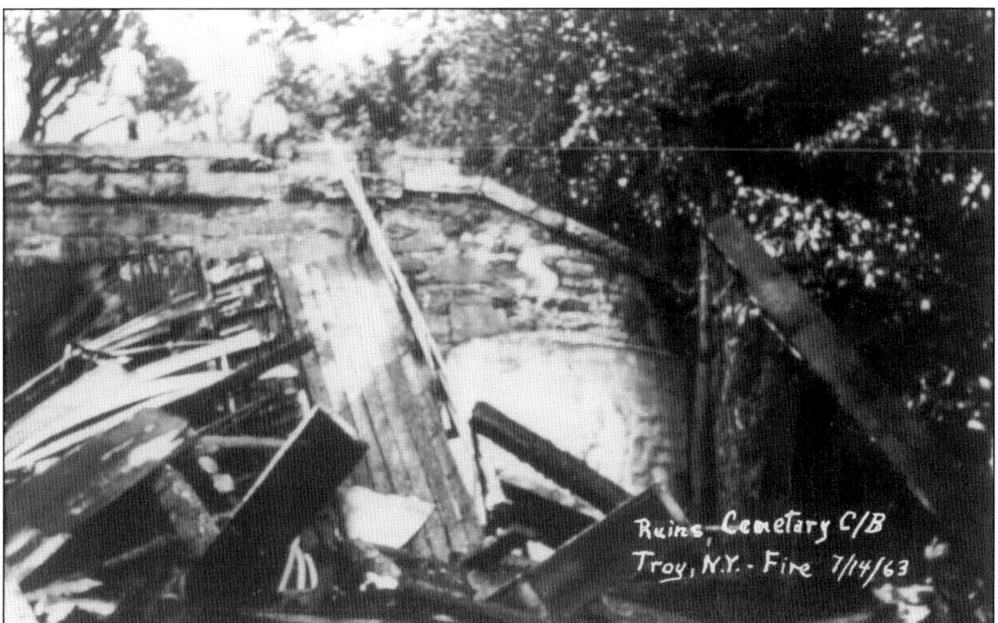

THE CEMETERY COVERED BRIDGE RUINS. This bridge, which used to span the railroad tracks, burned in July 1963.

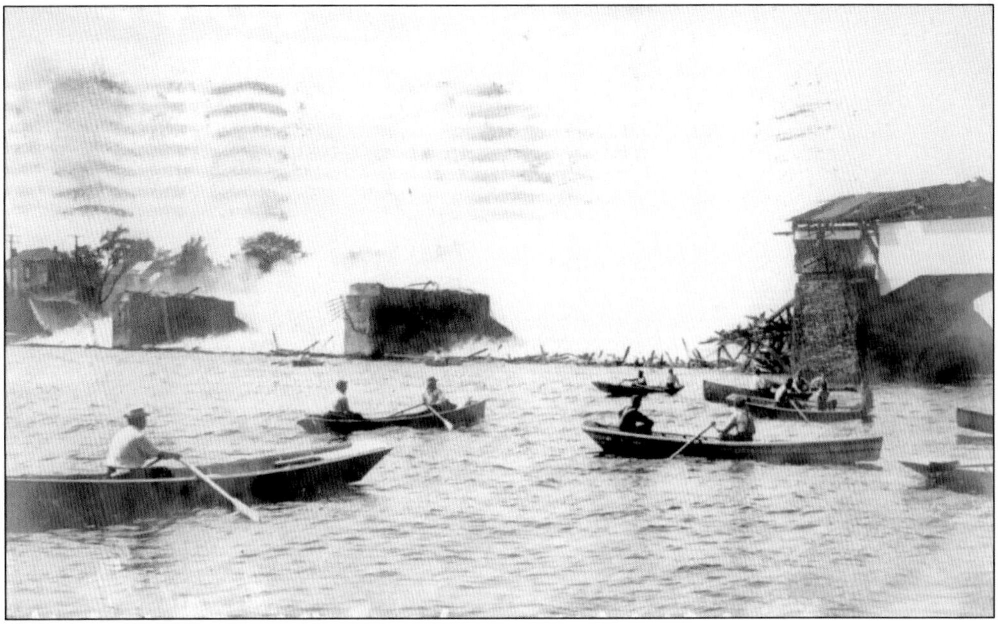

Waterford Fire. Disaster strikes the Waterford-Troy Bridge in North Troy. Fire destroyed this wooden covered bridge in July 1909. Over the years, Troy has had some horrific fires like the ones in 1854 and 1862. Many brave men tried their best to extinguish the flames. Some of the companies that the men came from were Good Intent Engine Company and Rough and Ready Engine Company. Today, this tradition still carries on.

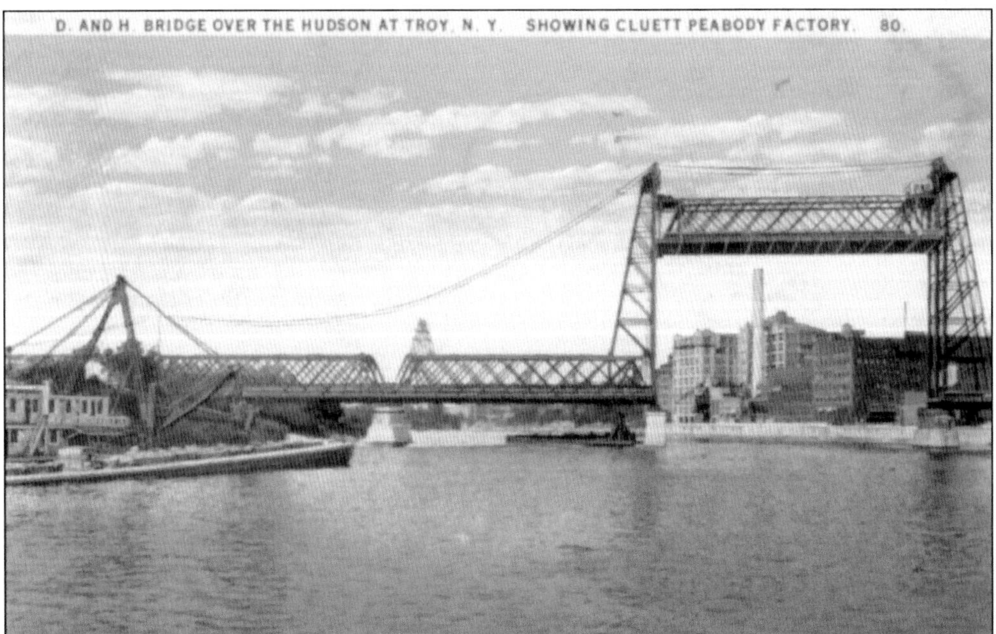

The Delaware & Hudson Bridge over the Hudson. This bridge was better known as the Green Island Bridge. It took tolls up to the 1930s. When the bridge was lifted to let a boat pass through, a traffic jam was caused.

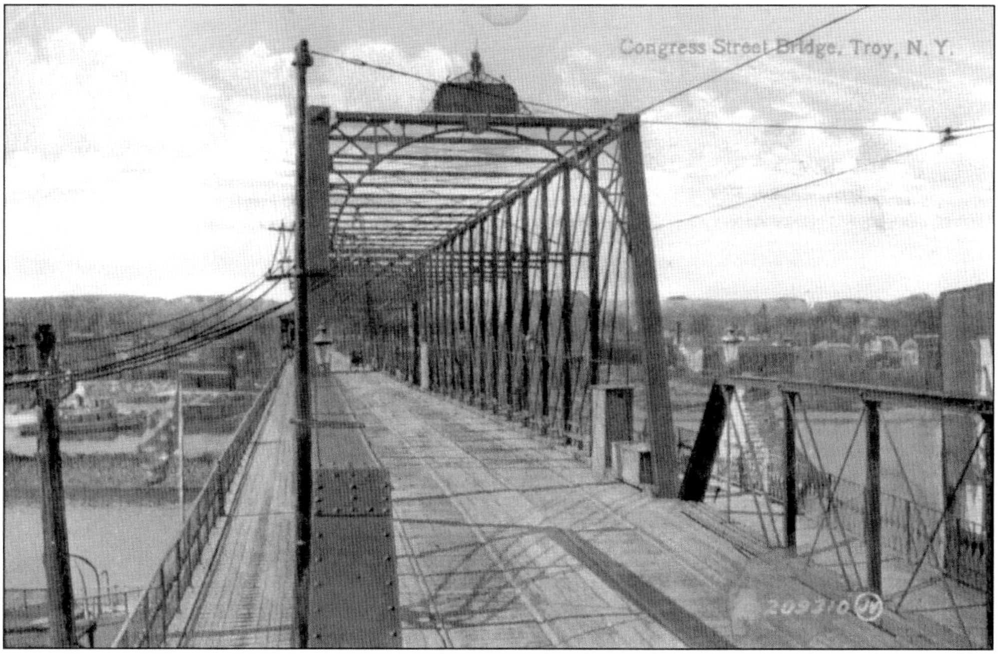

THE CONGRESS STREET BRIDGE. This bridge was built in the 1870s at a cost of $350,000. It spanned the Hudson River and connected with West Troy, which later came to be known as Watervliet.

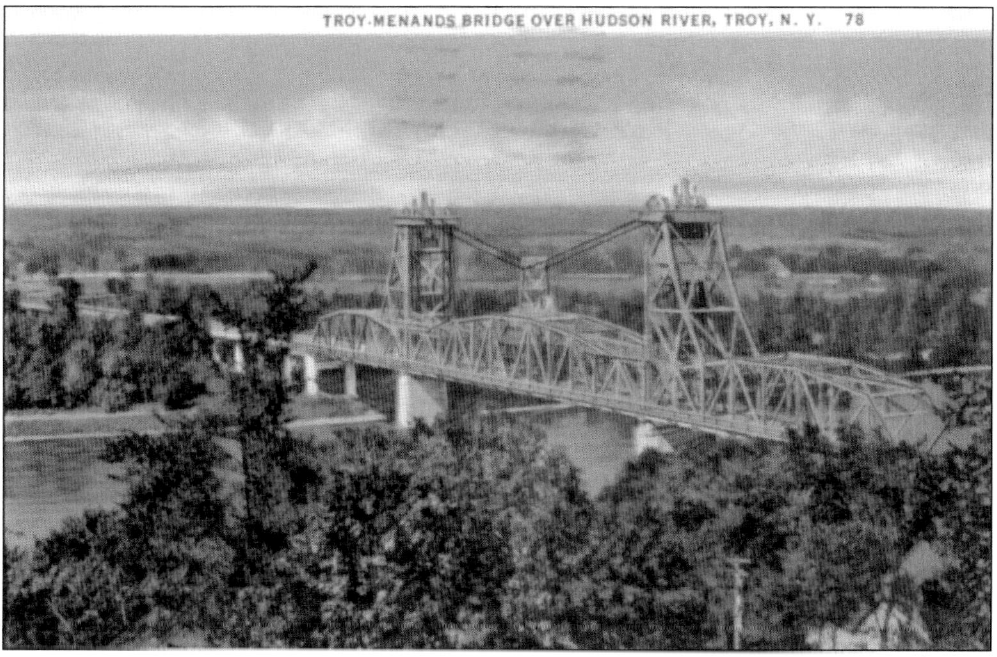

"TROY-MENANDS BRIDGE OVER HUDSON RIVER." The Troy-Menands Bridge, built in 1933, connects South Troy to Menands.

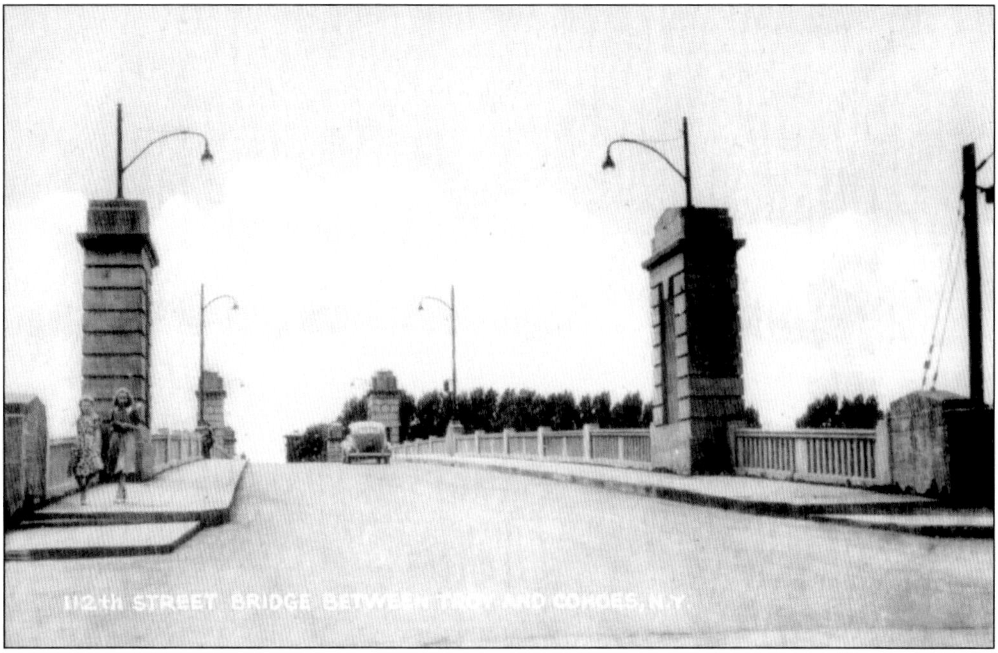

THE 112TH STREET BRIDGE. Seen in this view is the 112th Street Bridge over the Hudson between Lansingburgh and Cohoes. A newer bridge has since replaced it. The original bridge burned in 1920.

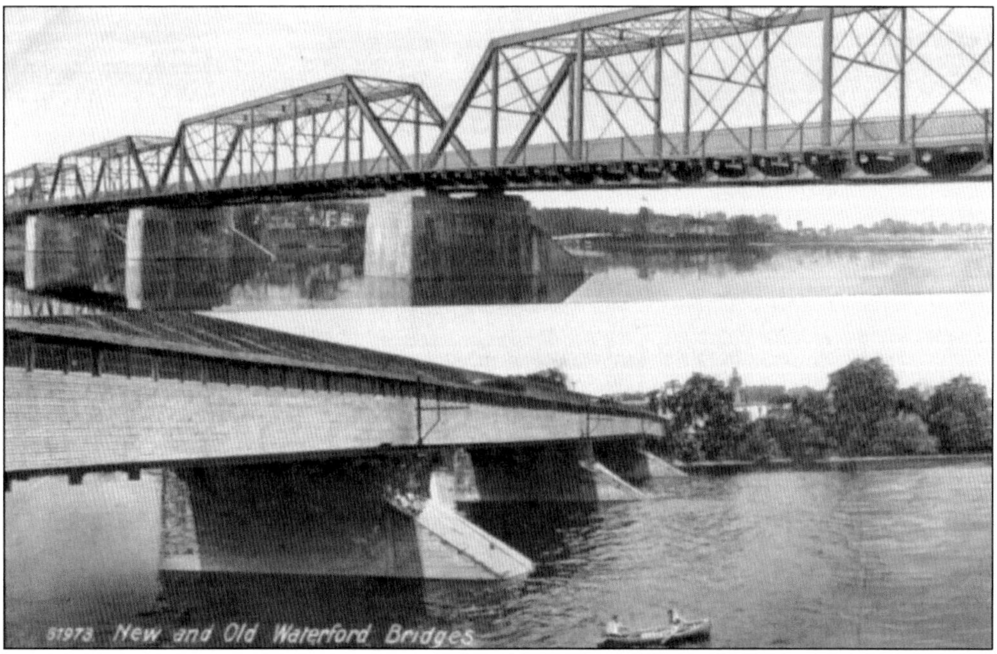

THE WATERFORD BRIDGES. The new (top) and old (bottom) Waterford Bridges are shown in this unique view. The wooden covered bridge opened in 1804. Its 800-foot span cost $50,000 to build.

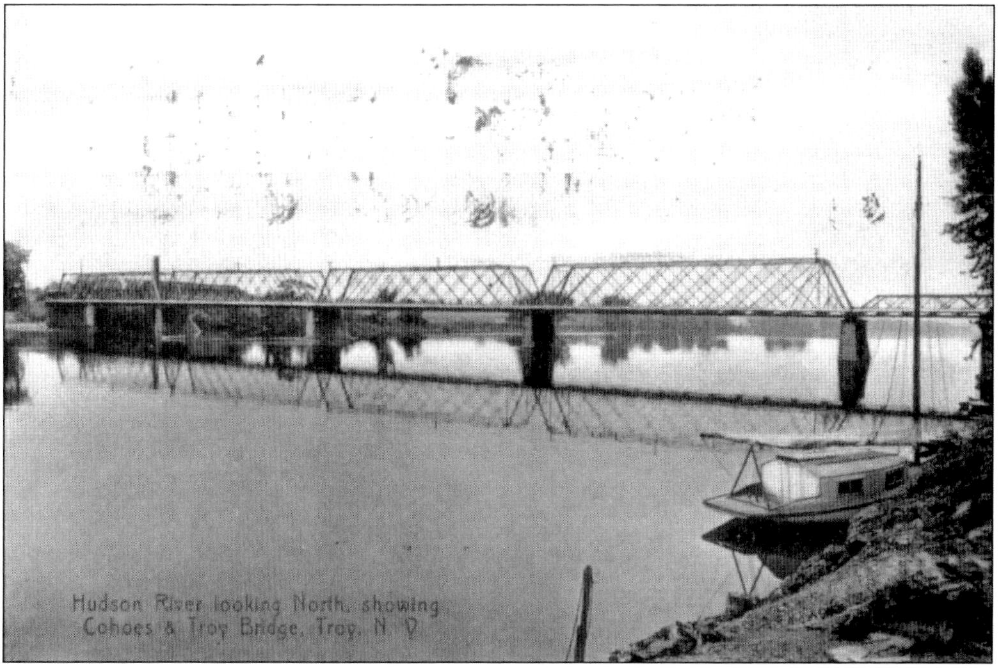

"HUDSON RIVER LOOKING NORTH." This is another view of the Waterford Bridge. Boating was not the only activity enjoyed on the Hudson. Folks would ice-skate, harvest ice, and fish. Unfortunately, you can not do any of these activities today because of all the pollution in the water.

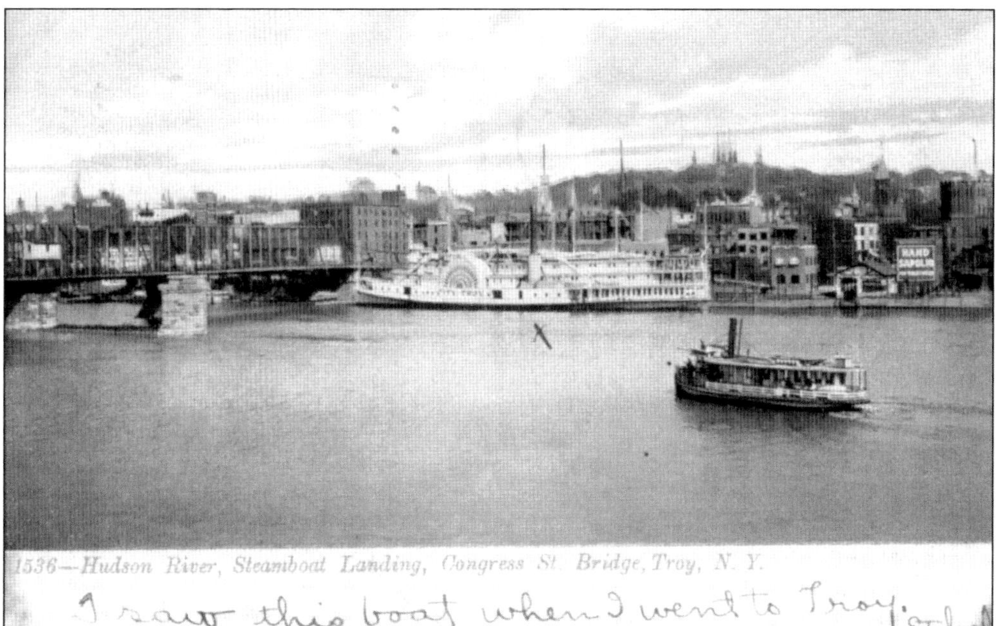

"HUDSON RIVER, STEAMBOAT LANDING." The *City of Troy* and the *Saratoga,* from the Citizen's Steamboat Company, traveled from Troy to New York City at night. Often called floating palaces, they were very luxurious, with state rooms, a dining room, and electricity. The boats could make the 150-mile trip down the Hudson in about 10 hours.

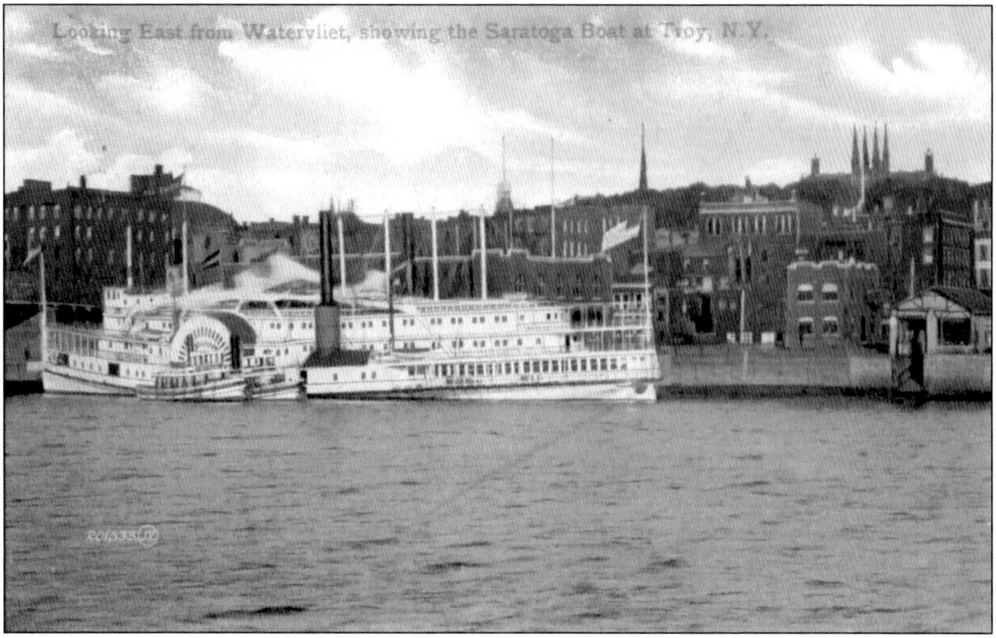

"LOOKING EAST FROM WATERVLIET." Note the *Saratoga* steamboat and the Troy skyline in this postcard.

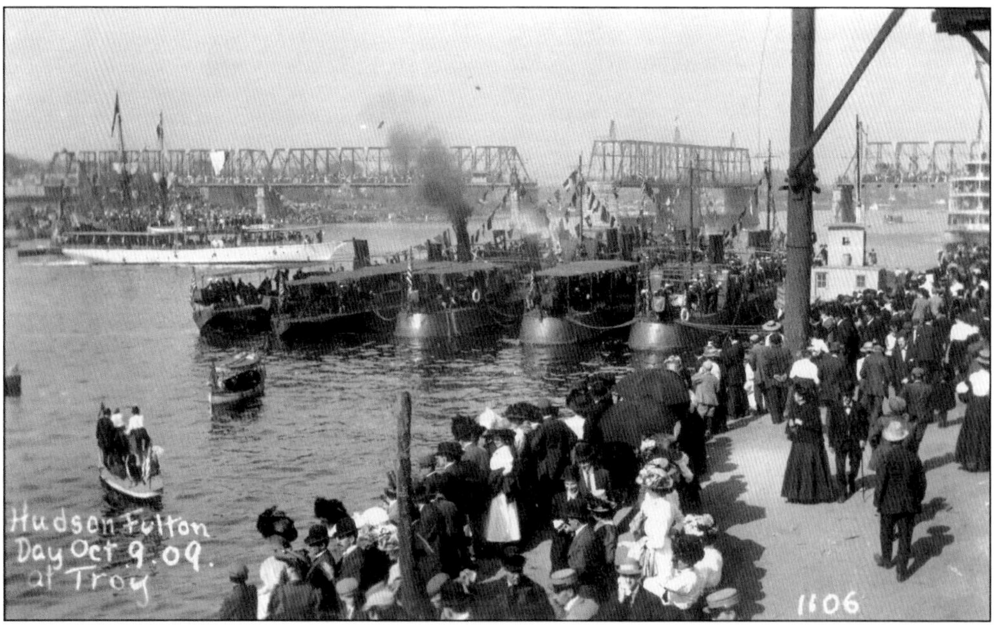

HUDSON FULTON DAY. Celebrated on October 9, 1909, Hudson Fulton Day was the 300-year anniversary of Henry Hudson as well as the 102-year anniversary of the invention of the steamboat by Robert Fulton. This was a week-long celebration with replicas of Fulton's *North River* and Hudson's *Halfmoon*. This is when people would dress up for an occasion.

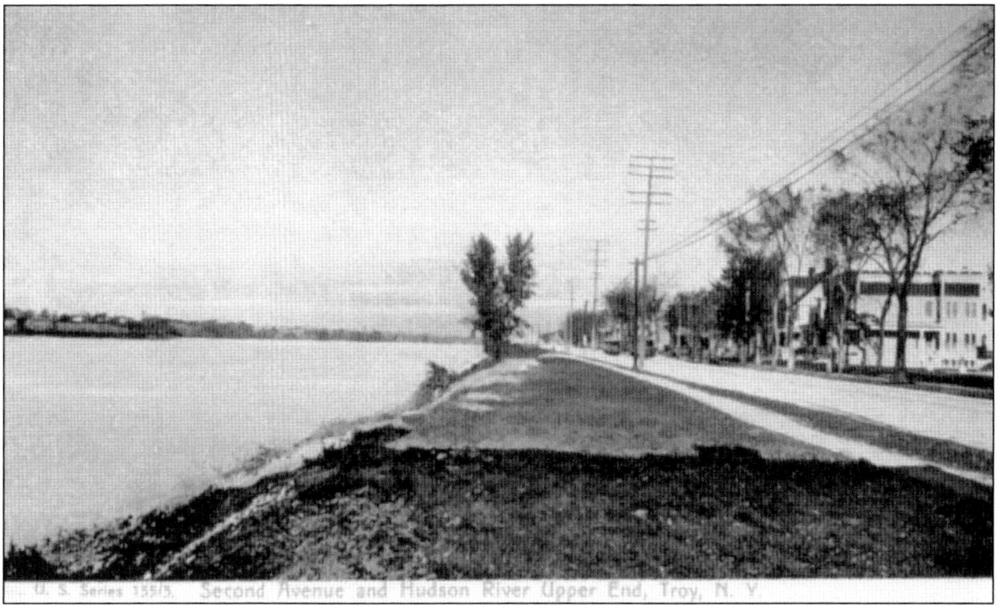

"SECOND AVENUE AND HUDSON RIVER." Here we see the Hudson River running along Second Avenue in the south part of Lansingburgh. With only a few buildings on this stretch, not much has changed at all.

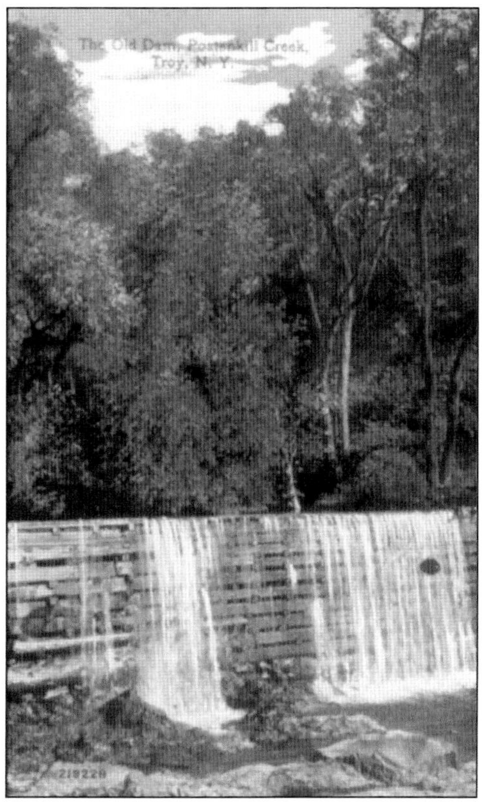

THE OLD DAM. In Dutch, the word *poestenkill* translates to "foaming or puffing stream."

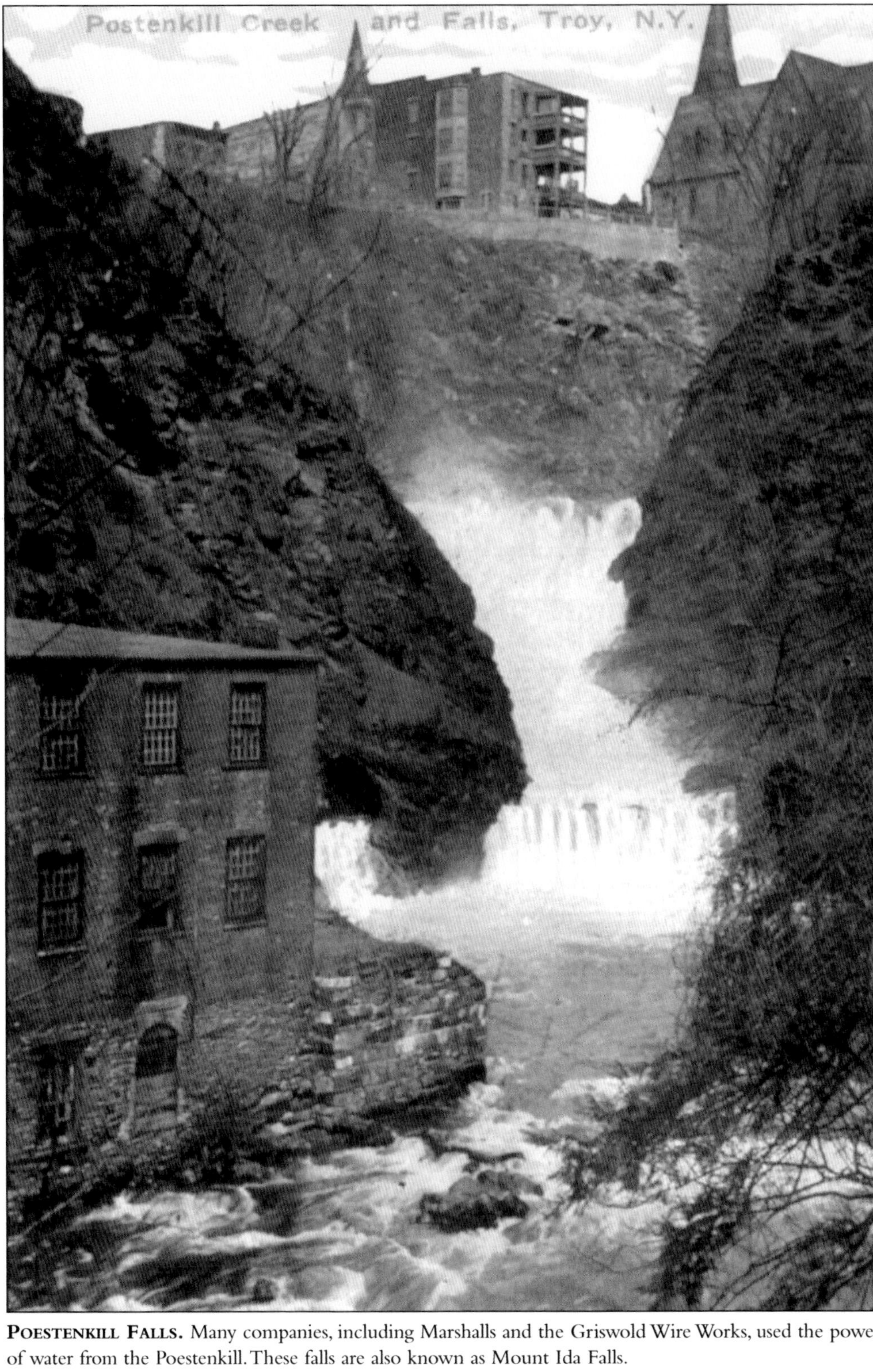

POESTENKILL FALLS. Many companies, including Marshalls and the Griswold Wire Works, used the power of water from the Poestenkill. These falls are also known as Mount Ida Falls.

Seven

Enjoying Life's Pleasures

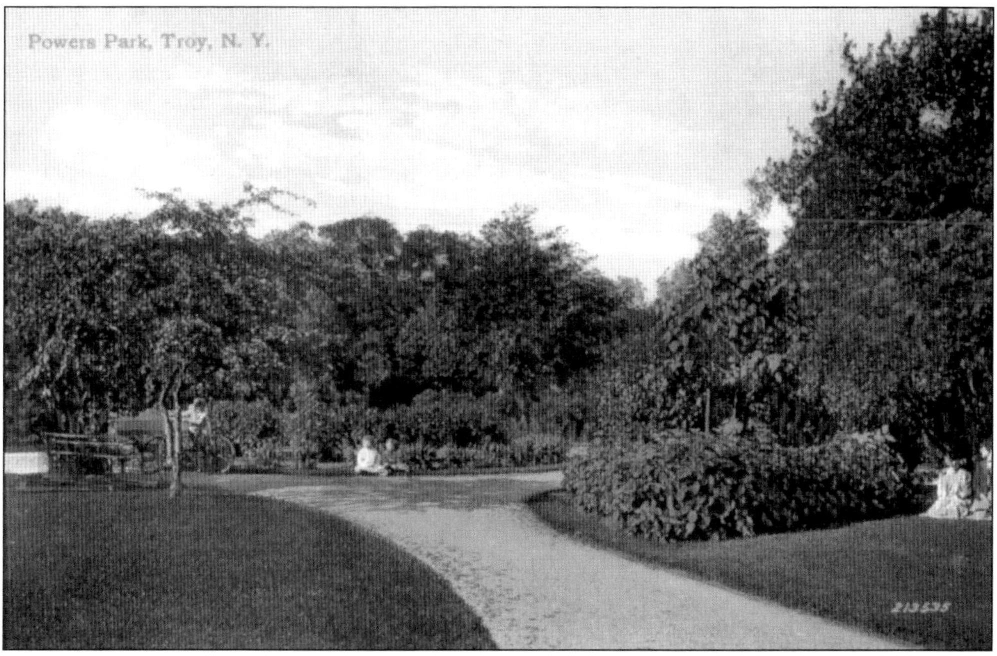

Powers Park. Powers Park was built between 110th and 111th and Second and Third Avenues in Lansingburgh. It was lush with trees, park benches, and a beautiful wrought-iron fence. It was called the William and Deborah Powers Memorial Park. William and Deborah Powers were from the famed Powers Oil Cloth Business.

RULES—Continued from Front Page

yond and out of distance before playing.

Do not talk while your opponent is playing.

Don't call out to a friend playing on another hole; it may disturb some other player.

Don't play your approach shot while anyone is on the putting green.

Don't tarry on the putting green when through playing; others may be behind you.

This Score Card furnished through the courtesy of

Benson's Radio & Sport Shop

14 KING STREET

YOU WILL SAVE MONEY HERE ON YOUR

SPORTS EQUIPMENT

A FREAR PARK SCORECARD. This 1930s scorecard is from the Frear Park Golf Course. Frear Park's beginnings started when the Frear family donated 22 acres of their land next to 90 acres of city-owned

Frear Park Golf Course

Troy Recreation Dept.

RULES

Out of bounds: all paved roads.

Player should lay the flag rod down when removed from the hole. Do not stick it in the turf.

No player should play from the tee until the party in front have played their second strokes and are out of range, nor play up to the putting green till the party in front have holed out and moved away.

When ball is on putting green, other than the one being played, it should be lifted and dropped, no nearer hole, without penalty.

The etiquette of Golf is as important as its rules. Matches playing slowly should let faster players go through and wait until they are be-

property. In 1931, the golf course opened as a nine-hole course. Today, it has grown to 18 holes and 200 acres.

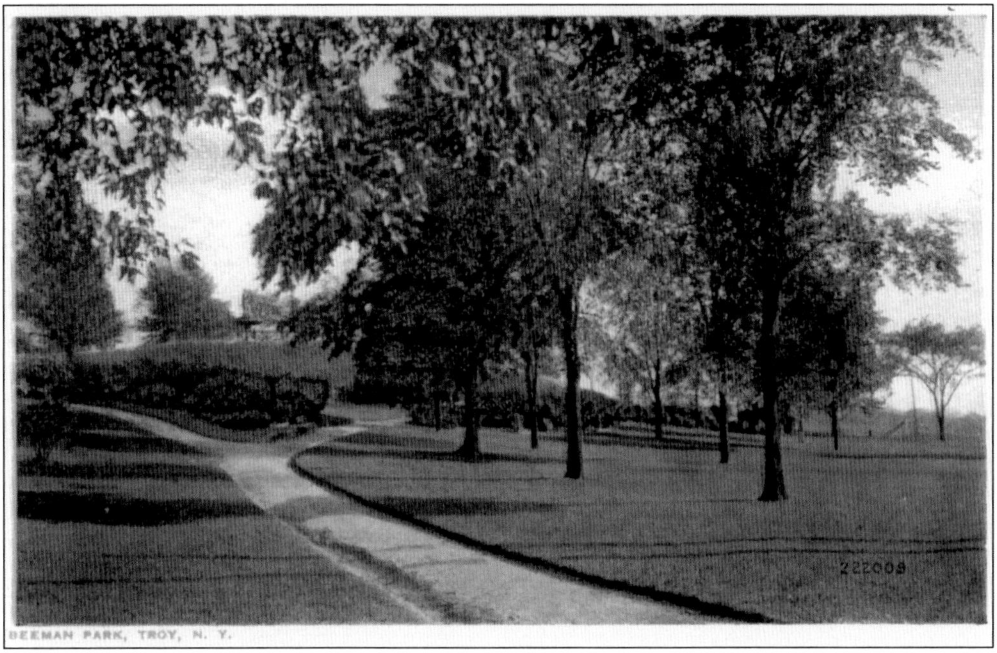

BEMAN PARK. John and Sarah Sherry donated Beman Park to the city of Troy in 1878. John Sherry was a partner in a wholesale grocery firm.

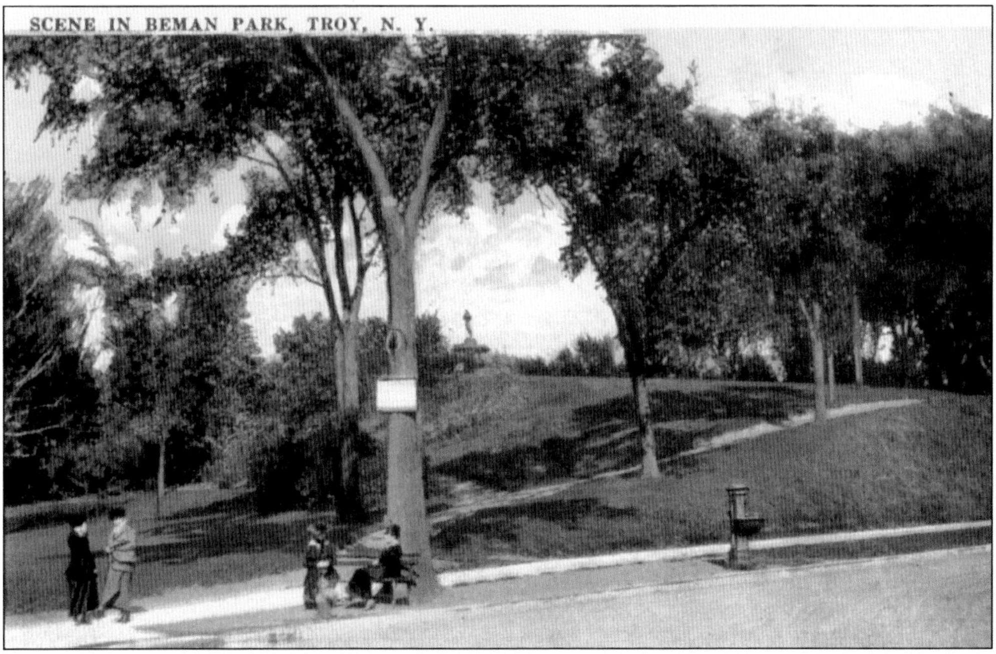

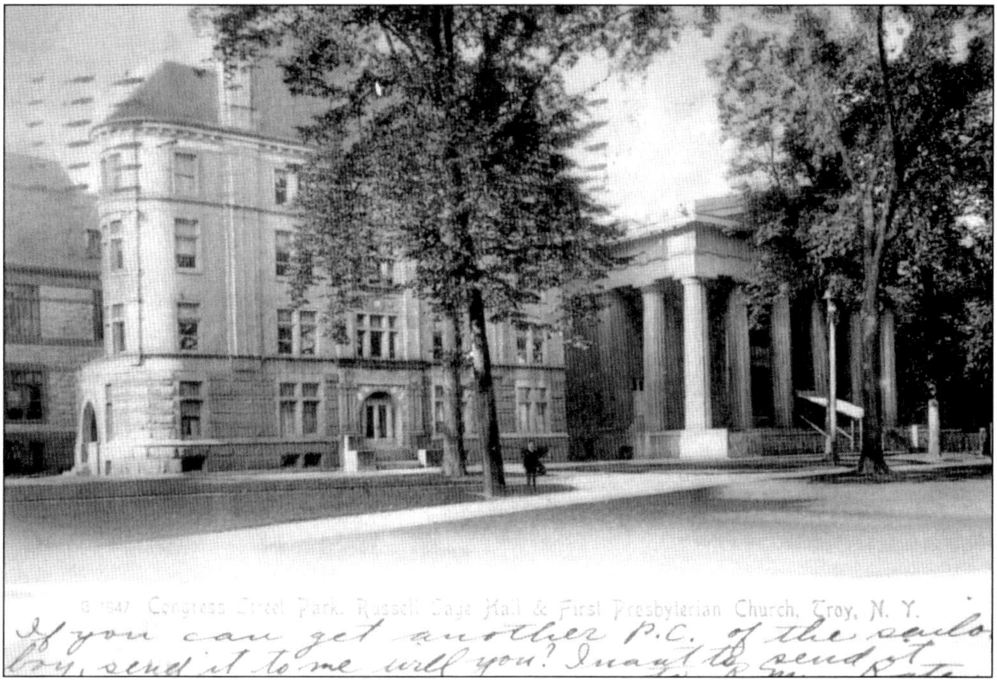

THE CONGRESS STREET PARK. Seen here is the Congress Street Park (Seminary Park), Russell Sage Hall, and the First Presbyterian Church. Today, there are a few more trees and park benches. However, not much has changed since the time of this *c.* 1906 view.

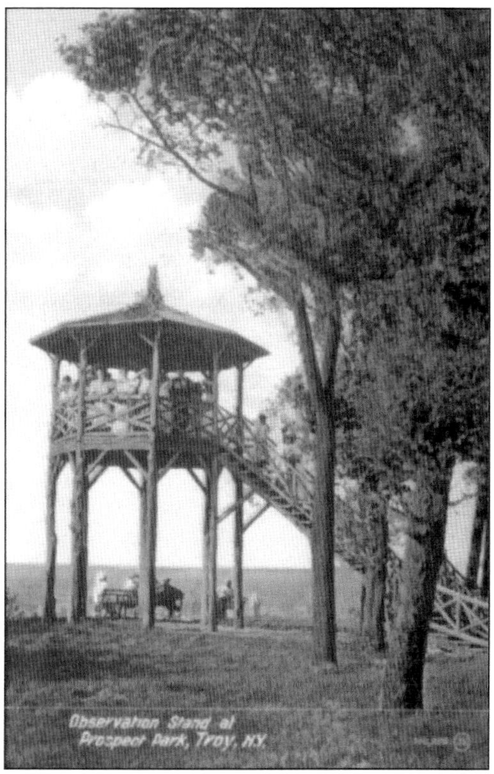

THE PROSPECT PARK OBSERVATION STAND. This beautifully constructed observation stand in Prospect Park gave sightseers an excellent view of the area.

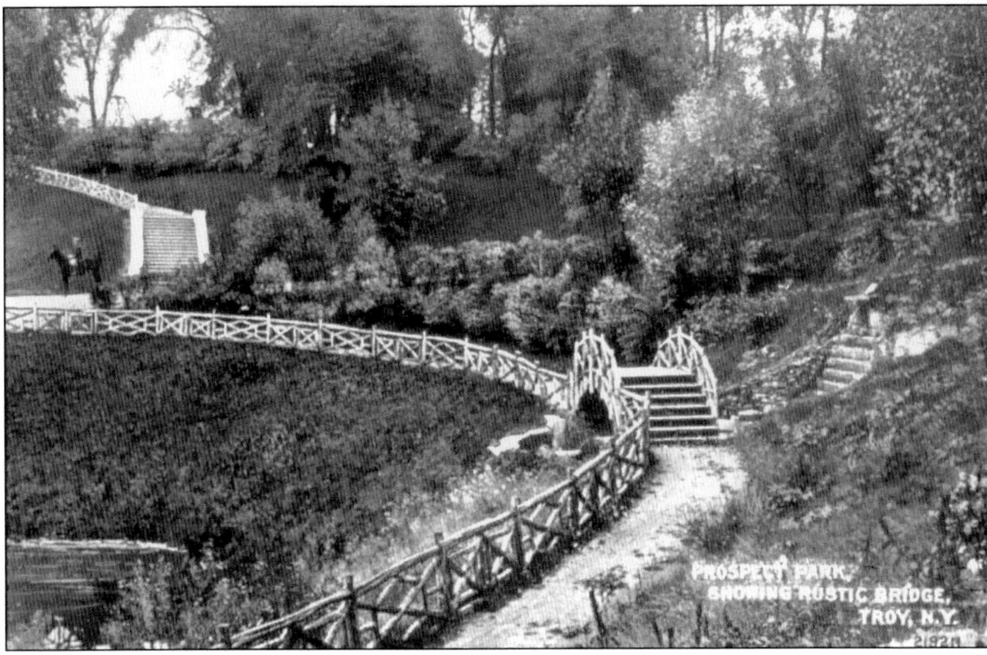

"Prospect Park, Showing Rustic Bridge." The park has trails with bridges and lakes with boats. Prospect Park is a fun place, especially for a picnic.

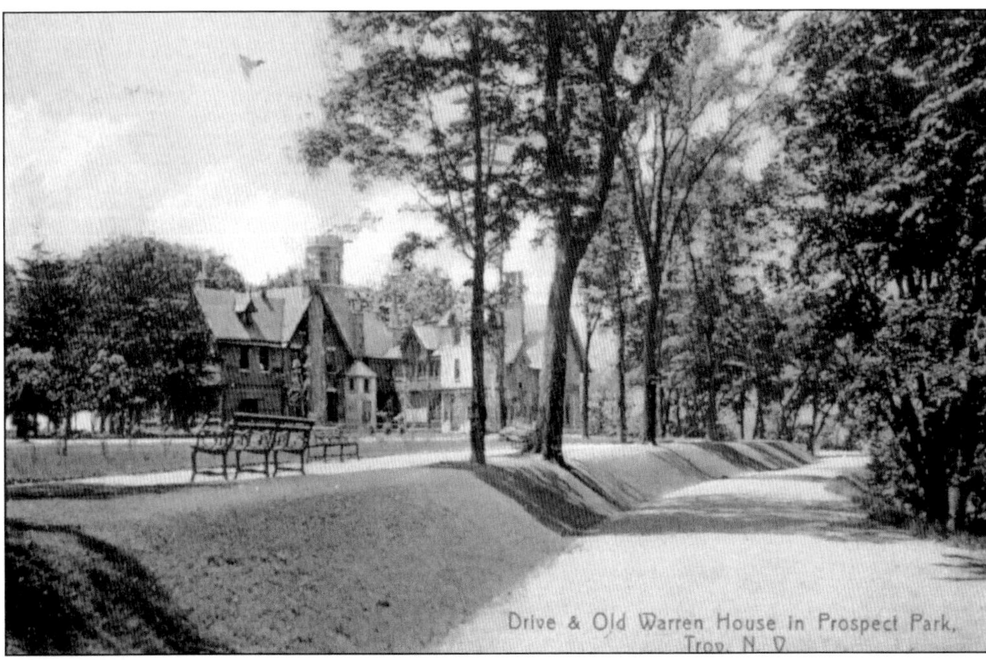

"Drive & Old Warren House in Prospect Park." Prospect Park was built on 84 acres of the Warren family's land. The family is from the Fuller & Warren Stove Company.

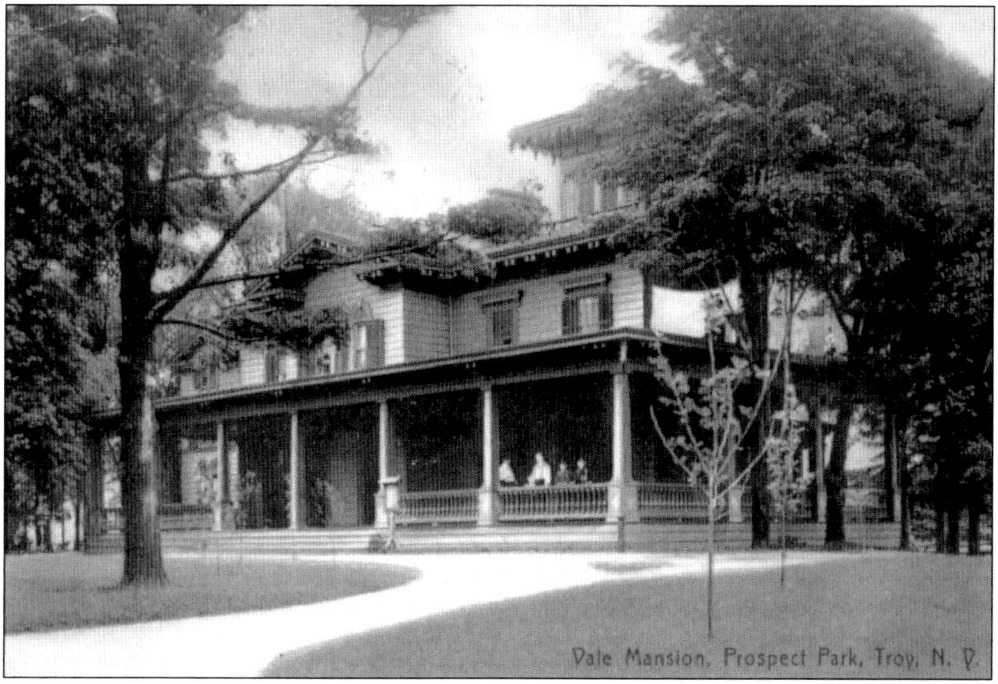

The Vale Mansion. Originally Vale and Warren property, the Warren House was used as a museum until the 1930s.

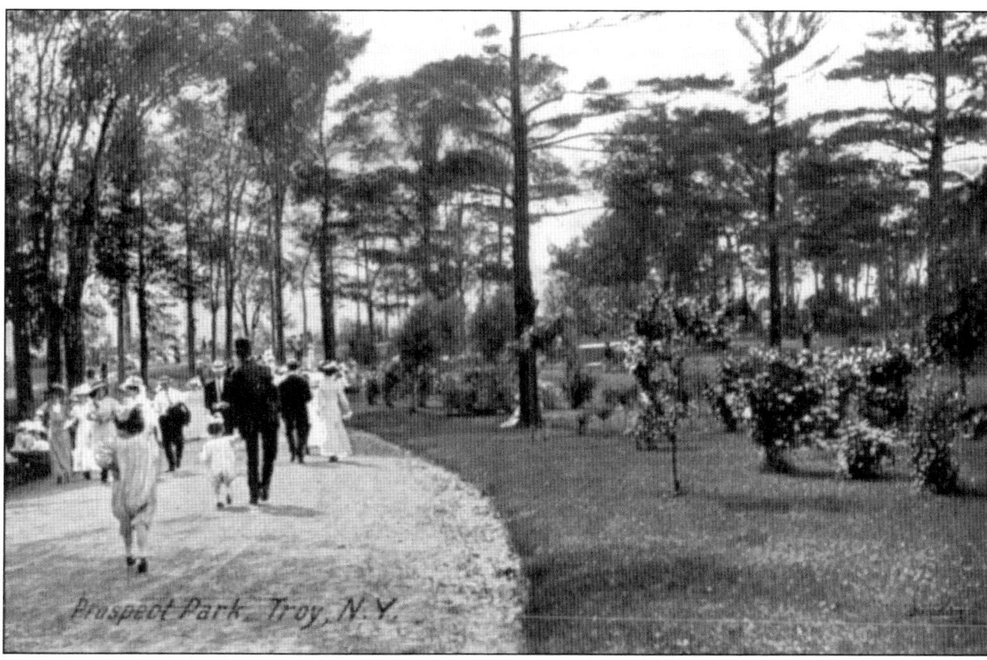

Prospect Park. Tree-lined paths wound their way through the park.

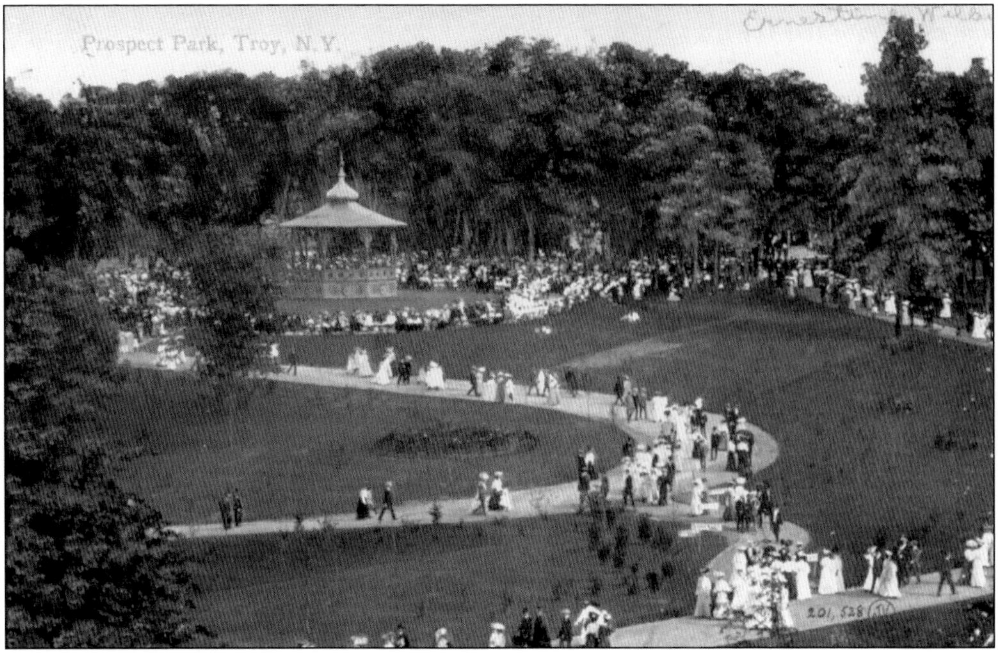

The Bandstand in Prospect Park. Many Sunday band concerts were held here in the summertime. People took the trolley to the park and made a day of it.

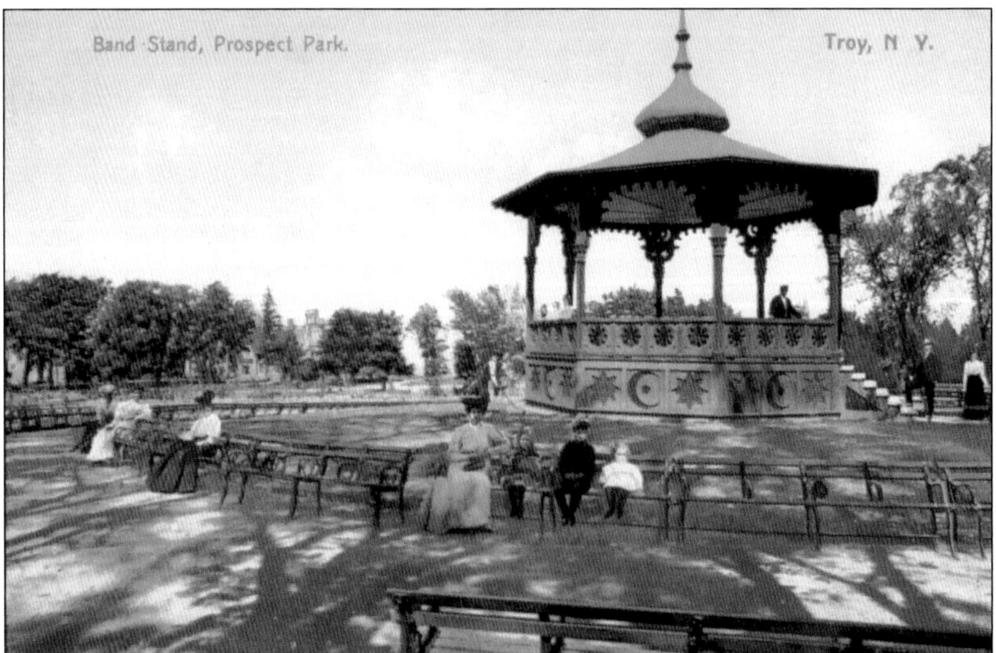

The Bandstand. These early birds are waiting for the concert to begin. It appears that they have a long wait ahead of them.

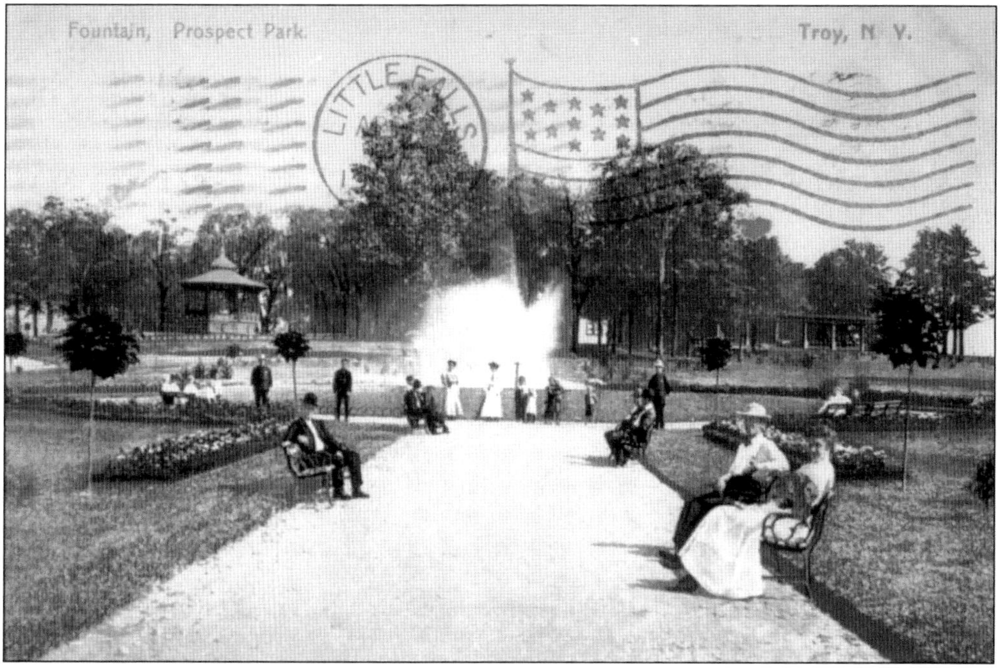

THE FOUNTAIN IN PROSPECT PARK. Seen here are people enjoying the fountain while sitting on some of the many benches in Prospect Park.

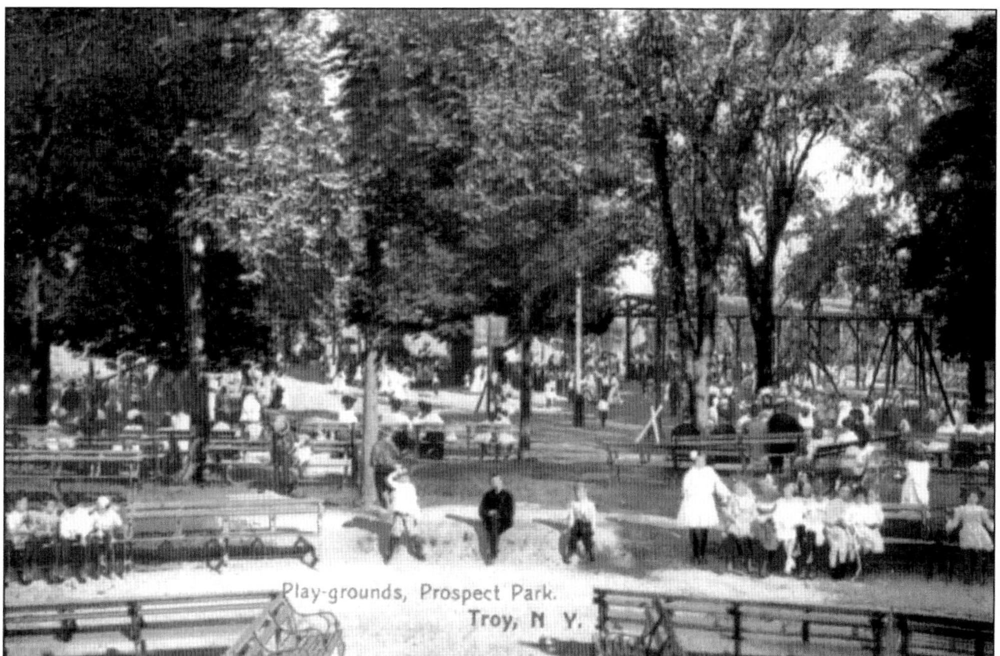

THE PLAYGROUNDS IN PROSPECT PARK. Over the years, generations of families enjoyed Prospect Park, which is just off Pawling Avenue.

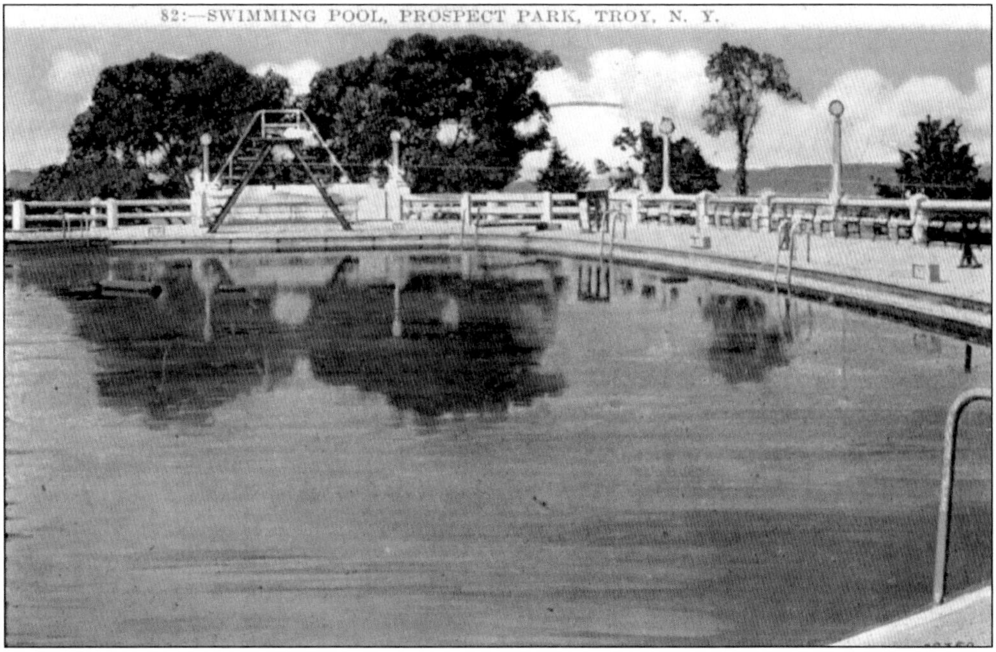

THE SWIMMING POOL IN PROSPECT PARK. In the 1930s, a municipal swimming pool was added to the park. Swimming lessons were given to the young and old alike.

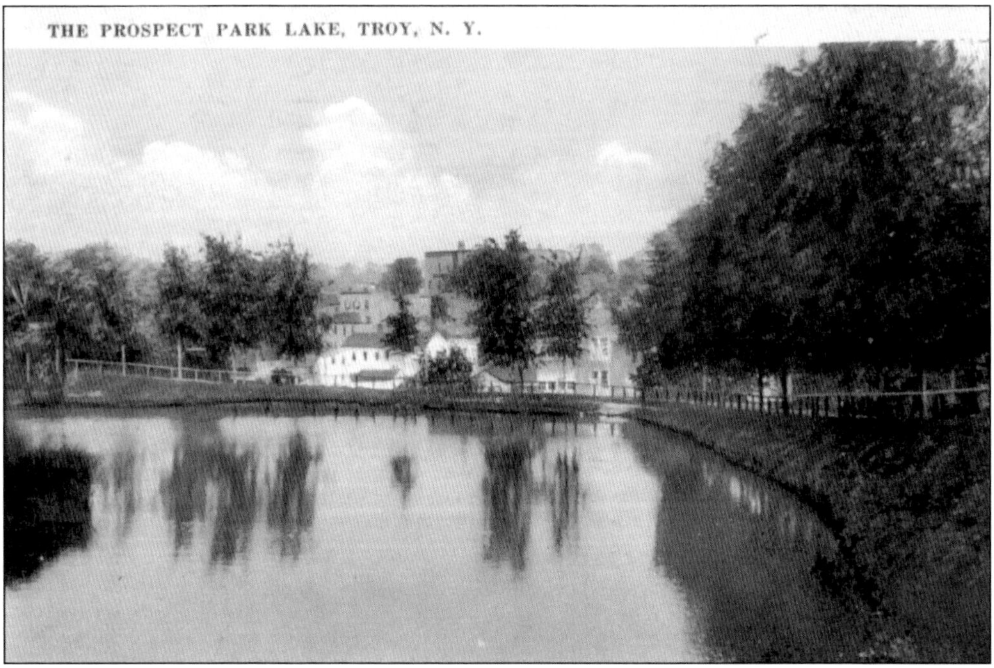

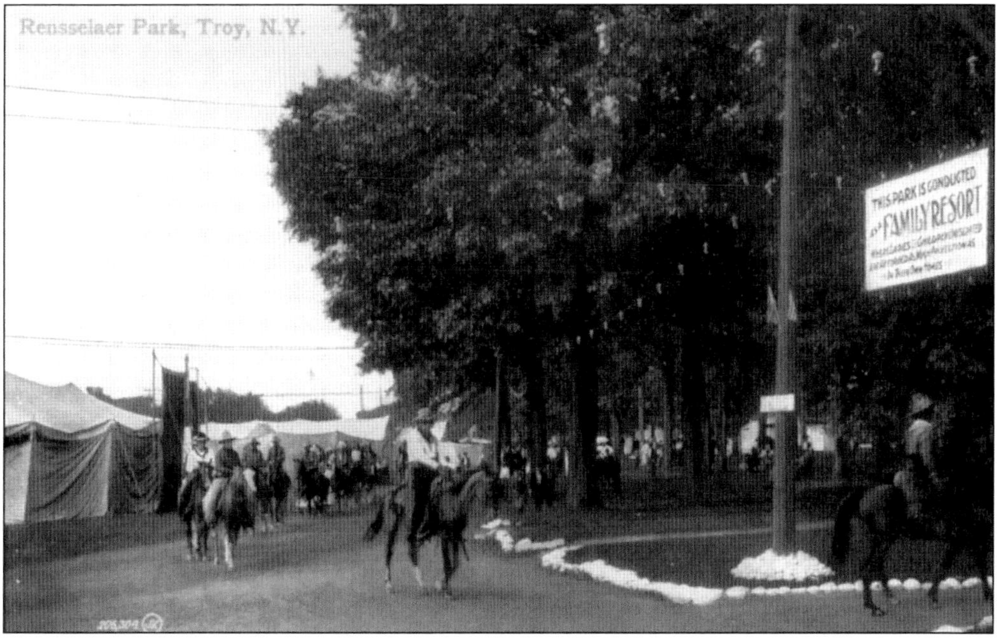

RENSSELAER PARK. The sign to the right reads, "This park is conducted as a family resort where ladies and children unescorted are afforded as much protection as in their own homes."

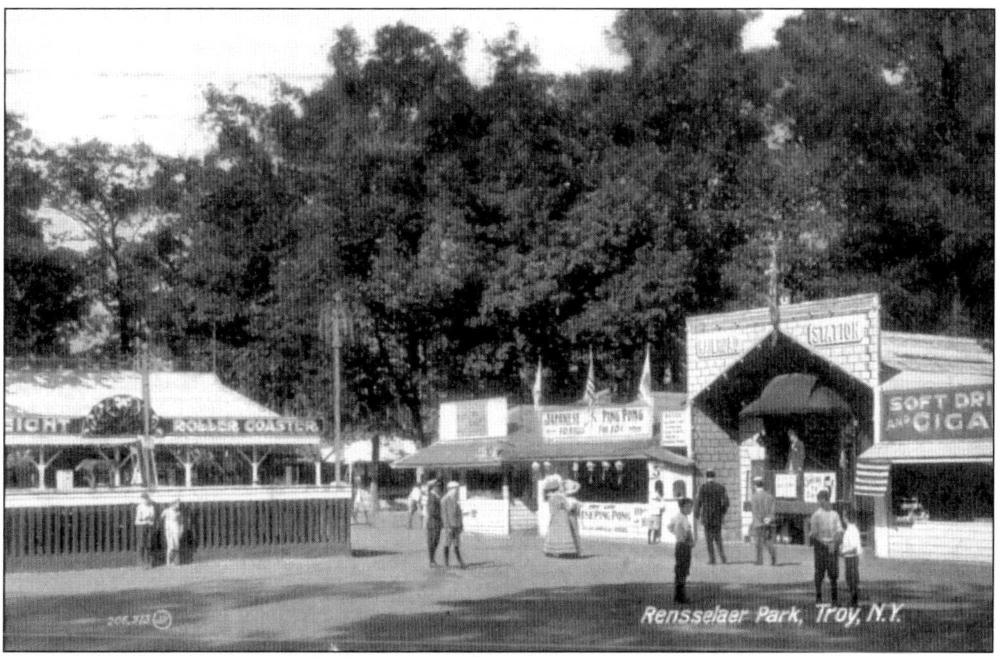

RENSSELAER PARK. Seen in this view are some of the park's attractions, such as electric-light photography for 10¢, Japanese Ping-Pong for 10¢, or train rides for 5¢.

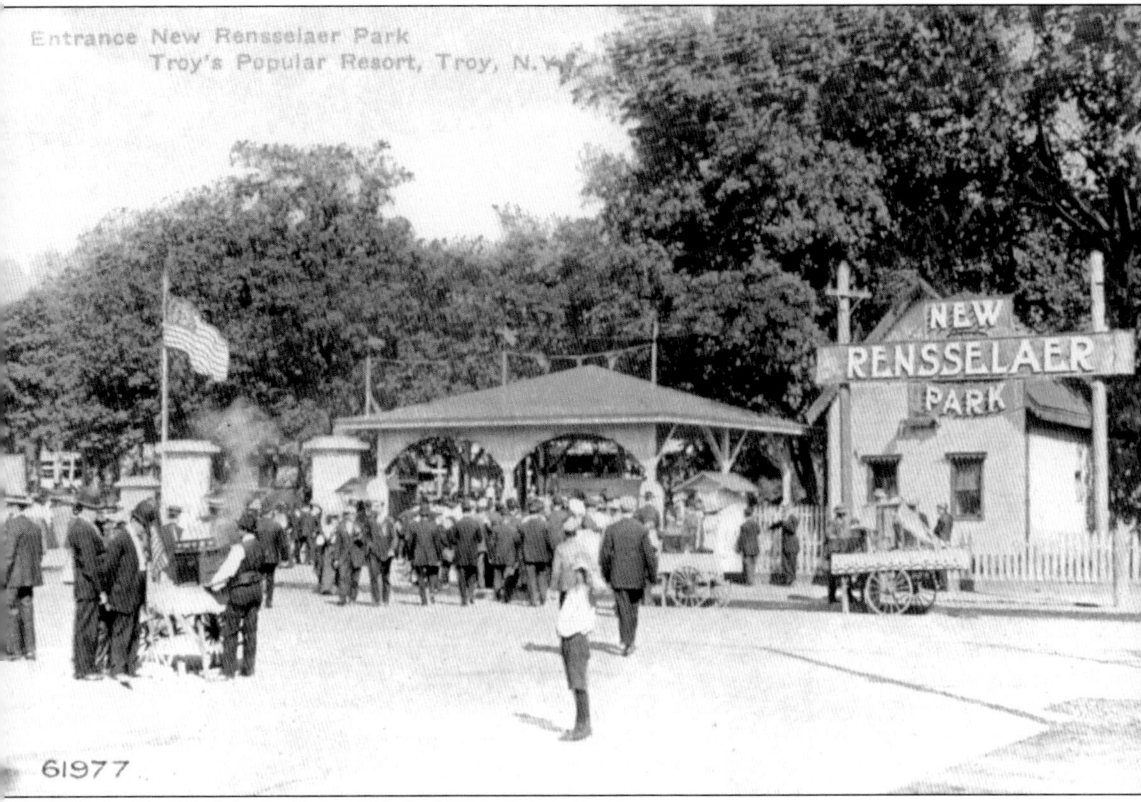

THE ENTRANCE OF THE NEW RENSSELAER PARK. It was not as big as the one at Coney Island, but Troy had its own wooden roller coaster. The park was up in the Burgh at Fifth Avenue and 108th Street. Along with the roller coaster were booths, a racetrack, a mechanical piano, and a carousel. Unfortunately, the park closed after World War I.

Eight

A Time to Worship

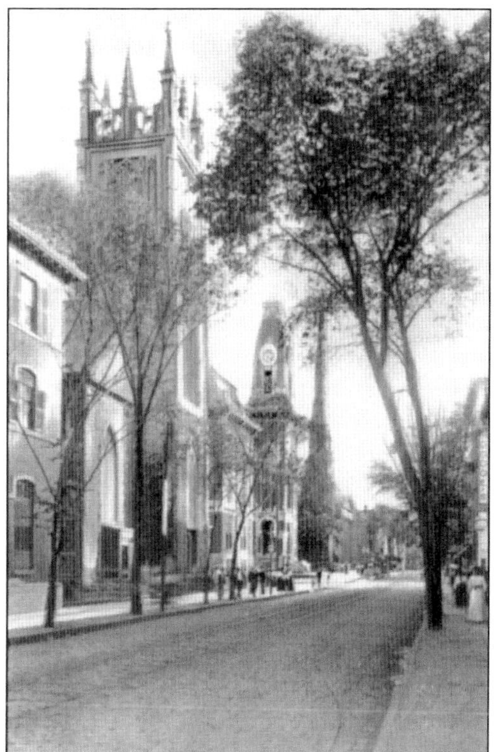

St. Paul's Episcopal Church. St. Paul's was built at Third and State Streets from Amsterdam limestone in 1828 at a cost of more than $40,000. Tiffany did this church's windows.

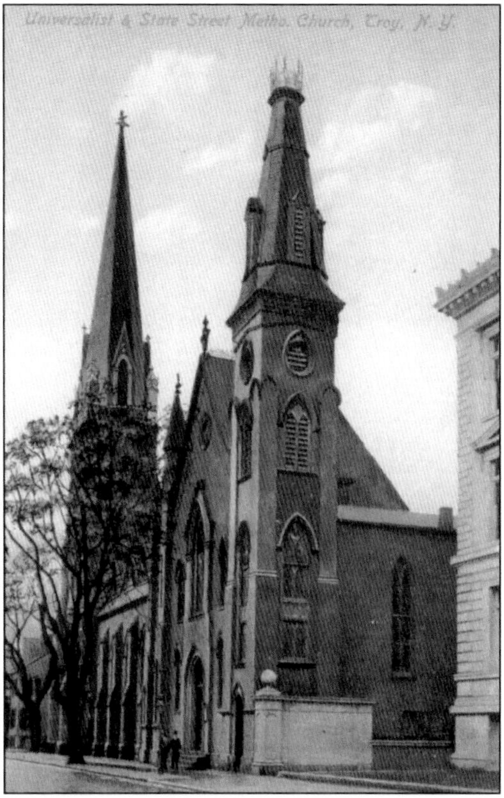

The Universalist and State Street Methodist Churches. First known as the First Restorationist Church of Troy, the name was changed to the First Universalist Church in 1829. The Methodist Church's beginnings go back to 1808.

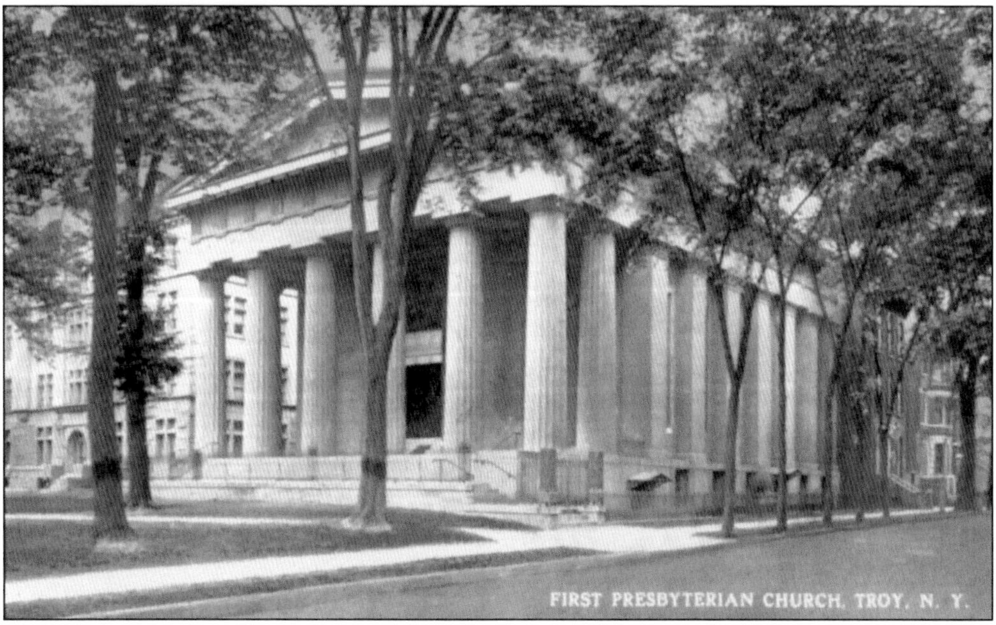

The First Presbyterian Church. On First and Congress Streets stands the First Presbyterian Church of Troy. This magnificent church was built between 1834 and 1836. The cost of the building was $45,000. Among the church's stained-glass windows, two were made by Tiffany.

THE SECOND PRESBYTERIAN CHURCH. Construction of the Second Presbyterian Church, located between Fulton and Grand Division Streets, began in 1826 and was completed the following year.

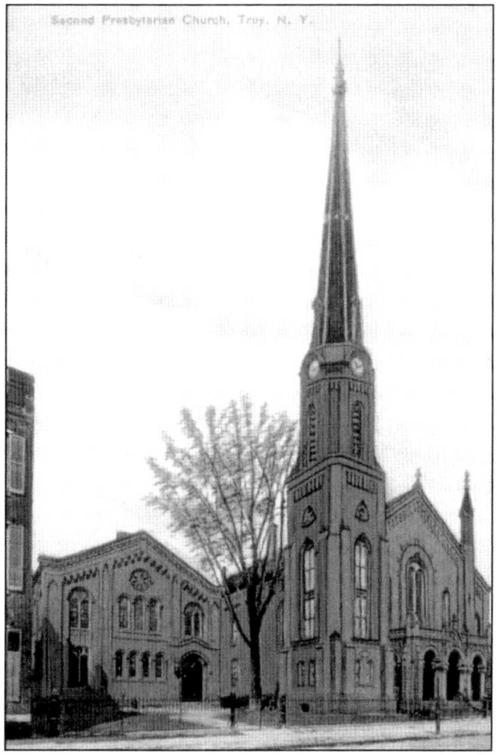

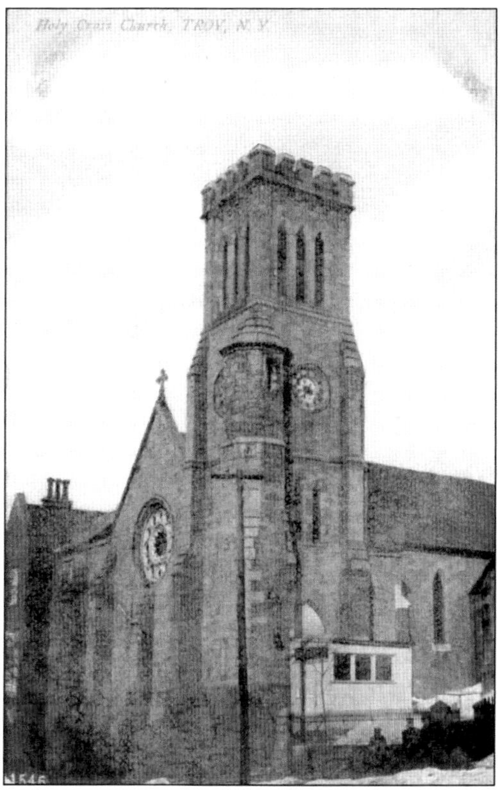

HOLY CROSS CHURCH. Mary Warren founded this church in April 1844 on Eighth Street. The first service was held on Christmas Day the same year. There are Tiffany windows at this church as well.

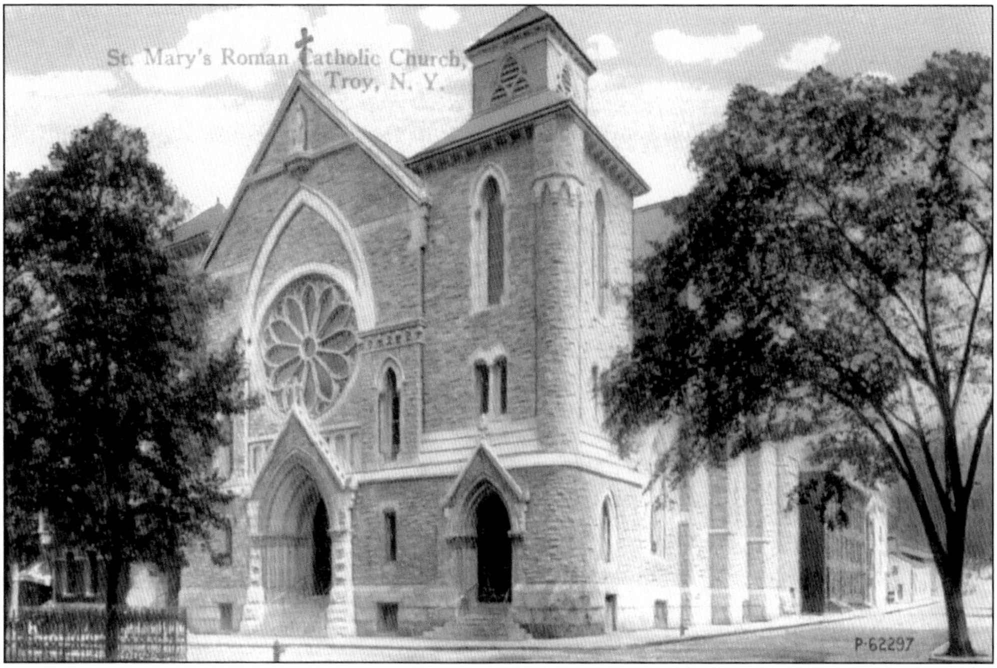

ST. MARY'S ROMAN CATHOLIC CHURCH. St. Mary's Roman Catholic Church is located on the corner of Third and Washington Streets. Land for the church was purchased in 1843, and it was built the following year.

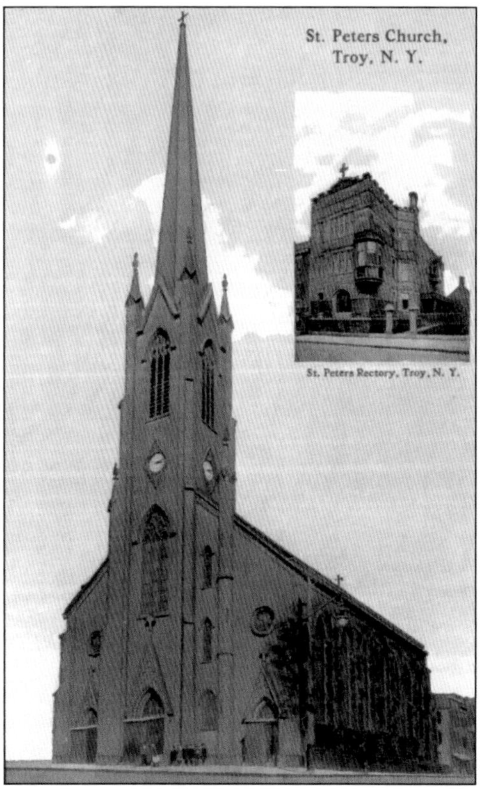

ST. PETER'S CHURCH AND RECTORY. The church seen here was built on Second and Hutton Streets, replacing the first St. Peter's, which was destroyed by fire in 1848. In the rebuilding, a tall steeple and a clock tower were added.

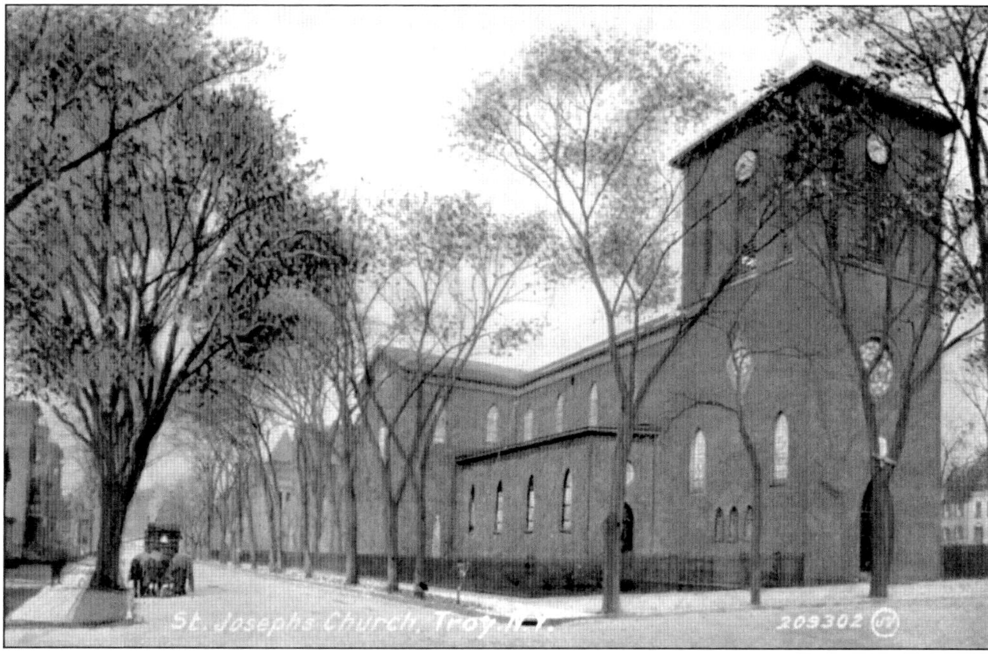

St. Joseph's Church. Located on Jackson Street, St. Joseph's was dedicated in 1853. It has been said that this church has more Tiffany windows than any other building in the world.

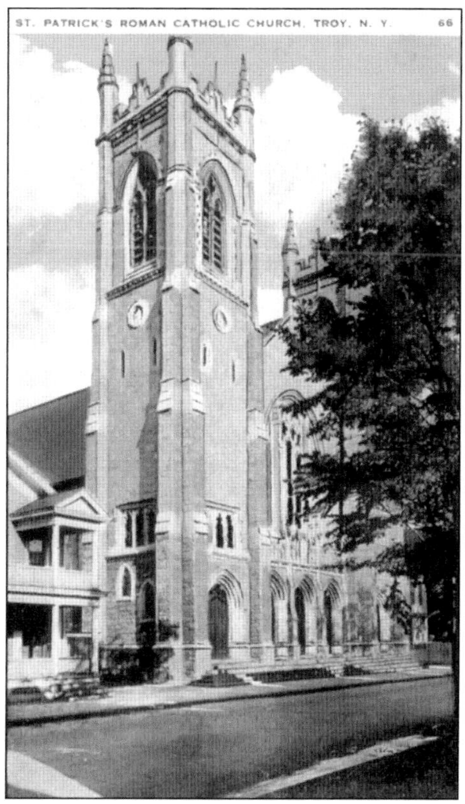

St. Patrick's Roman Catholic Church. St. Patrick's Roman Catholic Church was built in 1872 between Canal and Douw Streets.

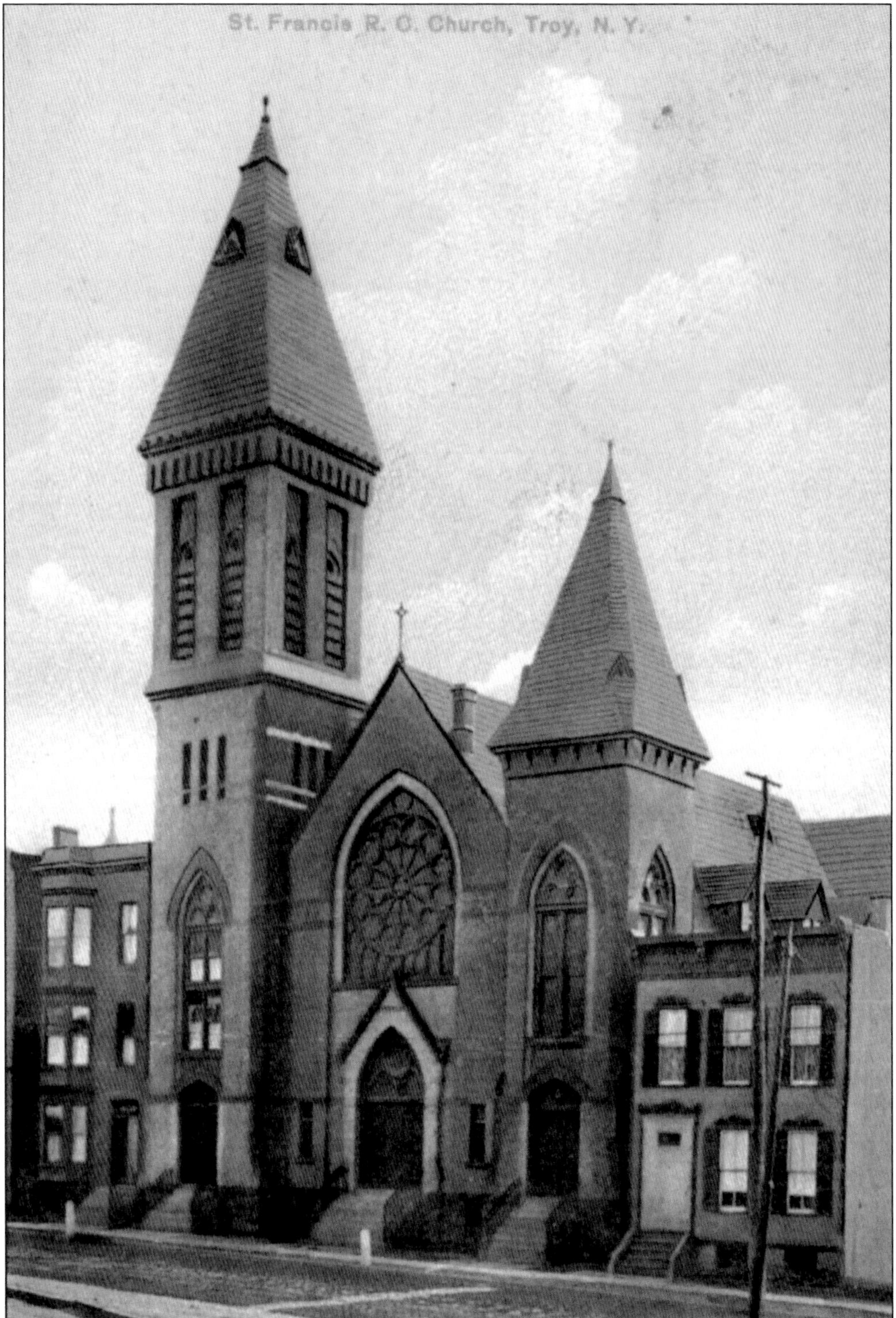

St. Francis Roman Catholic Church. Built in 1882, St. Francis Roman Catholic Church was located on the south side of Congress Street.

Nine

A Time to Mourn

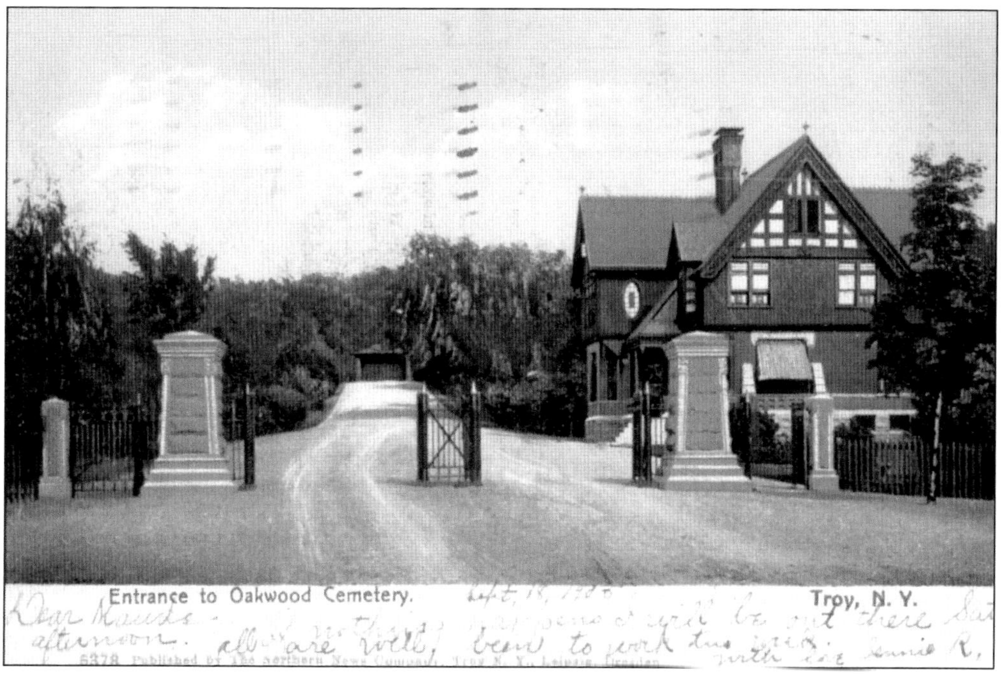

Oakwood Cemetery. Seen in this *c.* 1905 view is one of the entrances to Oakwood Cemetery. This entrance is located at 101st Street. The gatehouse is to the right.

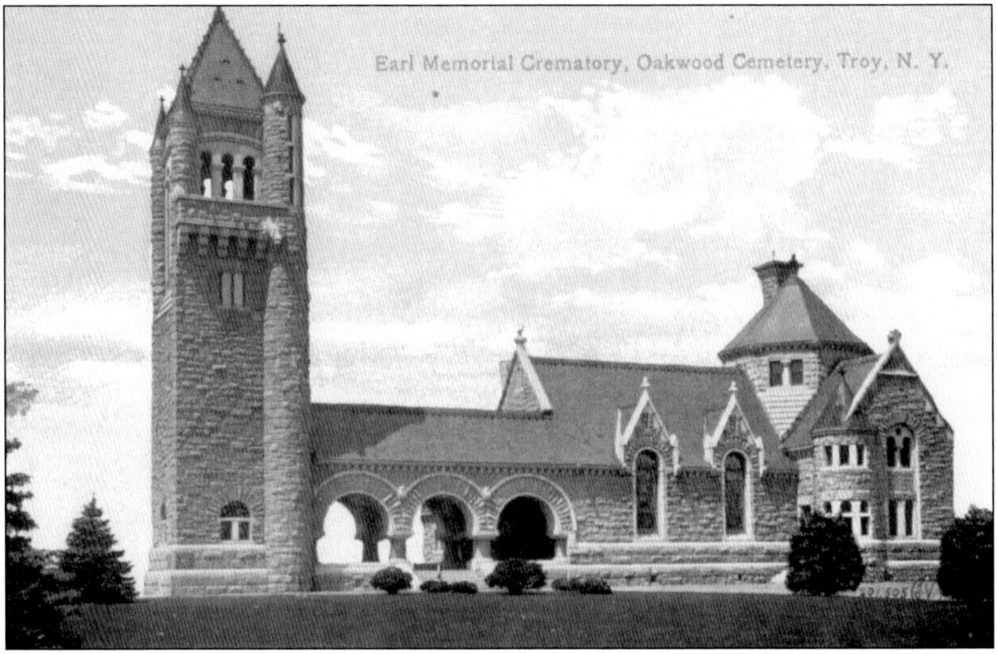

The Earl Memorial Crematory. William S. Earl and his wife built the Gardner Earl Memorial Crematory in memory of their son. It was built of Westerly Granite in Romanesque style. The tower on the crematory is nine stories high.

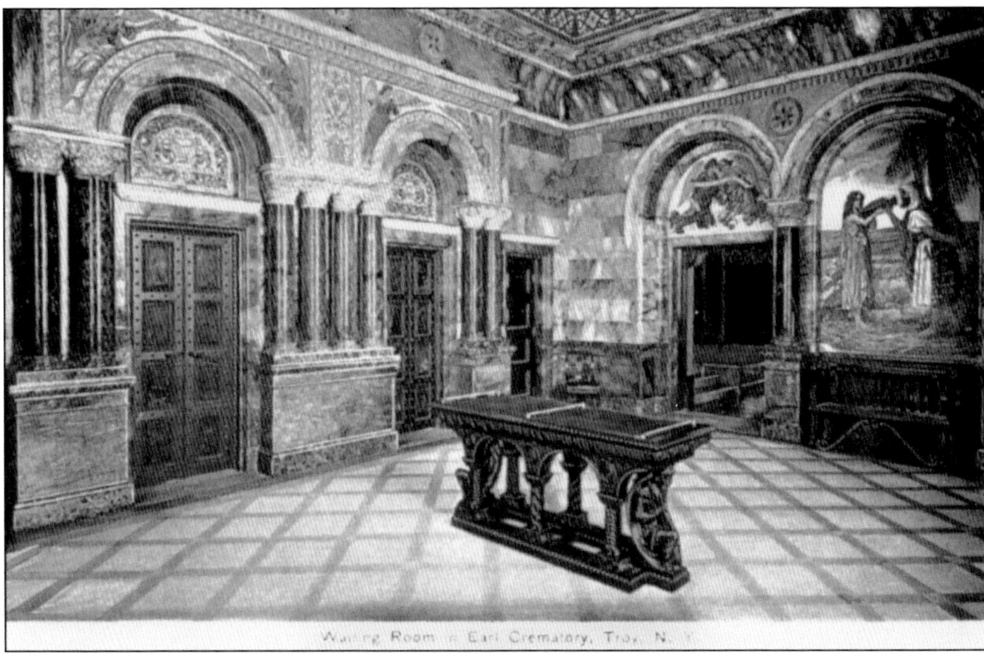

The Waiting Room of the Earl Crematory. Seen here is the waiting room in the Earl Crematory, which is located in the Oakwood Cemetery. The Earls were a very prominent family in Troy. The waiting room was built with Siena, Japanese, and African marble and was designed by its manager, James Inglis.

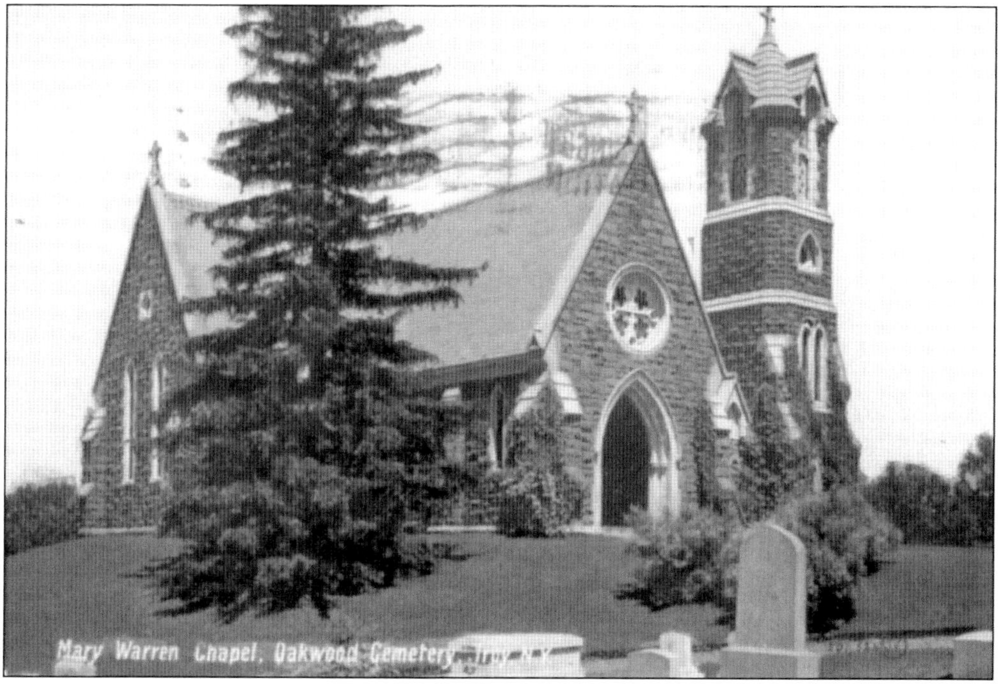

THE MARY WARREN CHAPEL. The Mary Warren Chapel was built in Oakwood Cemetery in 1860 in English Country Gothic design. Oakwood Cemetery celebrated its 150th anniversary in 2000. A nonsectarian cemetery, it accepts all faiths.

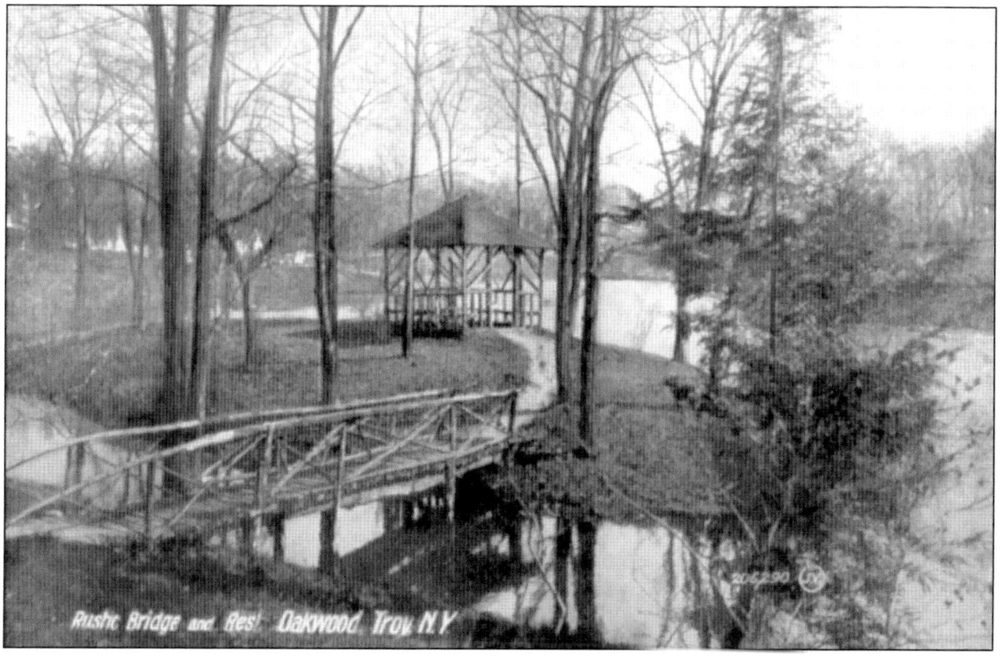

"RUSTIC BRIDGE AND REST, OAKWOOD." This wooded scene from the Oakwood Cemetery might make you think you were in the Adirondacks, not a cemetery in a small city.

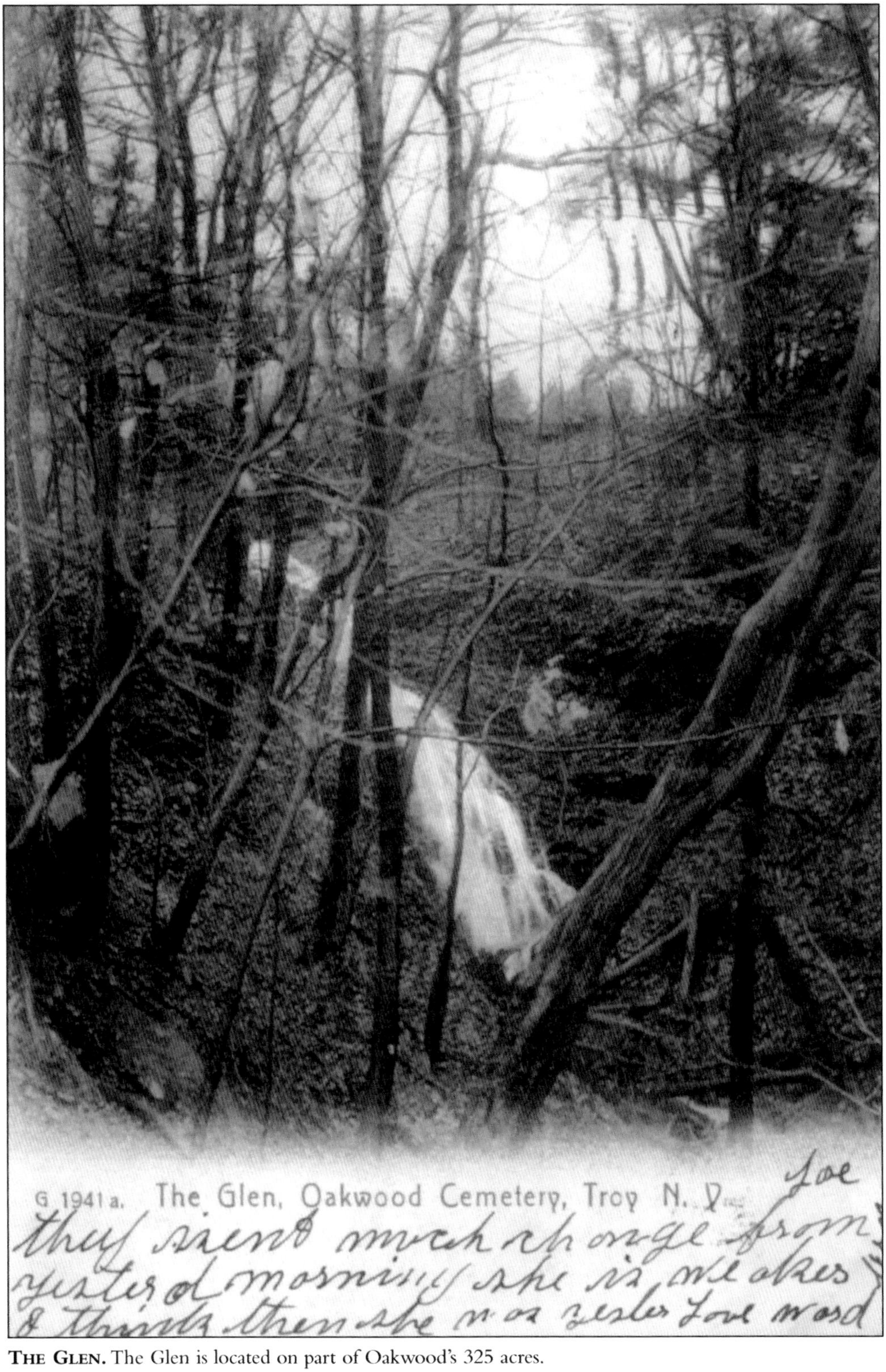

THE GLEN. The Glen is located on part of Oakwood's 325 acres.

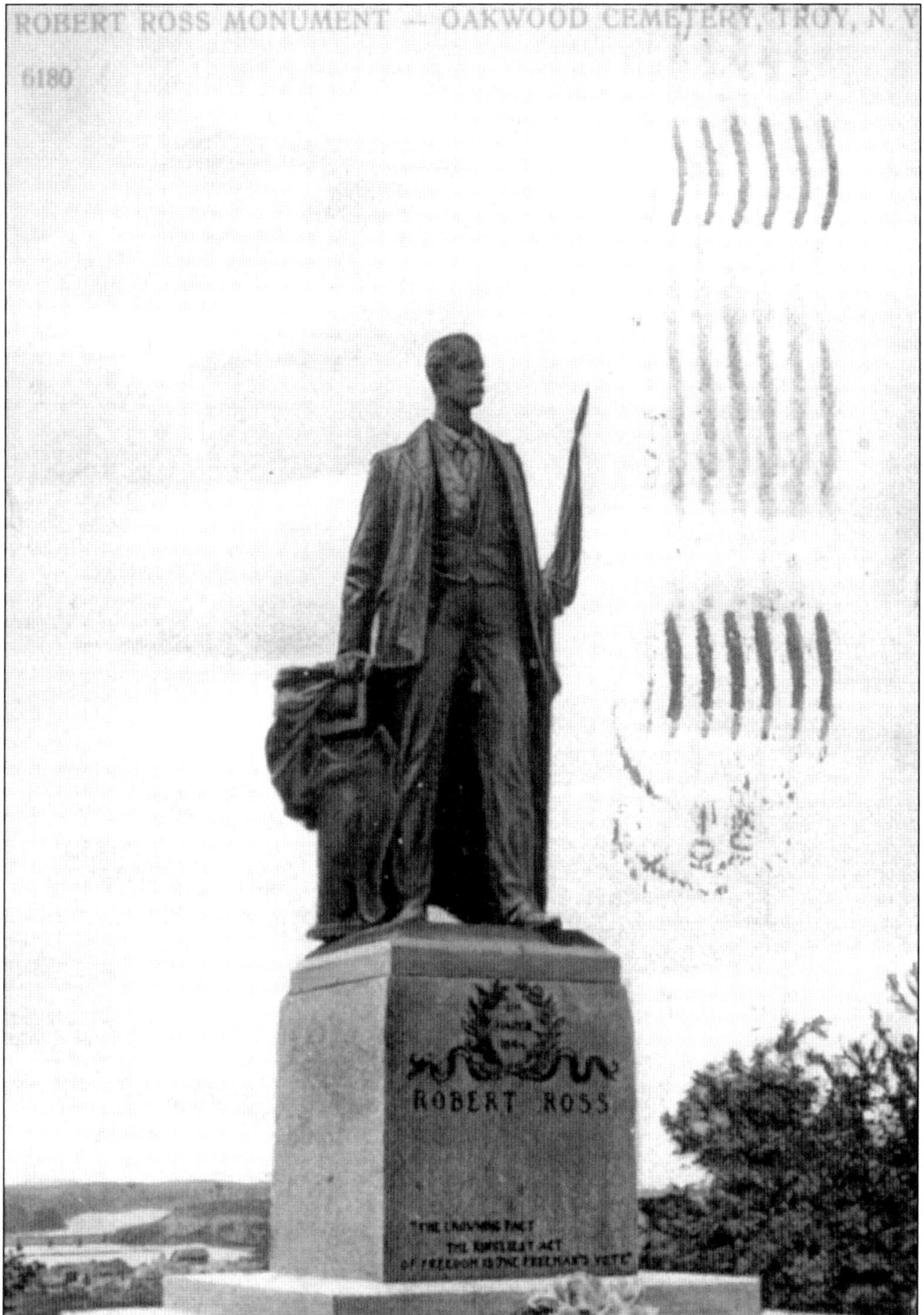

The Robert Ross Monument. This monument, which stands in Oakwood Cemetery, remembers Robert Ross. Ross was killed while fighting for election reform. Notice the ballot box and the flag in his hand. The monument reads, "The crowning fact, the kingliest act of freedom is the freeman's vote."

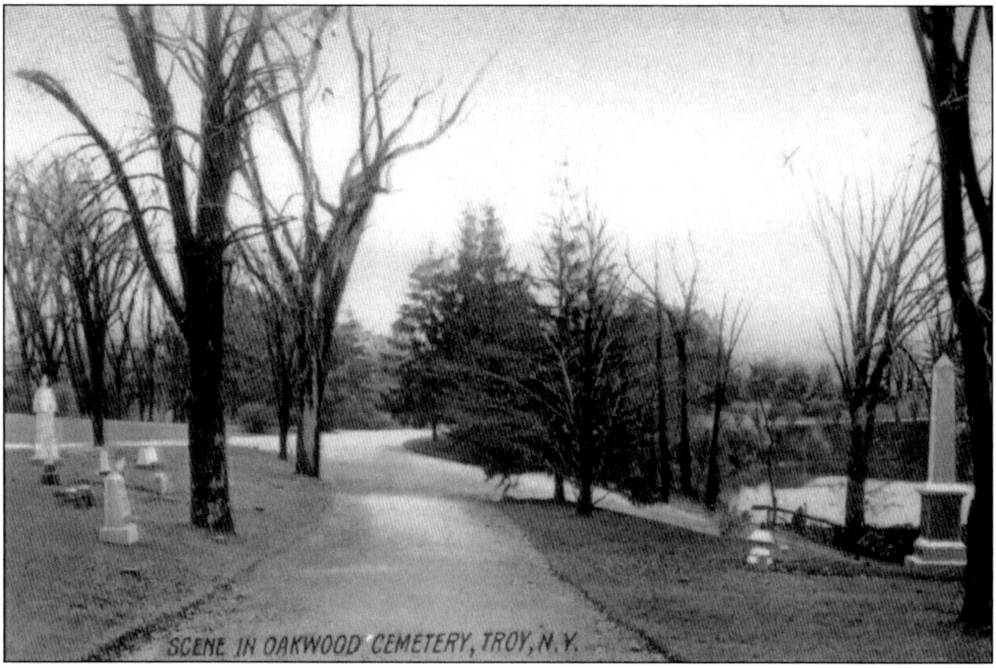

"SCENE IN OAKWOOD CEMETERY." Oakwood Cemetery has more than 55,000 graves and more architectural styles than some cities. These styles include Egyptian, Gothic, Greek Revival, and Neoclassical monuments. Several of Troy's most famous people are buried here, such as Mr. and Mrs. Russell Sage, Emma Willard, and Troy's favorite son, Uncle Sam Wilson.

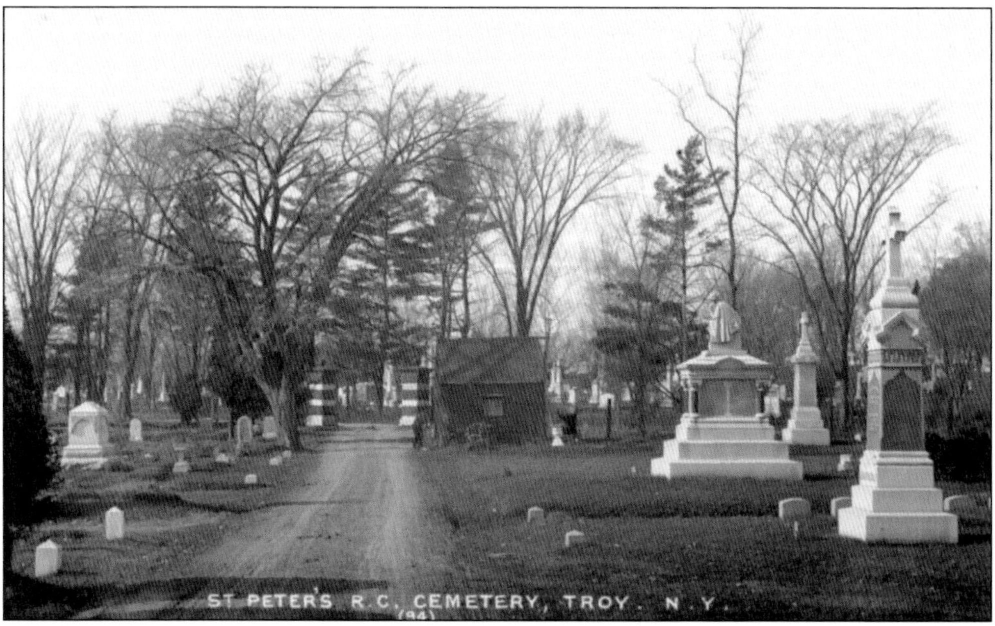

ST. PETER'S R.C. CEMETERY. Located just across from the Oakwood Cemetery, the land for St. Peter's R.C. Cemetery was purchased by the bishop of Albany in 1878.